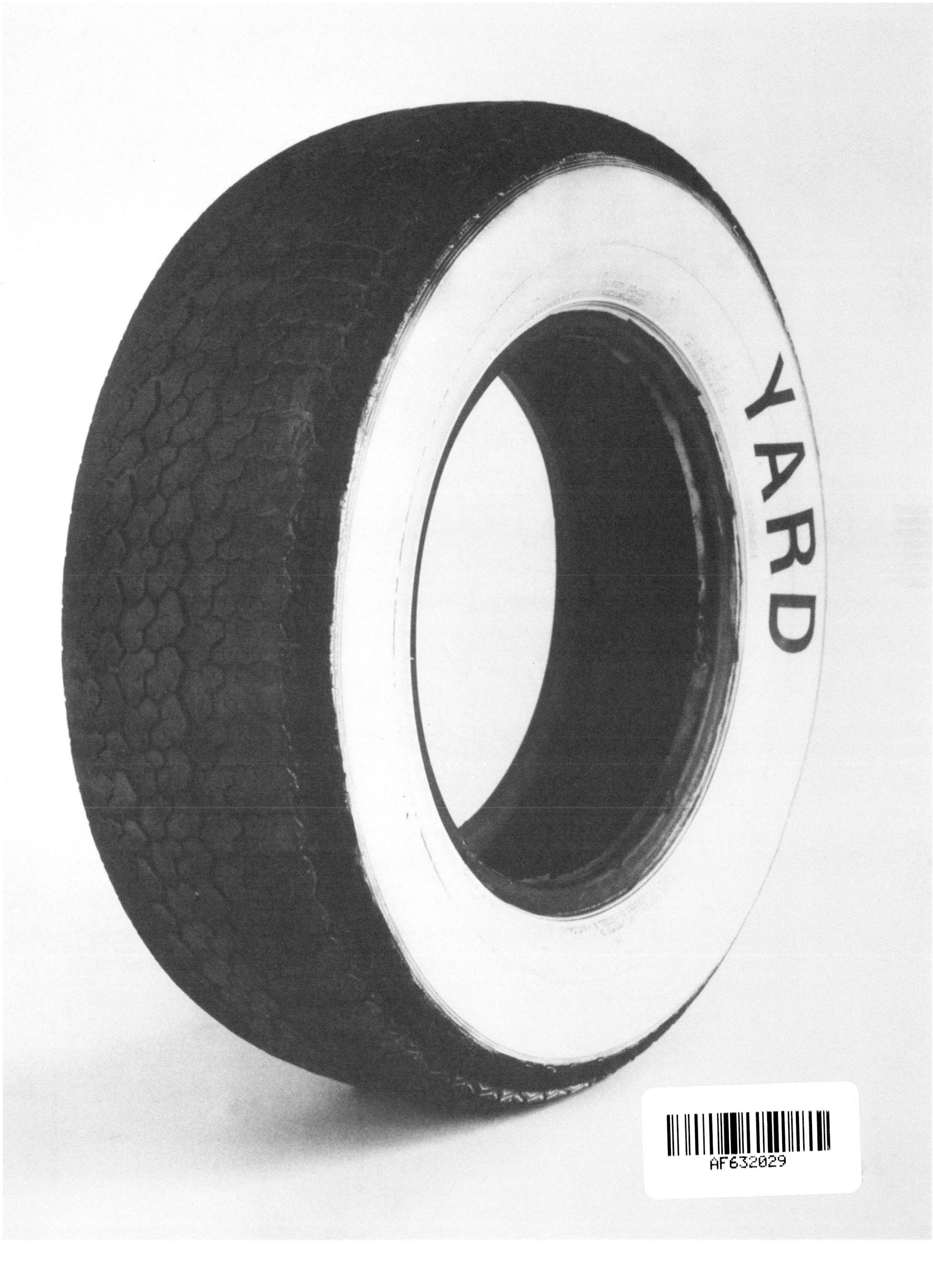
YARD

¶ *Yard* thus looks neither exactly like a junk pile nor ~~exactly like~~ any of the customary arts, nor even a fun-house (for in this, the themes and their form are fairly conventionalized). Yard could relate to any of them. ~~The principle question for me in making an Environment, or its natural extension, a Happening, is not whether it is good or bad because it is part of art or part of life, but, whatever it is, whether it keeps me involved and a few others involved in a living give-and-take~~

My feeling is that so long as this ambiguity holds, the life-line remains intact. ~~For the rest, the old verities still apply: The power of the image, the depth of one's feelings and the strength of one's convictions. And some art may come out of it, for that is my objective.~~ Some Art may be the result, and that is fine, but for me the principle objective is to derive from what I make as high a degree of involvement and rapport as I do from things "outside" of art. I do not think that either art of any value or a life-situation of any intensity could result if I were to start off and end up with a purely aesthetic problem in mind.

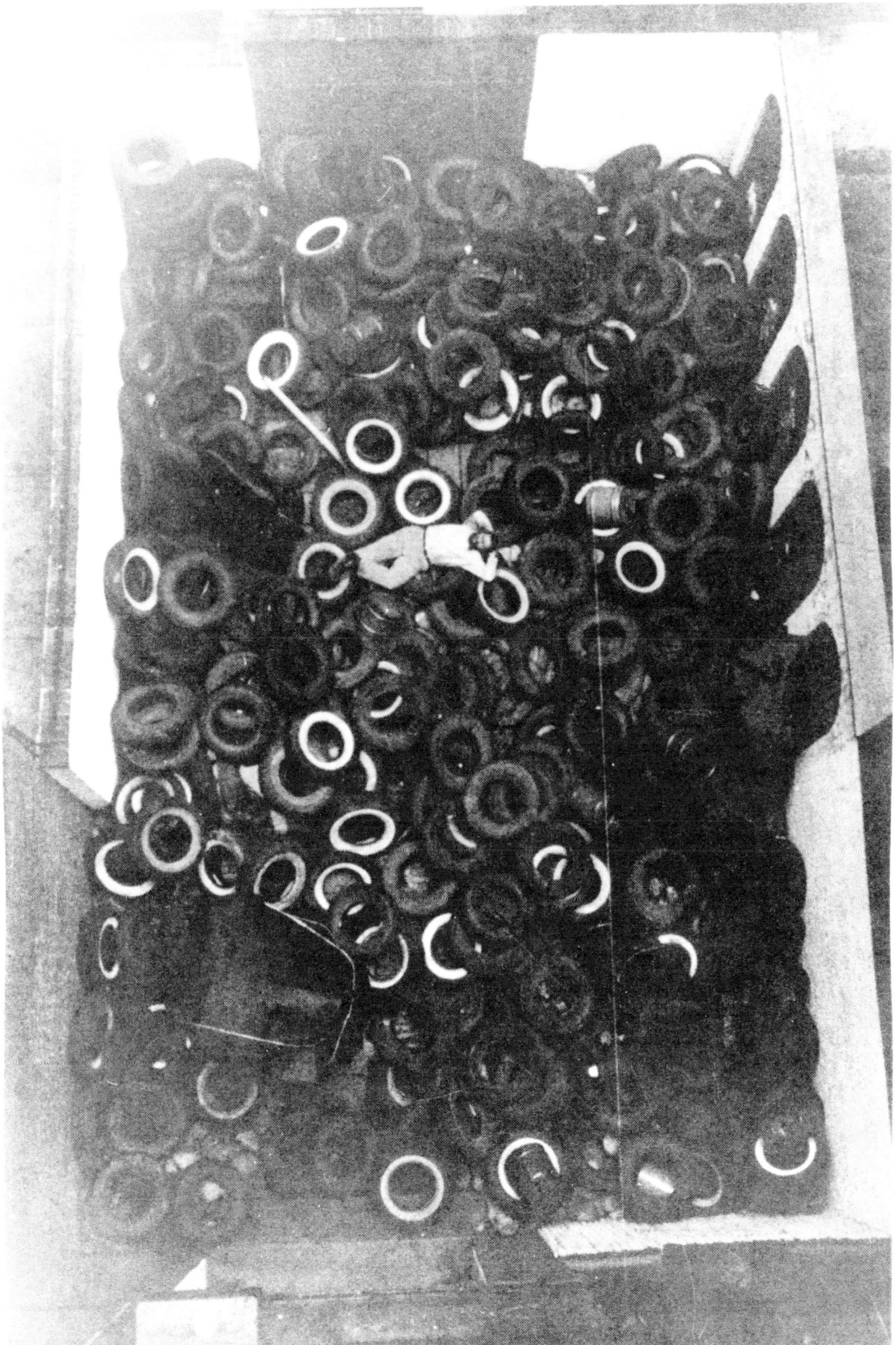

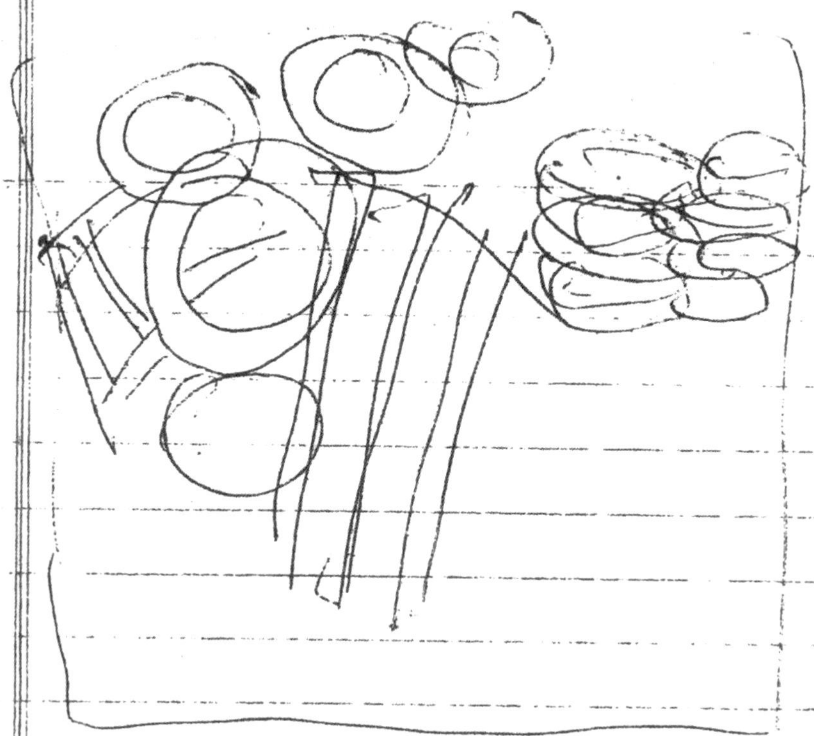

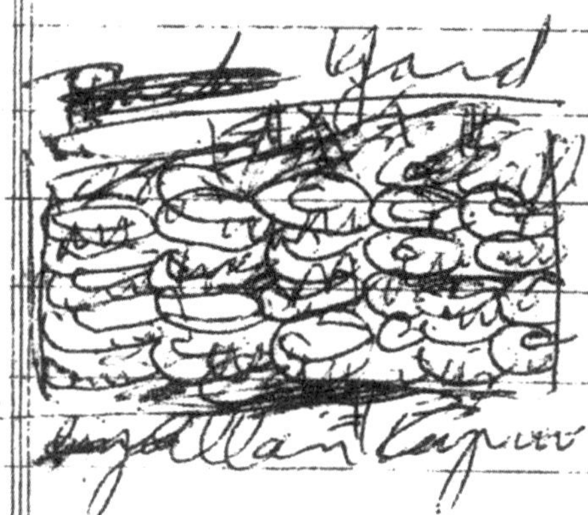
Yard

Among the things I have felt to be important in the conception of my work is the idea that it could be called art, or ordinary nature. I devote great effort to balancing what I do as precariously as possible on this tightrope of identities. I find here a certain drama. And then, more crucially, life and art begin flowing together in an easy give and take.

YARD thus looks neither exactly like a junk pile nor any of the usual arts, nor even a fun-house (for in this the themes and forms are also quite conventionalized). Yet YARD could relate to any or all fo them.

Beyond this general objective, each Environment or Happening has its source in things I care deeply about. For instance, in this case, dumps, and the shanty-huts built by those strange madmen who divide their world with rats....

MARTHA JACKSON GALLERY and DAVID ANDERSON GALLERY
32 east 69 street
new york

P R E S S   R E L E A S E

EXHIBITION OPEN TO PRESS
THURSDAY, May 25, 1961

10:00 AM to 5:00 PM

ENVIRONMENT - SITUATIONS - SPACES

Six Artists
May 25 through June 23

Once again THE MARTHA JACKSON GALLERY and THE DAVID ANDERSON Gallery affirm their commitment to significant but unestablished art movements in an exhibition made up of works by six younger artists, entitled ENVIRONMENTS - SITUATIONS - SPACES. The exhibition, opening May 25 and continuing through June 23, is unique in that it is the first group show by artists working within the totality of physical space creating environments which demand full and active participation from the viewer.

The exhibiting artist, GEORGE BRECHT, JAMES DINE, WALTER GAUDNEK, ALLAN KAPROW, CLAES OLDENBERG AND ROBERT WHITMAN, have all shown their work previously in New York and all, with the exception of Walter Gaudnek, have created "happenings." These can, perhaps, be best described as art of the five senses and have generated considerable international comment. The May issue of Art News carried a well documented and informative article on "happenings" by Allan Kaprow, whose book Paintings, Environments and Happenings, is soon to be published.

The growing awareness on the part of today's artist of the unlimited scope of expression available through the utilization of new materials as well as the reuse of society's material castoffs, was first brought to the attention of the viewing public in the exhibitions' NEW FORMS, NEW MEDIA, VERSION I AND II show held at THE MARTHA JACKSON GALLERY in June and September of 1960. Most of the artists in the current exhbition took part in this pioneering effort.

Each artist, though highly individual, aims at complete utilization of all facets of environmental space; achieveing, thereby, a new and profound form of art expression. Walls, ceilings and floors lose their confining identity, merging into this recreated space. The viewer finds himself within the artist statement, forcing him to forego his passive objectivity.

Titles of the individual events are:

ICED DICE...............George Brecht
SPRING CABINET..........James Dine
UNLIMITED DIMENSIONS.....Walter Gaudnek
THE YARD................Allan Kaprow
THE STORE...............Claes Oldenberg
UNTITLED................Robert Whitman

A group of drawings and paintings by the contributing artists will be shown in a separate exhibition space. Due to the nature of the exhibition, it will be necessary to review the show only after installation. A modest admission fee will be charged for this exhibition only.

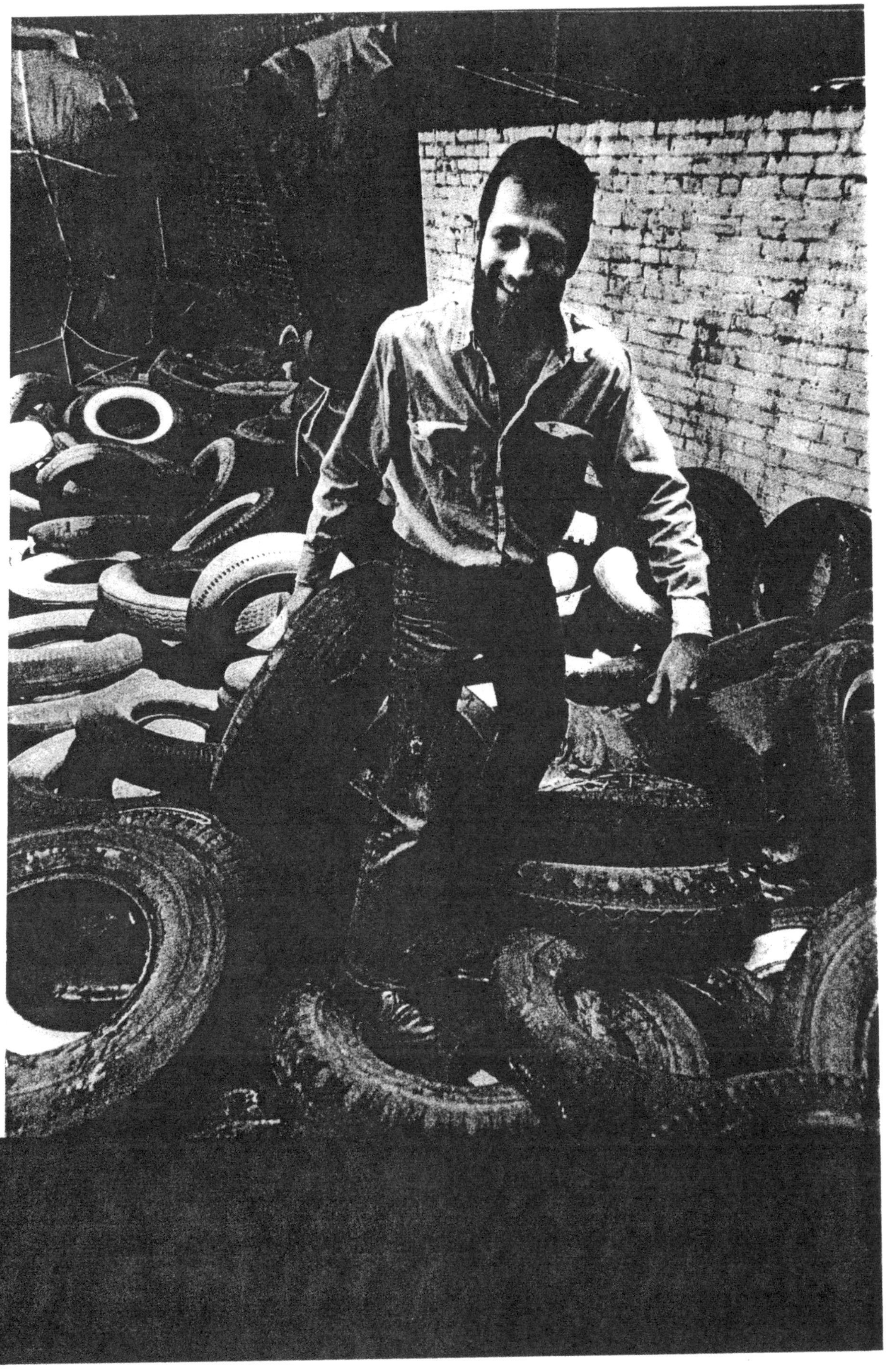

108. ALLAN KAPROW.

Yard. 1961. Environment

RECALLING THE ACT

109. ALLAN KAPROW. Yard. 1961. Environment

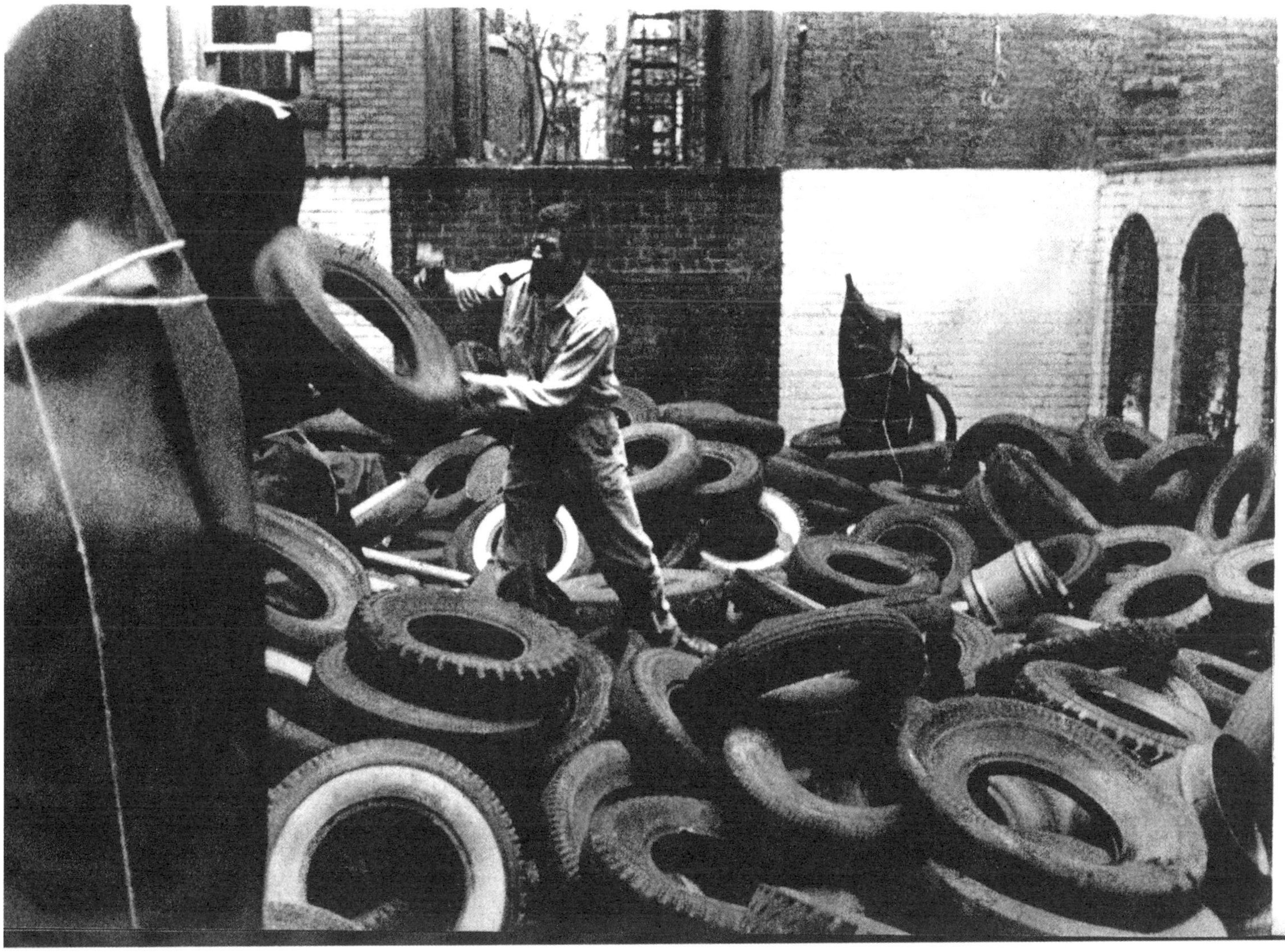

the village VOICE, *July* 6, 1961

'ENVIRONMENTS' at MARTHA JACKSON's

The "terrible children" invaded Martha Jackson's Gallery last May and June with more of those baffling non-commercial commodities, things youn can't use or sell or label even, which nobody could be too clear about why they should be encouraged or endured much less considered the prestige items they obviously a.e, or else why would Miss Jackson (whose commercial acumen is well known) clutter up her fashionable yard with a bunch of junky car tires that she permitted Alan Kaprow to put there?

No Dark Meanings

I don't know what Miss Jackson thought about those tires. I didn't think much myself. I mean I perceived a bunch of tires there in the yard and then asked my son if he wanted to stay and play around in them while I went upstairs to see the rest. I know Mr. Kaprow is against people finding dark serious meanings, commentaries on the state of the union, etc., in these situations, and I agree, there seems no pressing reason to find anything other than what you see; in fact the cultural references are usually a dodge and a distraction right off, a way of trying to account for what seems incomprehensible—how, say, Art and a mess of old tires could possibly be related. (And I don't mean to imply that they are, although they might be.)

Well, this was an unusual show. The gallery put out a fine brochure, tall and thin, called "Environments, Situations, Spaces," containing "statements" by each artist preceded by their handsome autographs. George Brecht is always clean as a clipped wing, airy, cheerful, and self-disappearing. He has a little white room just off the yard with a nice white chair in it, comfortable for a Cape Cod porch and adjoining Jim Dine's "Spring Cabinet." Brecht's autograph in the brochure is an inch wide. His first two statements are: A. nothing-special; b. no theory.

Inexhaustible List

Whereas Claes Oldenburg sears his page with a mud-luscious Whitmanesque catalogue of the materials of art, and for Oldenburg the list is inexhaustible because he is for an art that is everything, everything that is "that does something other than sit on its ass in a museum," and preferably everything that is *not* self-consciously refined, in other words that is raw, quick, smelly, holy, many small "sweet and stupid" acts of ungracious side-splitting, nose-blowing living that are supposed to be left for keeps in dirty abandoned corners. Oldenburg's "Store" has that unkempt look; the items hang in blobbish disregard for civilized order; the store articles are sculptured in relief with muslin strips dipped in plaster and placed over chicken wire, then painted with enamel to give the business a high dripping festive gloss.

These environments, situations, spaces are not going any place; they're not on the market for immortality; they're just not negotiable at all, except for tempting traffic with the eye and heart that is looking for more or less anything, or ready to stumble on something; and even that is saying too much, or too little, and no doubt Robert Whitman is right when he says that "this whole business has been complicated by people who say all smart things . . . "

—Jill Johnston

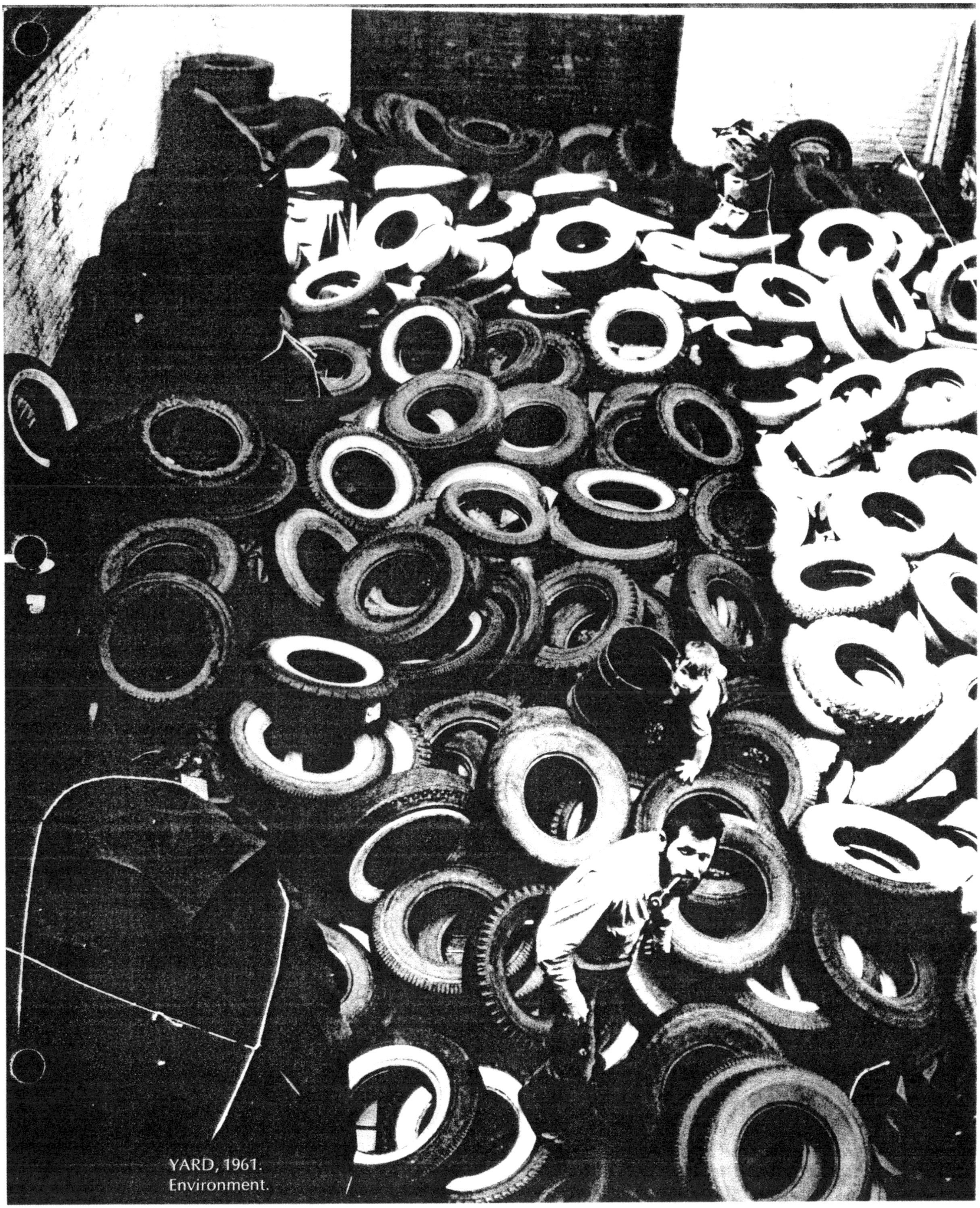

YARD, 1961.
Environment.

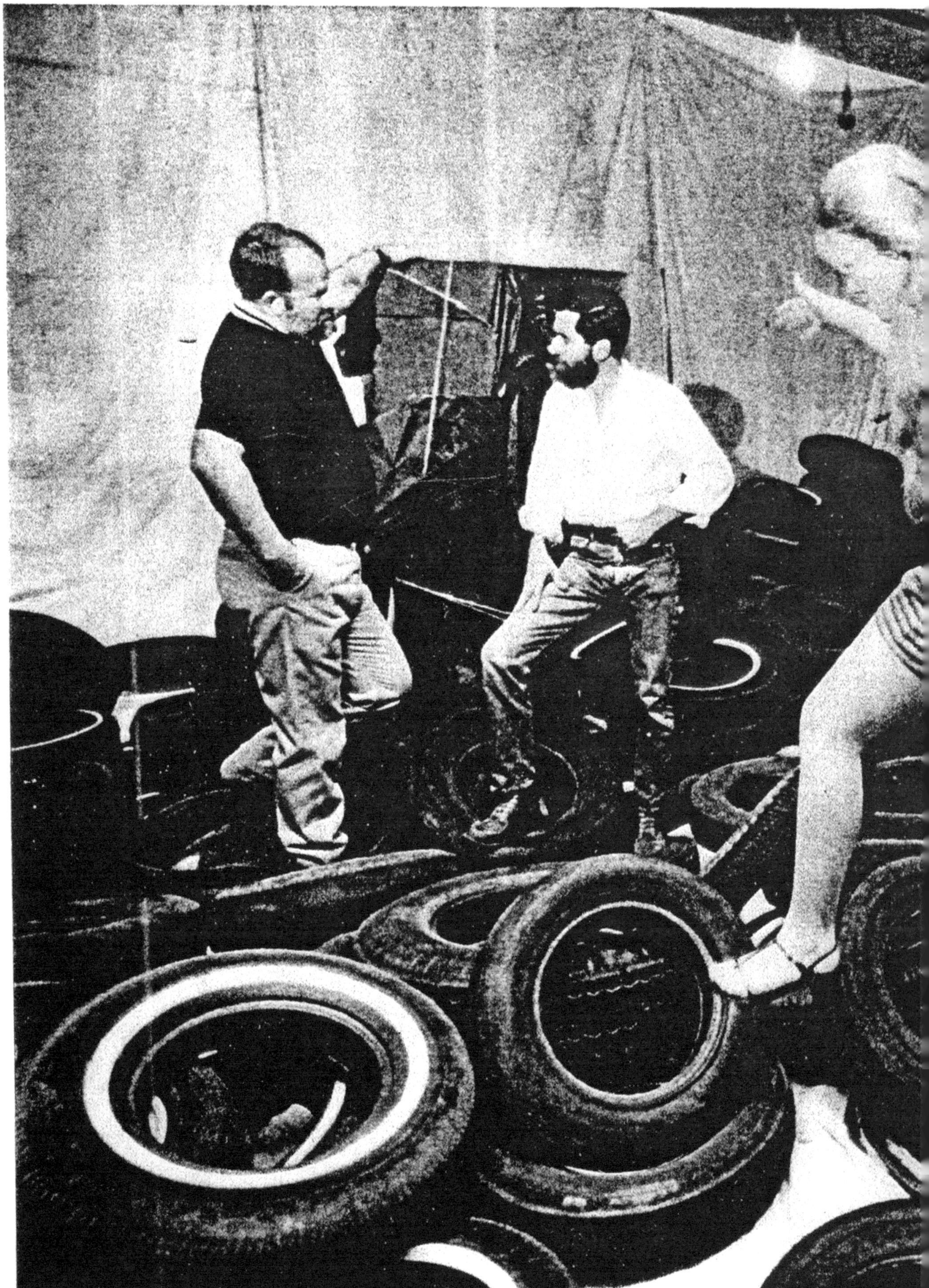

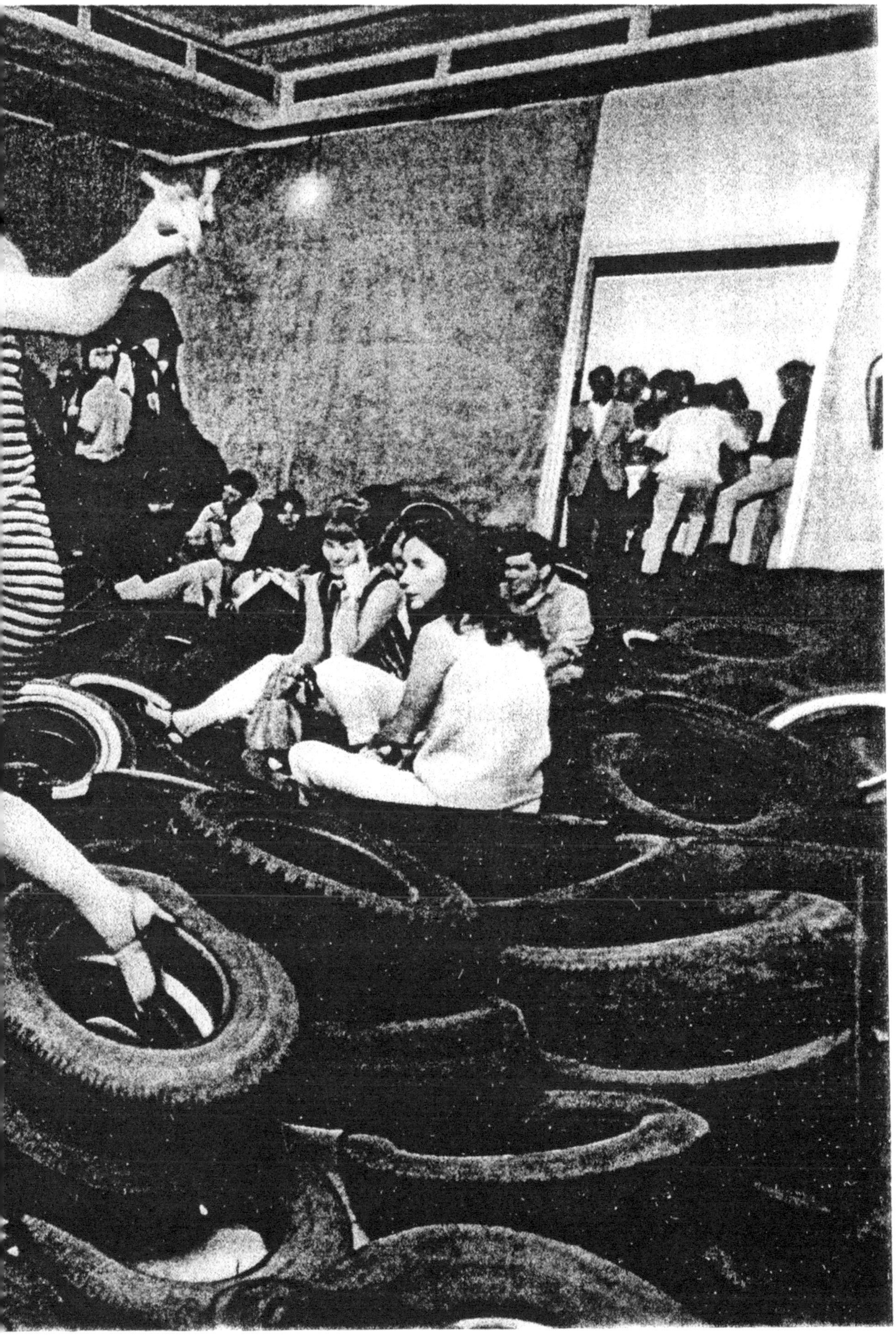

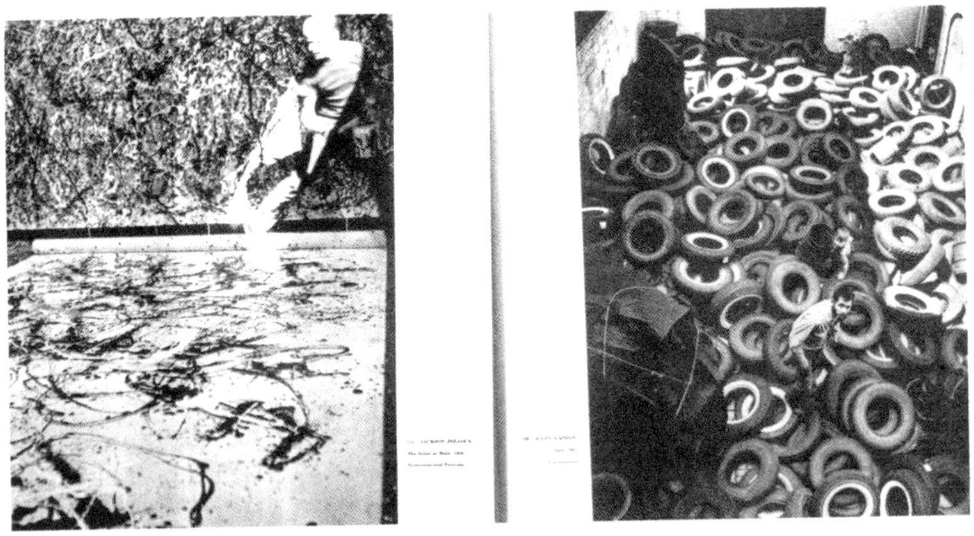

Spread from Allan Kaprow's *Assemblage, Environments and Happenings*, 1966. Photograph on left: Hans Namuth. Photograph on right: Ken Heyman/ Meridian Photographics.

ALLAN KAPROW

An Exhibition sponsored by the Art Alliance
of the Pasadena Art Museum

Pasadena Art Museum, September 15 through October 22, 1967
Washington University, St. Louis, February 1 through March 3, 1968
University of Texas, Austin, March 17 through April 28, 1968

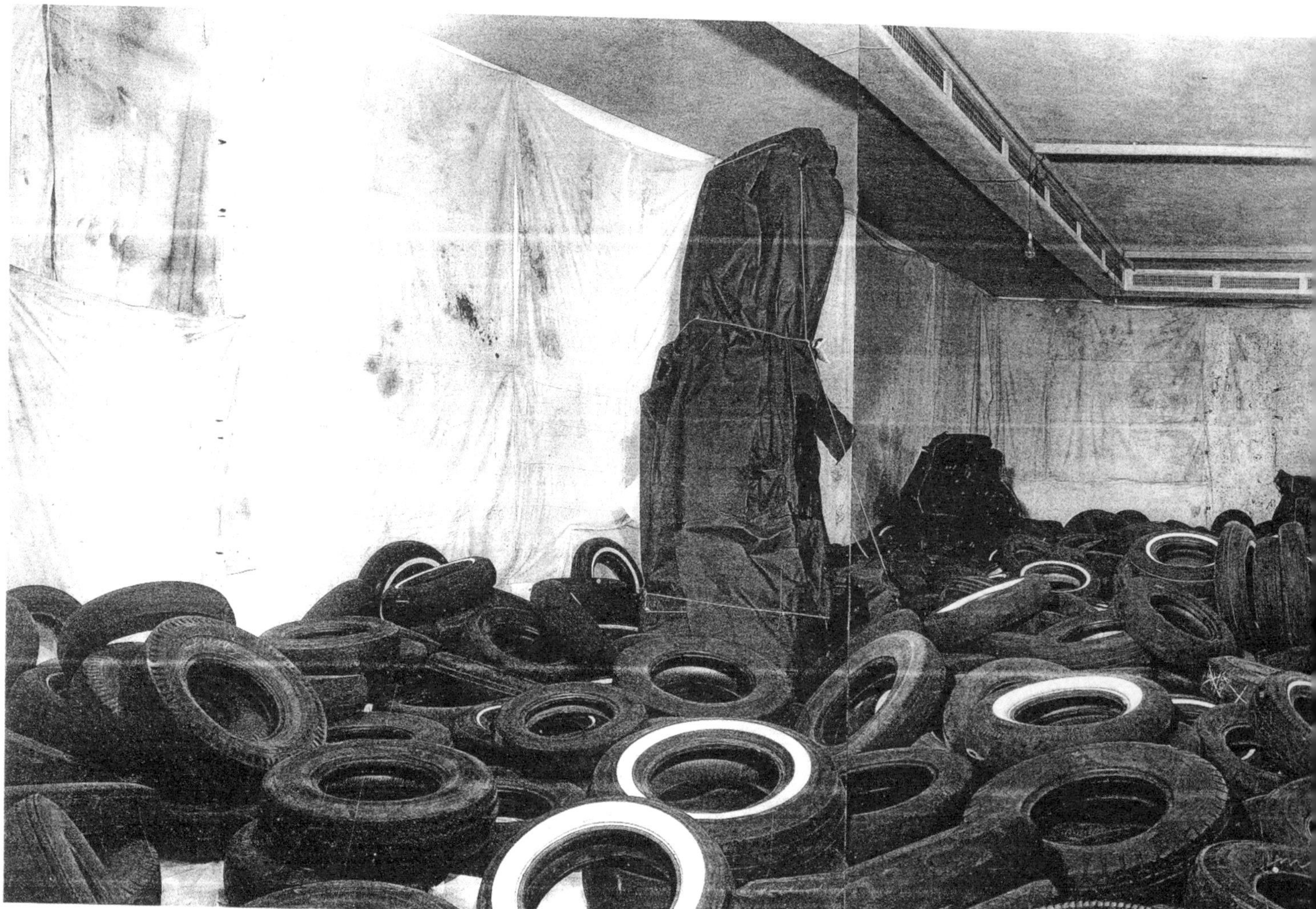

Yard, Pasadena Art Museum, 1967

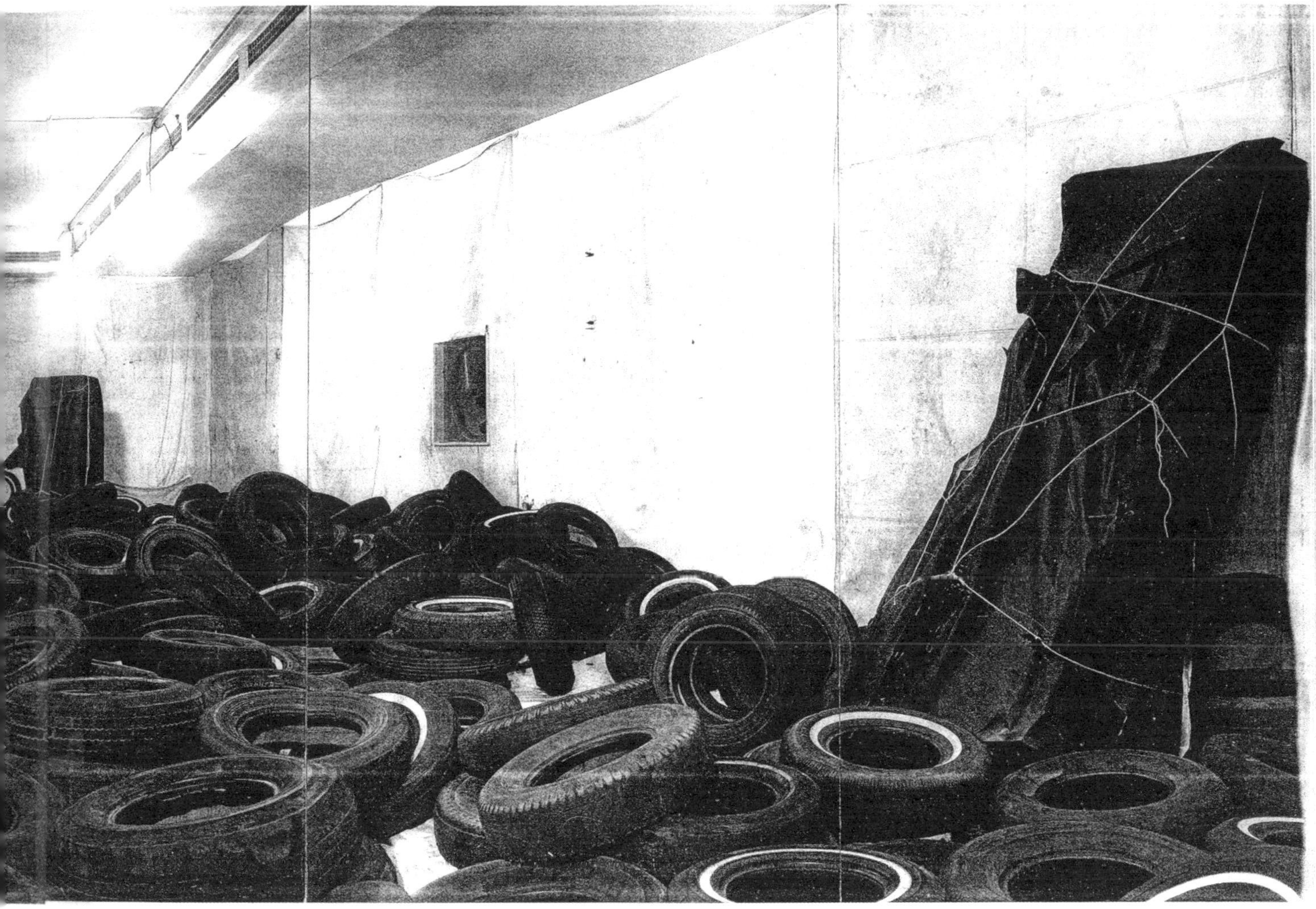

Art Gallery Encourages Rolling Tires

PASADENA, Calif. (AP) — The Pasadena Art Museum says its patrons can write on the walls, roll a few tires through the gallery and, if they feel like it, move some furniture.

At least they can in the new exhibit by Alan Kaprow—the man who created "happenings."

The 40-year-old New York artist opened his one-man show by turning one gallery into a tire dump, another into a lower middle-class living room and a third into divided enclosures of paintings about words and sound.

The galleries are like settings for happenings, and that's what Kaprow hopes they will turn out to be. He wants his viewers to participate in his art. The show, called "Environments," is a rebellion against a passive relation between art and the viewer, he said.

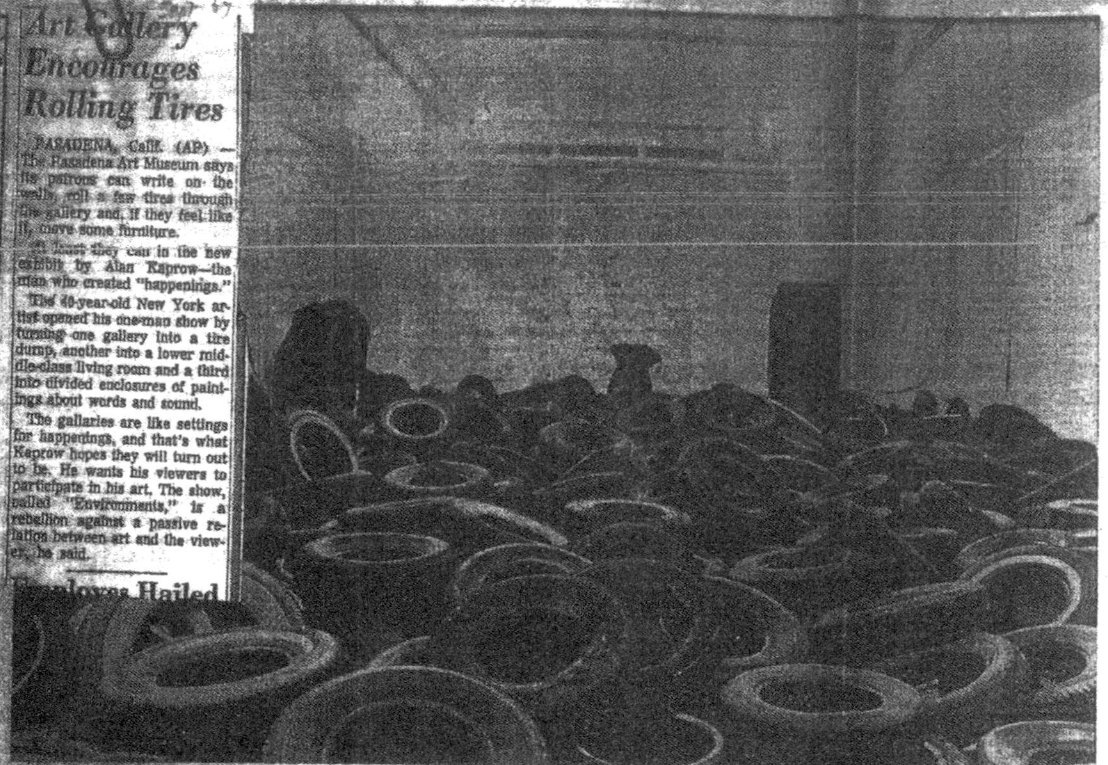

AN ENVIRONMENT—Included in artist Alan Kaprow's exhibit at the Pasadena Art Museum is this display of tires he calls An Environment. Times photo by Charles O'Rear

Kaprow Exhibition Yes, Charlie Brown You Can Call It Ar[t]

BY WILLIAM WILSON

Los Angeles Times
CC PART III
LETTERS—TV
SATURDAY, SEPTEMBER 16, 1967

Alan Kaprow seems to contradict himself a lot. For example, he doesn't altogether like museums, yet he is having an exhibition at the Pasadena Art Museum. He is concerned about people, yet his work is mainly abstract. Forms he has invented are supposed to create personal responses, yet they are public forms.

These evident contradictions are enough to bend a linear mind into a pretzel of confusion, yet Kaprow has an amazing and creative way of resolving these contradictions.

The Pasadena Museum doesn't look like a museum since Kaprow's exhibition opened there Thursday night. One gallery has been turned into a tire dump, another has become a lower-middle class living room, a third has been divided into enclosures containing words and sounds.

Unlike a Museum

Even the gallery that contains Kaprow's older, more conventional art looked very unlike a museum when I viewed the show before it was completely installed. A radio blared rock, an assistant lettered words, and Hal Glicksman and Barbara Berman of the museum bustled happily about amid ladders and sawhorses. Kaprow himself moved calmly as if to maintain the dignity of a full chestnut beard that adorns his youthful face.

At 40, the New York artist is world-famous as the inventor of the form called "A Happening." He seems to have created them partly out of disgust with the passive relation between art and viewer. The rooms in the museum are called "Environments." They are like settings for a Happening. In them, the viewer is encouraged to roll tires, move furniture, write on walls or just generally carry on any way that seems appropriate to the situation.

A Moral Jolt

The works are partly a tool directed against [illegible] ... amount of calculation that tends [to] manipulate the viewer into certa[in] patterns of action and thought th[at] is inimical to work that wants t[he] viewer to be creative.

Today everything from the Vi[et]nam War to cosmetics is bei[ng] called a Happening. Kaprow deni[es] that any event of which we becom[e] intensely aware or any action whi[ch] involves us deeply is a Happenin[g]. Kaprow's disguised art has been [so] successful in the deception that it [is] not art at all, that its popularity h[as] involved still another contradictio[n].

If anything is proved by t[he] present exhibition, it is that Kapro[w] makes art and does so out of [a] profound knowledge of its conte[m]porary history added to his ow[n] deepest feelings.

The gallery containing his pain[t]ings and collage of the 50s expos[es] aspects of an artistic character th[at] carries consistently into the enviro[n]ments. We see a concern for perso[n]al expression in a brushy figurati[ve] painting that recalls German E[x]pressionism, subjects that reveal [a] fascination with the life of the city, [a] landscape made of the spontaneou[s]ly splashed expletives "Ha!", "Ah[!]" and "Oh!" reveal liveliness, wit an[d] a suggestion of concern with th[e] theoretical reality of words.

They Backed Their Creed With Action

BY ELLEN SHULTE
Times Staff Writer

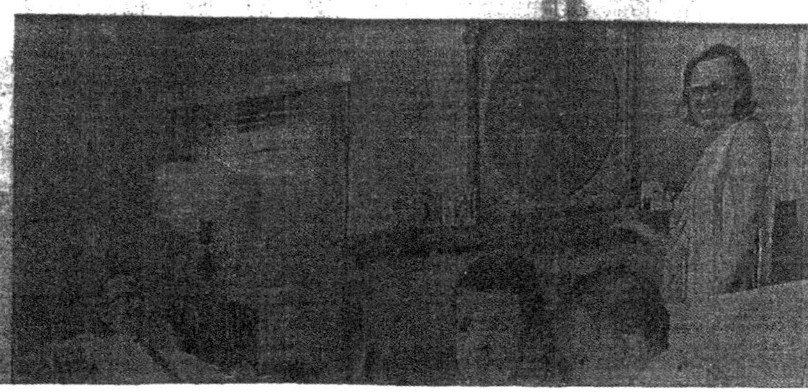

"This household welcomes neighbors of any faith, race or nationality. We ask only that they be good neighbors, as we shall try to be."

This notice, which greets guests at the entrance to the J. Winter Cobb home in Eagle Rock, is more than just words. It is the key to the couple's philosophy of life—backed up by the most personal kind of action, namely by adoptions of children with mixed backgrounds.

These adoptions, moreover, [illegible] "second family" for the couple, [illegible] two children were already grown.

The [illegible]

Our Servicemen

. . . . Here and Abroad

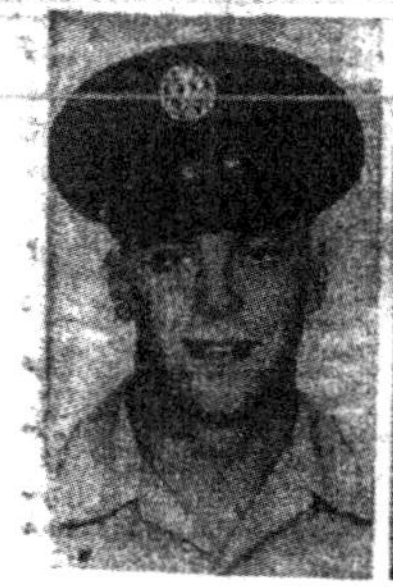

CALIO PATRONAGGIO

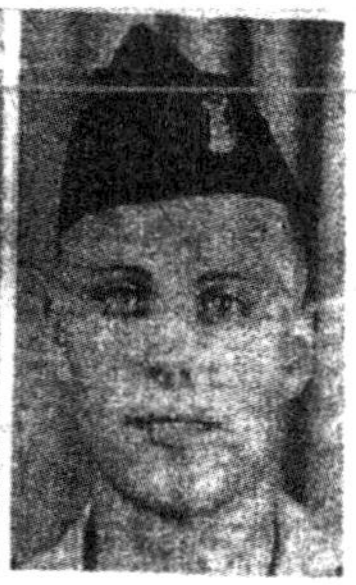

ROBERT McLINN

Airman Calio O. Patronaggio, son of Mr. and [illegible]rs. John L. White of 1621 S. Fifth St., Alhambra, [illegible]as been selected for technical training at Chanute [illegible]FB, Ill., as an Air Force missile facilities spe[illegible]alist.

Patronaggio is a 1966 graduate of Alhambra [illegible]igh School.

Robert L. McLinn, son of Mrs. Glory A.C. Hees [illegible]4556 Indiana Ave., La Canada, recently completed [illegible] six-week Air Force Reserve Officers Training [illegible]rps field training encampment at Fairchild AFB, [illegible]ash. He is a student at UCLA.

Thomas H. Kirkeby, 22, son of Mr. and Mrs. Wayne Kirkeby, 1505 Second St., Alhambra, has [illegible]en awarded the American Spirit Honor Medal at [illegible]e end of eight weeks of basic combat training at [illegible]t. Campbell, Ky.

The award is made to the trainee who best [illegible]emonstrates honor, loyalty and high example to [illegible]is fellow soldiers during basic training.

Army Spec. 4 Alan W. Lenaburg, 20, son of Mr. and Mrs. William A. Lenaburg, of 11112 W. Hondo Parkway, Temple City, has been assigned to the 11th Armored Cavalry Regiment near Long Giao, Vietnam.

Pvt. Richard Domholt, 20, son of Mrs. Gladys Domholt, 407 N. Mentor Ave., Pasadena, has completed a five-week course at the Army Aviation School at Ft. Rucker, Alabama, as a Flight Operations Specialist.

Domholt, who took his basic training at Ft. Ord, [illegible]s a 1965 graduate of Pasadena High School and attended Pasadena City College.

Airman Joseph R. Saldana, son of Mr. and Mrs. [illegible]oseph S. Saldana of 200 San Miguel Road, Pasadena, has been selected for technical training at [illegible]owry AFB, Colo., as a supply specialist.

The airman, who recently completed basic training at Amarillo AFB, Tex., is a 1965 graduate of John Muir High School and attended PCC.

Marine Maj. Royal N. Moore Jr., whose wife, Patricia, resides in Pasadena, has been presented his 4th Air Medal while serving with the 1st Marine Aircraft Wing in Vietnam.

He was awarded the Air Medal for outstanding achievement in aerial flight and for courage and devotion to duty in the face of hazardous flying conditions.

Airman Joel E. Bursdall, son of Mr. and Mrs. Edmond J. Bursdall of 2209 Brigden Road, Pasadena, has been selected for technical training at Chanute AFB, Ill., as a missile equipment repairman.

Bursdall, who is a 1965 graduate of Pasadena

Crime War Gets Support

Petition Asks Police Pay Hike

By WANDA TUCKER
Staff Writer

First major public reaction to Police Chief Sam Addis' plea last week for an aroused citizenry and higher pay for Pasadena police to combat crime in Pasadena came at Tuesday's Board of City Directors meeting, as board members accepted a petition.

The petition asks that Pasadena's policemen receive the highest pay in Los Angeles County "in order to secure for our city the best possible law enforcement officers in adequate numbers and to keep for the city its present experienced law enforcement officers."

The petition signed by 50 persons, was presented by Mrs. Robert Kegel of 65 Malcolm Drive, a private citizen, who said she [illegible] that additional petitions will be filed soon.

[illegible] Kegel later told this newspaper that she acted after reading a story detailing Chief Addis' view and after talking to several police officers whose morale, she said, is extremely low, partly because of the pay issue.

Mrs. Kegel said that she spent last Friday on the phone, talking to about 100 persons who promised to send letters on the subject to Mayor Boyd P. Welin, who was absent Tuesday.

Monday, she added, she secured the signatures on her petition in between getting her children off to and home from school. She found, she reported, a widespread feeling that steps must be taken to correct Pasadena's police problem.

In addition to paying Pasadena policemen the highest salaries in the county, the petition requests "that the Pasadena City Police Department shall not be subjected to undue restraints in the performance of its duties in the enforcement of the law, the keeping of the public peace, and the protection of the person and property of the people."

The petition also asks the city, through its various agencies, to "establish an intensive public relations campaign with the object of securing a better understanding and increased cooperation between the people and the city Police Department.

"In particular," the petition adds, "efforts should be made through the public school sys-

POLICE: See Page B-4

STAR-NEWS
SOUTHERN CALIFORNIA'S [illegible] EVENING NEWSPAPER
A-5-H PAGE B-1—PASADENA, CALIF., WEDNESDAY, SEPT. 13, 1967

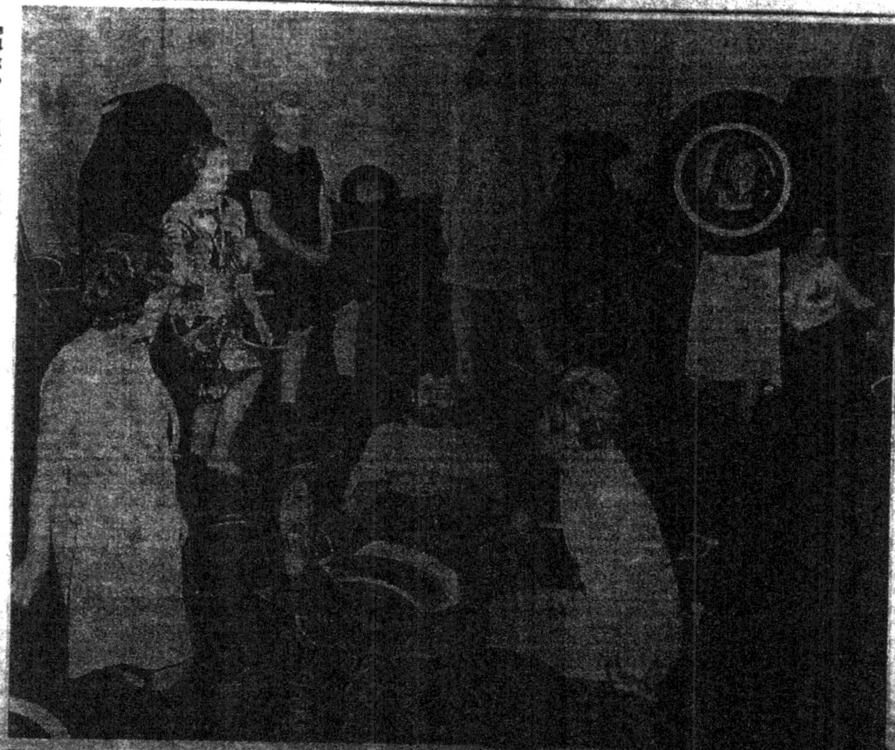

ENVIRONMENTAL RECAP—The Docents, who provide free guided tours of Pasadena Art Museum exhibitions, may [illegible] exploring Allan Kaprow's environment called "[illegible]" Kaprow and museum curator [illegible] [illegible]

Board Endorses New Community Stabilization Plan

Pasadena's Board of City Directors Tuesday gave its endorsement to the citizens' volunteer group known as PRIDE and approved the general concept of a community stabilization program.

Earlier, the board had approved a related item, asking City Manager John D. Phillips and City Attorney Wendell Thompson to prepare the necessary documents for a police-community relations advisory committee, with the understanding that it will not be a police review board.

The police-community relations advisory duties may become a function of the city's Human Relations Committee, as may the community stabilization program. One of PRIDE's aims, as outlined by Chairman Albert Lowe, is community stabilization.

The community stabilization program, designed to maintain the racial balance of the community as various neighborhoods integrate, is already in use in Inglewood, where a Community Stabilization Committee has that duty plus others similar to those now held by Pasadena's human relations group.

Referred to Phillips

Director Robert W. Oliver, who first mentioned the program, made the motion approving the general concept and referring it to Phillips to recommend how the function can best be carried out.

Vice Mayor C. Bernard Cooper expressed his hope that the end result would be a broadening of the powers of the Human Relations Committee and an increase in its size, getting [illegible]

Veterans To Receive Unit's Aid

By BRENT BOWELL
Staff Writer

Pasadena's Human Relations Committee Tuesday night decided to go ahead with original plans to send a letter to veterans' organizations calling for "an appropriate community acceptance of returning servicemen."

But the committee will add a paragraph inviting veterans' organizations to join with the Human Relations Committee in furthering community acceptance of returning servicemen regardless of race.

In another matter, the committee took note of the Board of City Directors' action Tuesday in approving the principle of a "Police - Community Relations Advisory Committee" and [illegible] particular stress on the importance of future appointments to the Human Relations Committee being made with attention to the qualifications of appointees in dealing with [illegible]

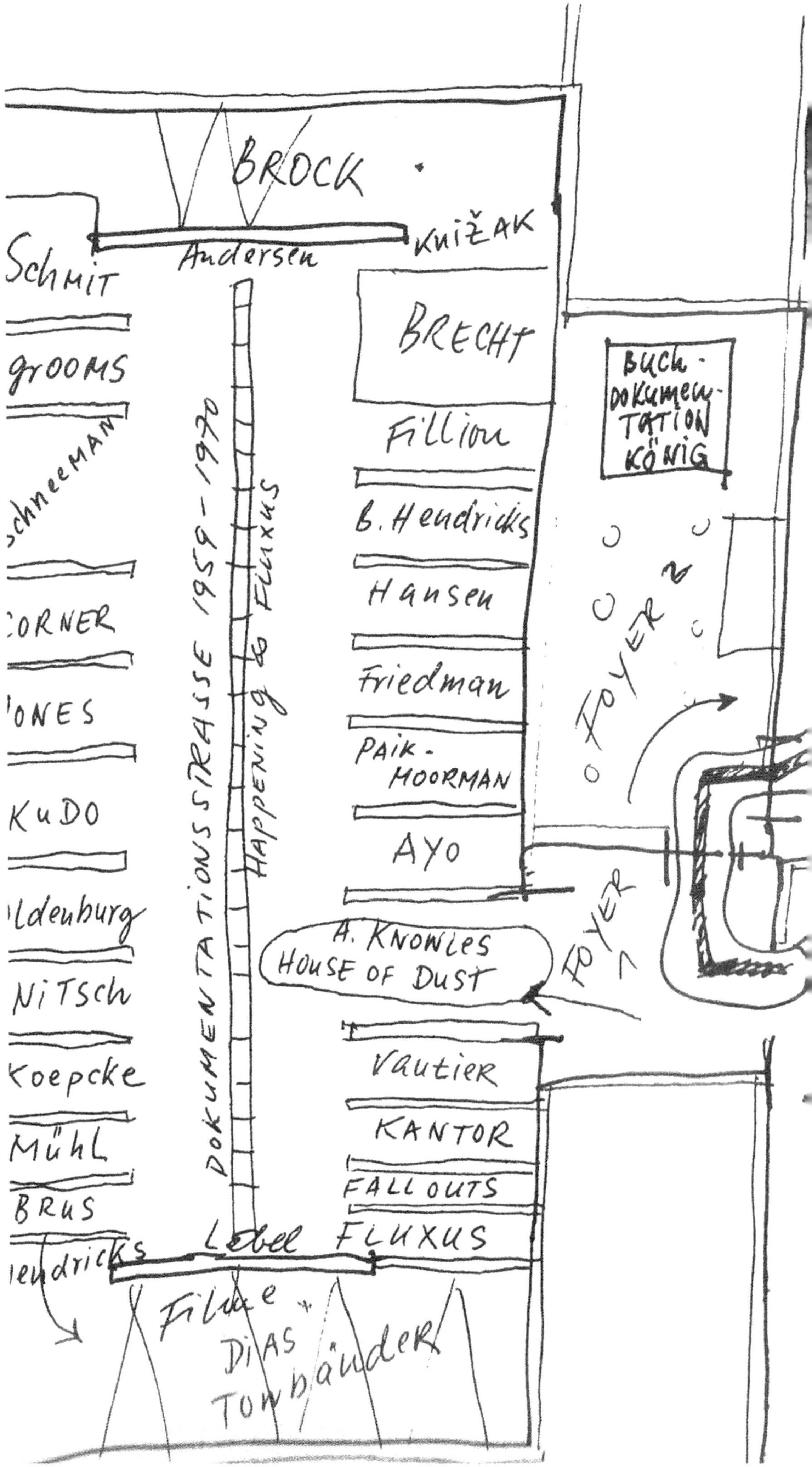

BROCK
KNIŽAK
Andersen
Schmit
BRECHT
grooms
BUCH-DOKUMENTATION KÖNIG
Schneeman
Filliou
B. Hendricks
CORNER
Hansen
JONES
Friedman
DOKUMENTATIONSSTRASSE 1959–1970
Happening & Fluxus
FOYER 2
PAIK-MOORMAN
KuDO
AYO
Oldenburg
A. KNOWLES HOUSE OF DUST
FOYER 1
NiTsch
Vautier
Koepcke
KANTOR
Mühl
FALLOUTS
BRUS
Lebel
FLUXUS
Hendricks
Filme + DIAS TONBÄNDER

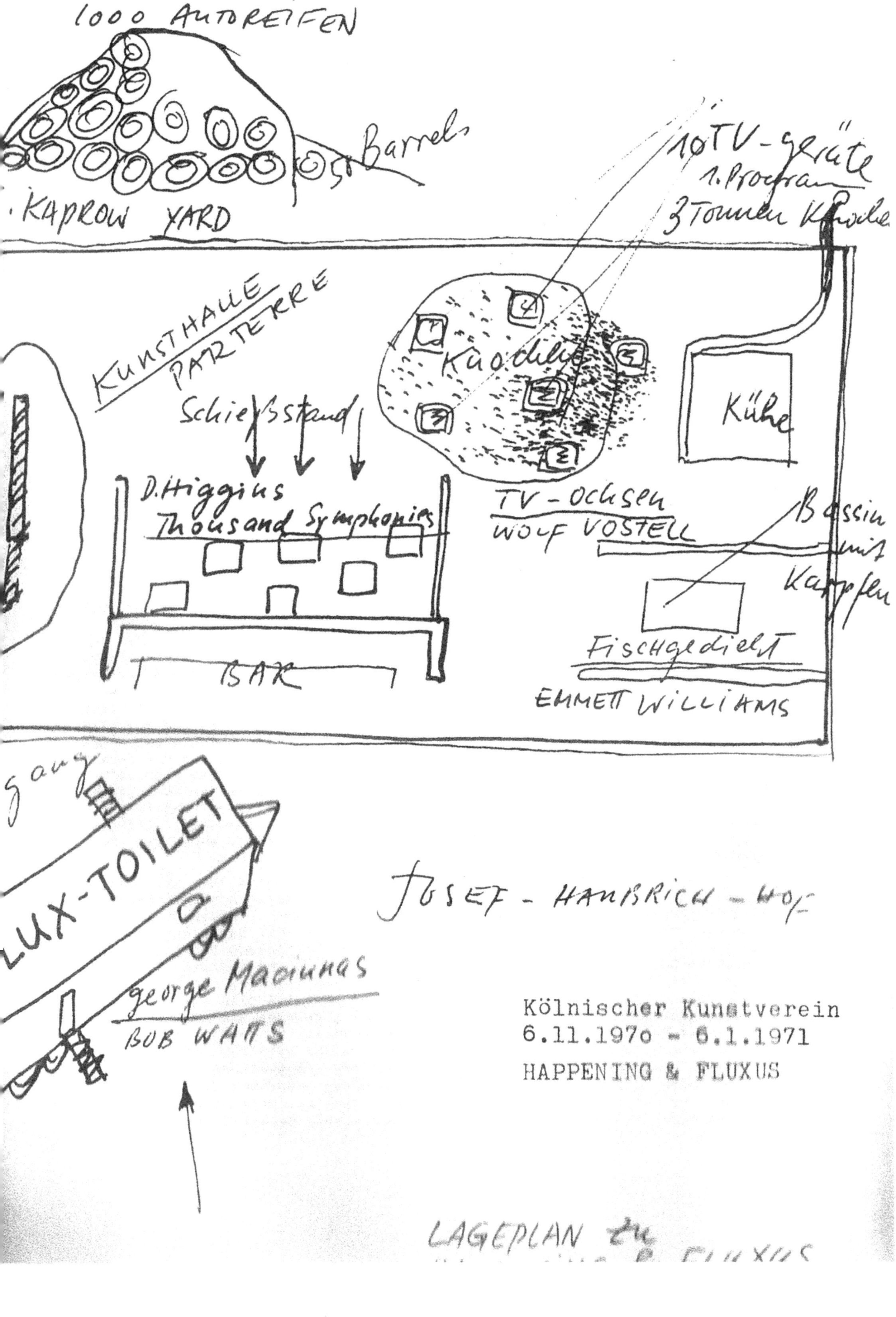

Kölnischer Kunstverein
6.11.197o - 6.1.1971
HAPPENING & FLUXUS

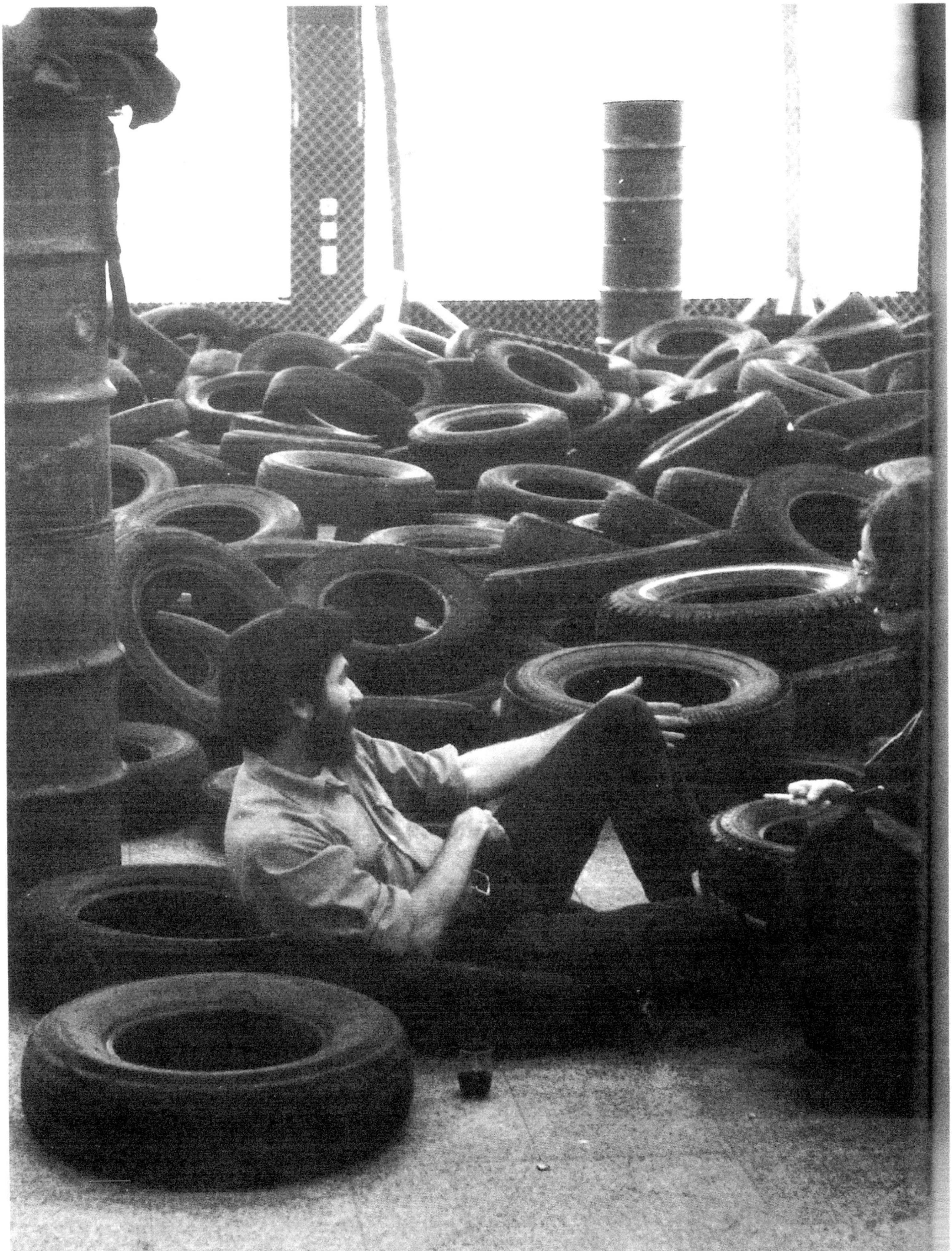

YARD

This version of my 1961 Environment was made for the "Happening - Fluxus" retrospective in Cologne (1971). It was inside the Kunstverein instead of outside; it was surrounded by a wire fence and metal barrels, instead of stone walls. And old wooden crates were buried among the tyres instead of small blue barrels. Otherwise, visitors had the freedom to climb around the tyres and rearrange them at will.

- ALLAN KAPROW
Allan Kaprow
Photos: Dick Higgins
(copied 1975)

SCHWARZ

16. Oktober – 29. November 1981

herausgegeben von Hannah Weitemeier
in Zusammenarbeit mit der
STÄDTISCHEN KUNSTHALLE DÜSSELDORF
Direktor Jürgen Harten

Inhalt

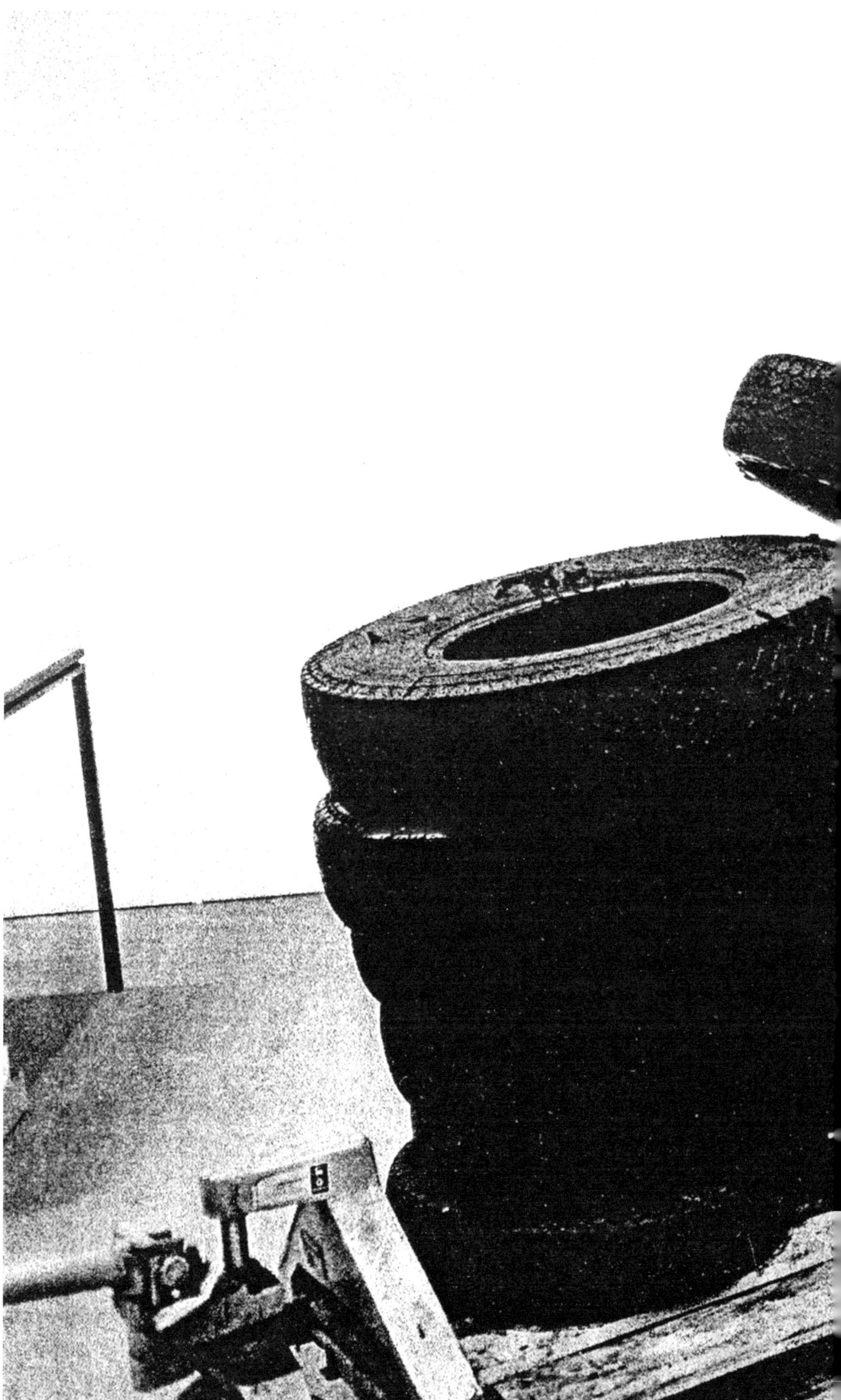

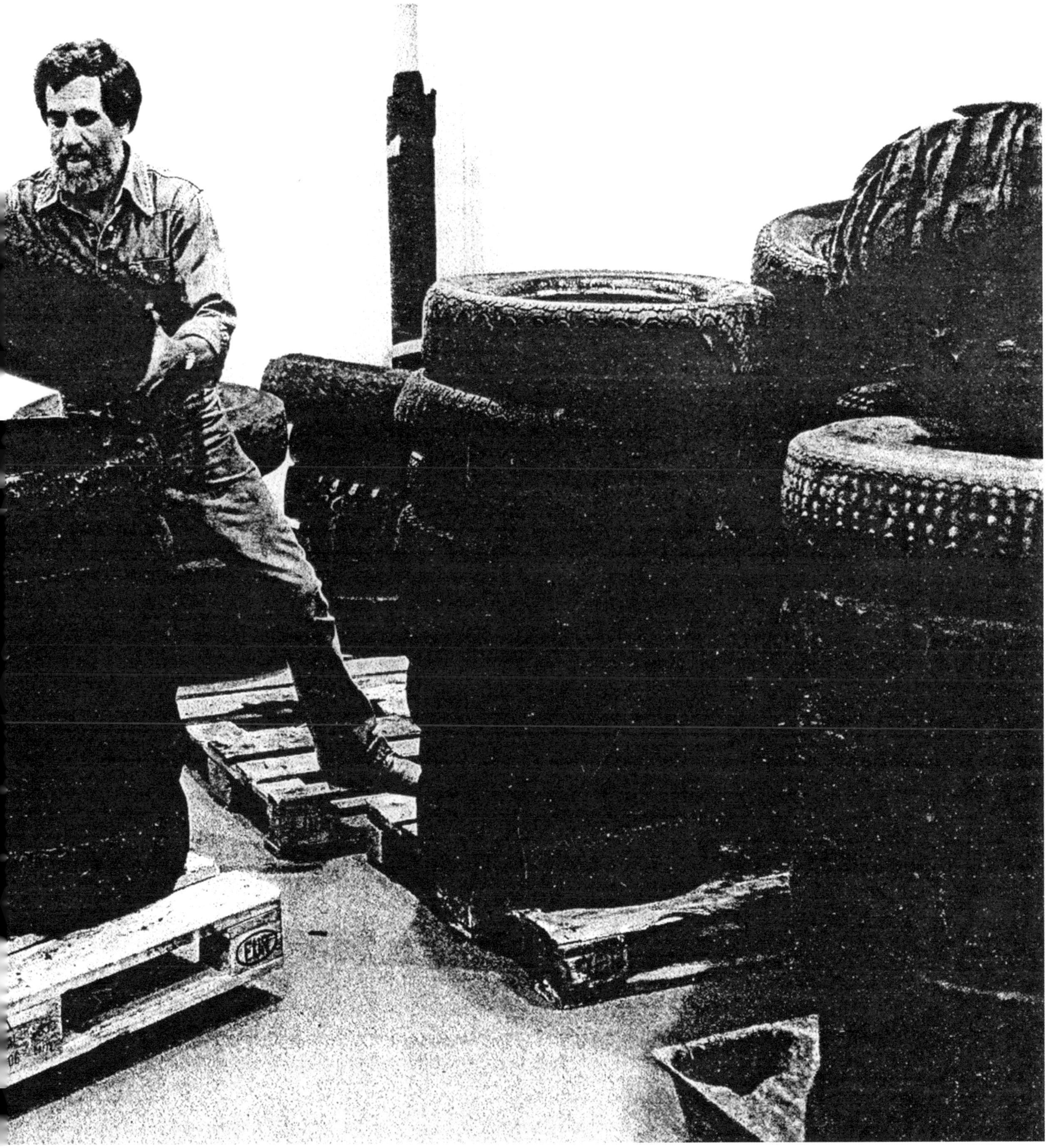

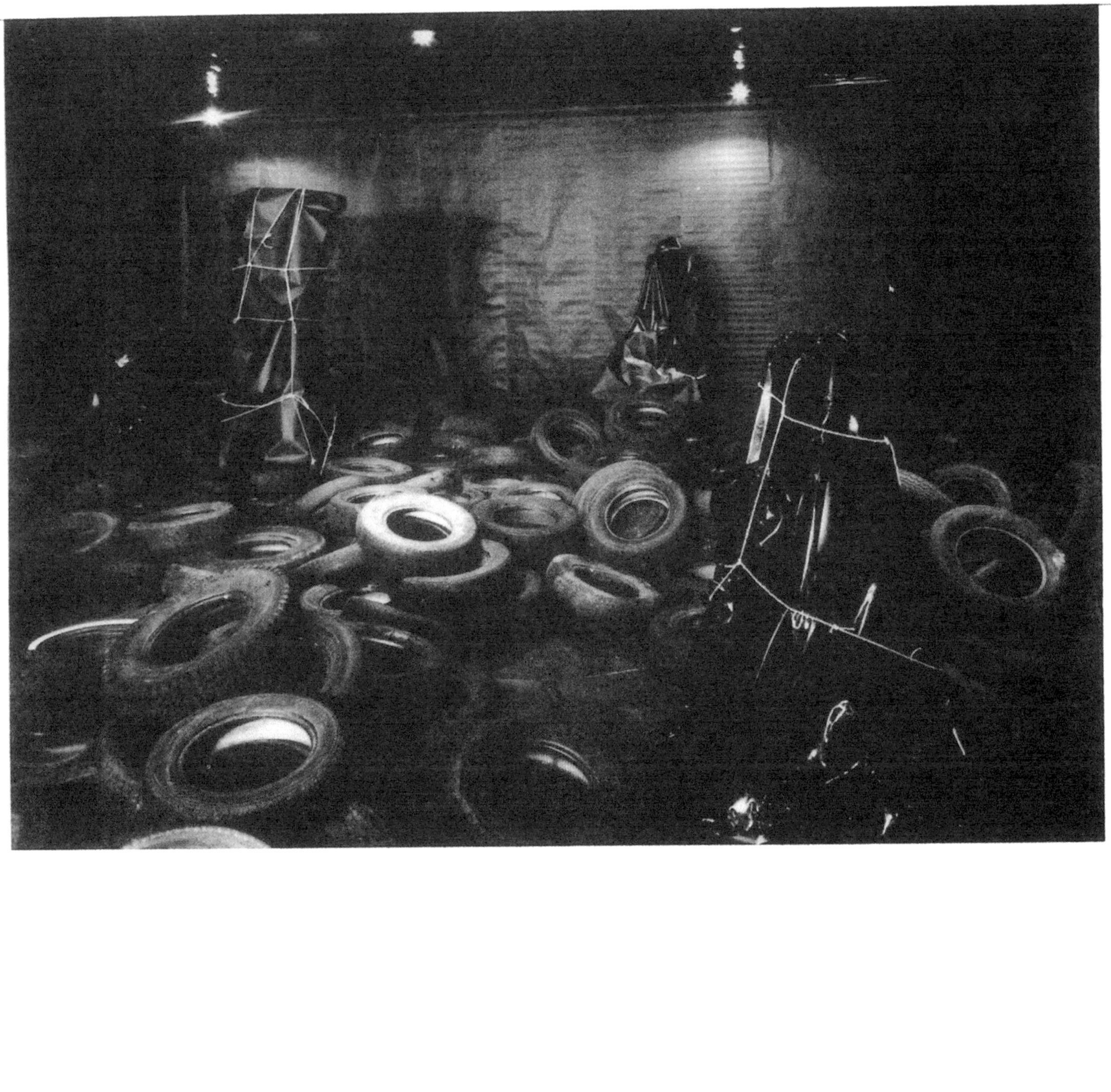

Städtische Kunsthalle
Düsseldorf

4 Düsseldorf 1
Grabbeplatz 4
Postfach 1120

(02 11) 8 99 — 62 43 / 62 44

Mr. Allan Kaprow
Box 2336
Rancho Sta. Fé
California 92067
U.S.A.

December 9, 1981
SK/fd

Dear Allan:

As I have not been in Düsseldorf almost during the whole duration of the "BLACK" exhibition, you are hearing only today from me.

The exhibition terminated with an interesting and well attended panel discussion, on November 29, 1981.

According to the enclosed press reviews you can see that the reaction to this exhibition was quite controversial, as regards the art-critics. With the public it was similar, although part of the visitors reacted spontaneously. A lady from Bremen, who had visited the exhibition, sent us a completely burned cake, with the remark: "If that which you show is art, than this is housewife-art". We have shown all the reactions of the visitors in a show-case.

The visitors have duly played in your environment. Once, all the tires had been piled up to high towers, fortunately the towers resisted.

I had no news in the meantime from Dany Keller. I shall call her one of these days.

As you revealed your knowledge of German only very slowly, the enclosed cuttings will be a kind of exercise material for you.

Best wishes,

Klaus

Klaus Schrenk

Notes on "Yard"

The Environment "Yard" was first made for the backyard of the Martha Jackson Gallery of New York, in 1961. Put into the backyard, the heaps of old tires and tarpaper felt somewhat cut off from the aesthetic of the inside gallery, and from the other art works exhibited there. It reminded you less of art (in those days) than of an industrial dump. I was pleased.

The move to the outside of the gallery was part of a series of steps I had been taking since 1956. I wanted to develop an art which would depart radically from the art history and contexts we traditionally associate with art. It wasn't enough to make new kinds of painting or sculpture; it wasn't enough to invent new genres such as kinetic assemblage. What was needed, I believed, was to leave the galleries, museums, stages and concert halls, for the everyday world. (Later, I would include the inner "spaces" of our heads and bodies.)

By 1962, the break was completed. All my environmental and performative work since then (some 140 pieces has been carried out in the real world we live in: kitchens, trams, telephone booths, the countryside, freeways, our stomachs, minds, feelings, social interactions, etc.

Thus, when I do occasionally exhibit, it is not to show the work of the last twenty years, but earlier paintings and collages, or transitional Environments such as "Yard". Or I might exhibit documents of the

-o-outside events. These are appropriat for exhibition. The outside events themselves are not.

In recreating "Yard" indoors, I have camouflaged the space provided to create a strong contrast to the museum's normal clean, neutral look. So, while "Yard" was initially seen in daylight, here it is dark, and probably feels like a coal cellar rather than a dump. That's okay.

Otherwise it, is roughly the same. Visitors today, as in 1961, are invited to come into the Environment, to walk and jump on the tires, and to move them about if they wish. The five mounds are fixed elements; the tires are changeable.

As an historical note, when I first made "Yard" I thought of the mounds as rocks off a wild coastline; the tires as the sea. I also thought of that great Japanese rock garden in Kyoto: the temple of Ryoanji. But it became a dump. Now perhaps it has become a coal cellar...

– Allan Kaprow
1988

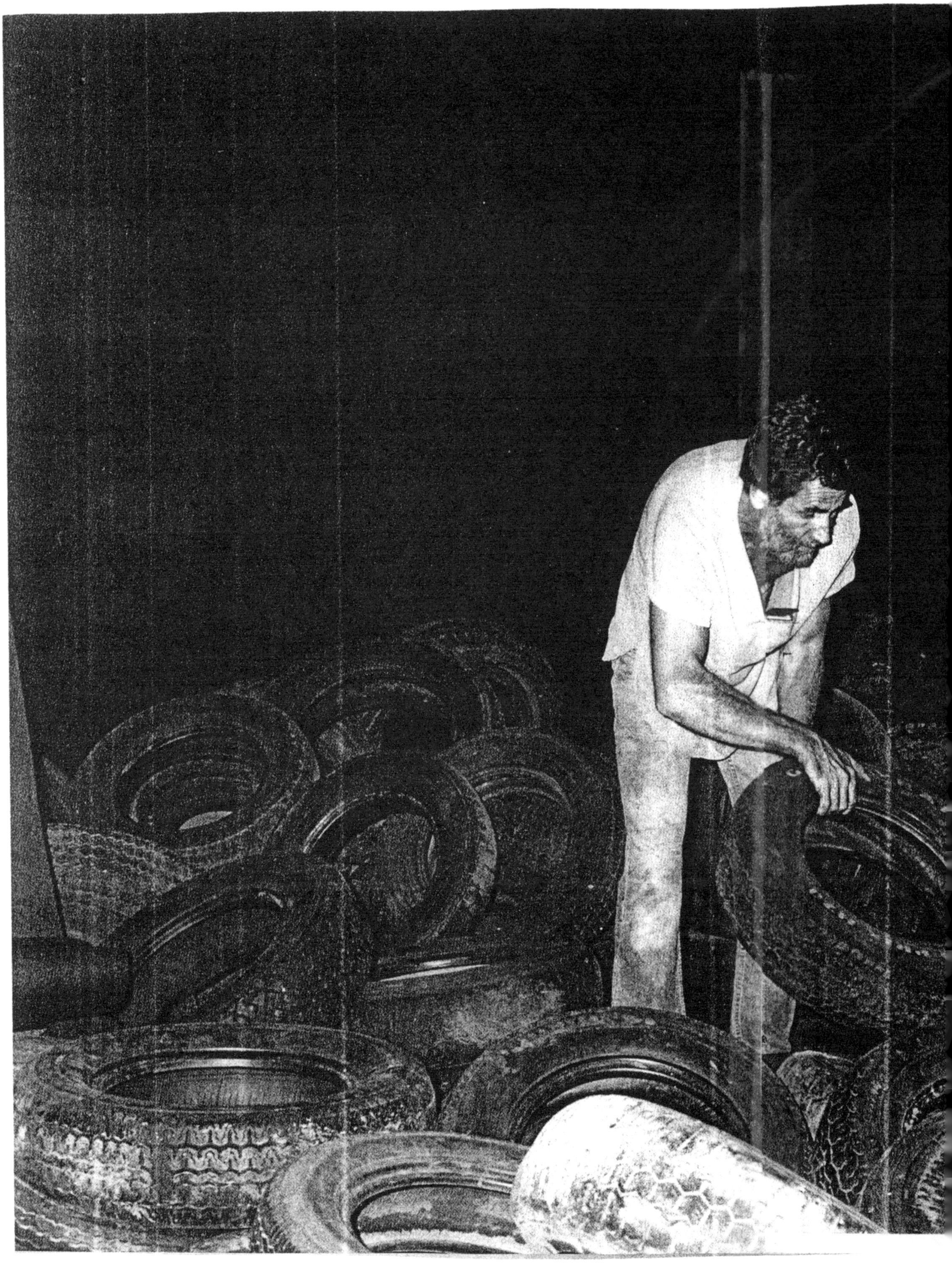

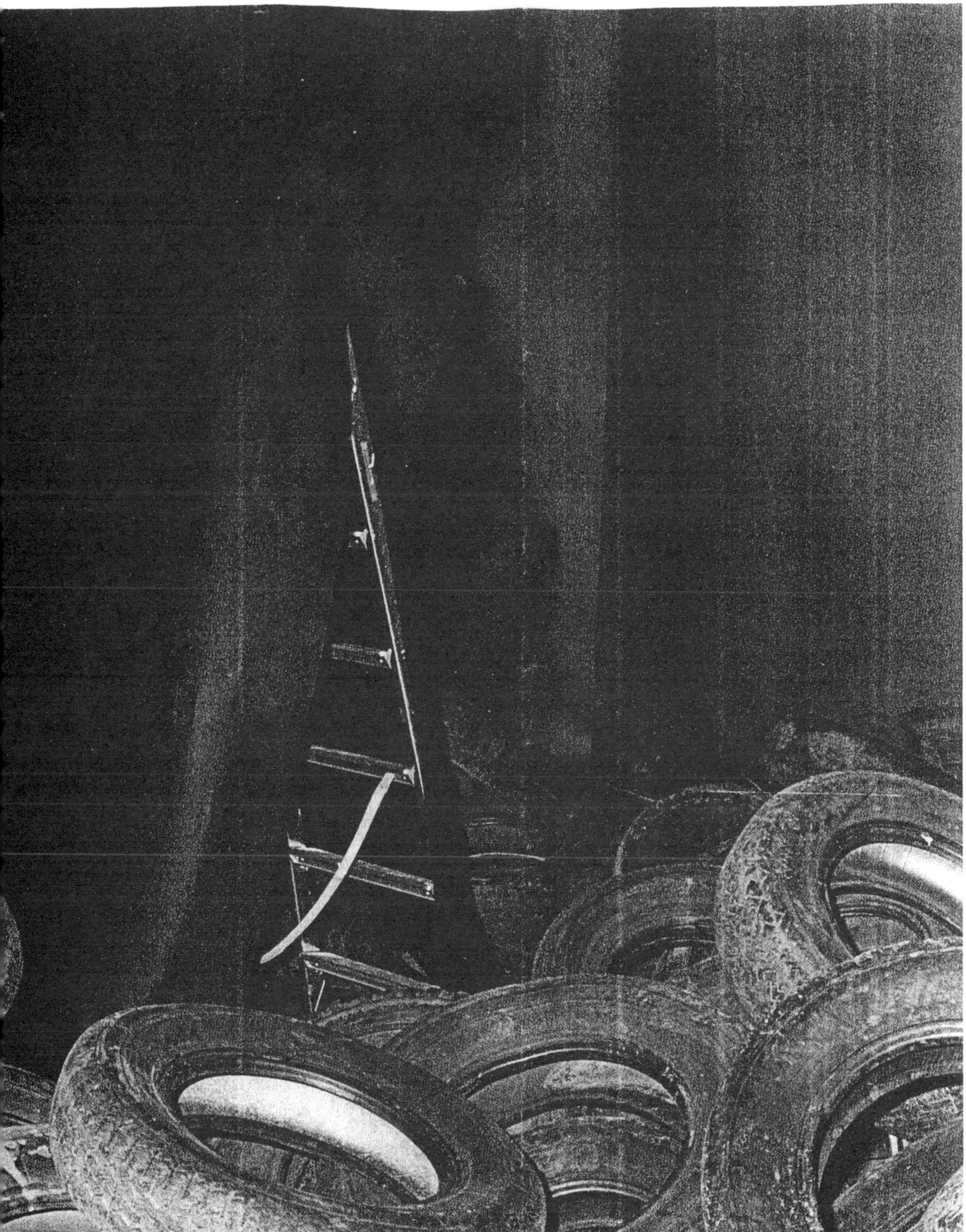

12:00 noon
Aug 12, 84
Corner B'way / Canal (@ City Bank) (!)
#6 Ave Lex line
RR also (only local)

Dear Barbara —

Your proposal is insane! but, as I telegrammed, it's possible if we all can work intensively well before the actual floor work begins. "Words" is of the most difficult piece to reassemble because there's so much hands-on work to be done. Here's the general plan.

First: "Yard" can be done in the pit. The proportions are different but can be an advantage for maximum impact. Entry should be from the side wall for appropriate feeling of the scale and mass of tires. A rough wooden fence should be made as sketched on plan, with 3'2" opening accessed by steps.

Inside, we'll need quite a lot of tires: easily 1,000 of them. The walls and floor should be completely covered with tarpaper (though when I see the space again this might be modified somewhat). Wooden inner forms to cover with tarpaper and rope will be constructed in the floor areas, as approximately indicated on plan, i.e.

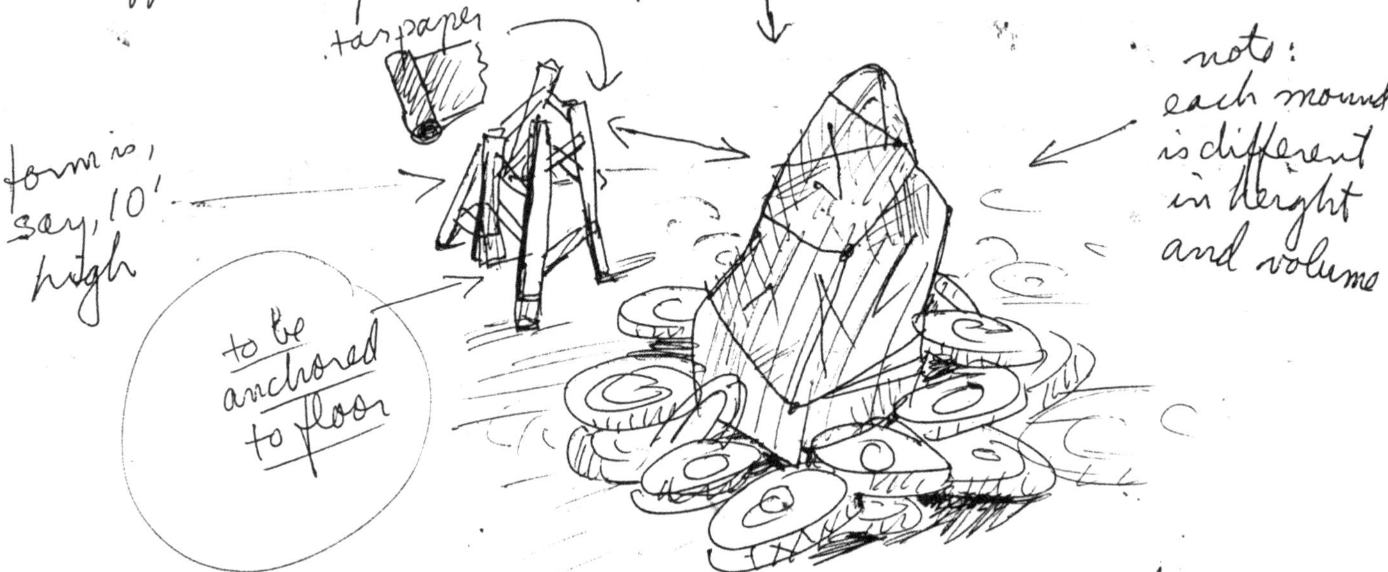

So, what must be arranged in advance are: used tires to be delivered and removed (dumps don't like to have them back!); enough rolls of tarpaper to cover space and mounds (3 rolls are sufficient, I think, for the mounds alone); 1,000 feet roll of heavy hemp twine 3/16" thick approximately; enough scrap wood (2"x4"s, 2"x3"s, 2"x2"s for the inner forms, plus anchoring tape to adhere to the floor [or equivalent method); rough construction lumber (used if possible) for the fence and steps; wire mesh for the fence, say, 8'x16' of it. (The fence will keep of/ the tires inside, since people will play with them and otherwise throw them outside into the galleries ....)

Second: "Words" was, and should be, small in scale; it needs psychological compression to make sense. It had two spaces: a "public" one full of "noise", auditory and visual; and a "private" one, smaller yet, darker, and quiet — both roughly equivalent to everyone's outer and inner experiences. So, I've reduced the space you've allowed by cutting off the triangle in it (as you'll see by the plan modification I'm sending back). That gives ~~us~~ us a room 9'x 10', and ~~[illegible]~~ one 10'x 7'; about the same as the original. Outside the entry was a cardboard sign ~~[illegible]~~ in the form of a 5' or 6' box of cartonboard lit from within with the cut-out words in freehand saying "Words" — see the photo in my book.

Inside the public room were word-strips randomly combined in rows covering the walls. ~~[illegible]~~ On the far wall separating the larger from the smaller room, were two flanking cloth rolls with words stencilled on them. (These were to be rolled and aligned, or not, ad lib.) Tacked to a center pole were stacks of additional word strips, to be taken by visitors and added (by staple guns provided along the walls) to those already there on the walls. Throughout the space were roughly torn cartonboard signs advising you to "make words!" "roll the rolls!" etc. A stepladder was provided for this process; at any moment three or four people could be tacking away.... ¶At the same time, around the center post (a 2"x 2") were small tables with three ~~[illegible]~~ children's record players; and signs advising one to play one or more of them at any time, singly or at once. These players had records of me saying words in various ways set upon their turntables.

Around the top edge of this public room were alternating red + white 25 watt bulbs flashing on and off (like a second-hand car lot, I thought). These added to the visual noise. (PLEASE SEE P. 6 FOR DRAWING)

The second, private, room was entered by a central doorway

BLAM!

THE EXPLOSION OF POP, MINIMALISM, AND PERFORMANCE 1958–1964

BARBARA HASKELL

with an essay on The American Independent Cinema
by JOHN G. HANHARDT

Whitney Museum of American Art, New York
in association with W. W. Norton & Company,
New York, London

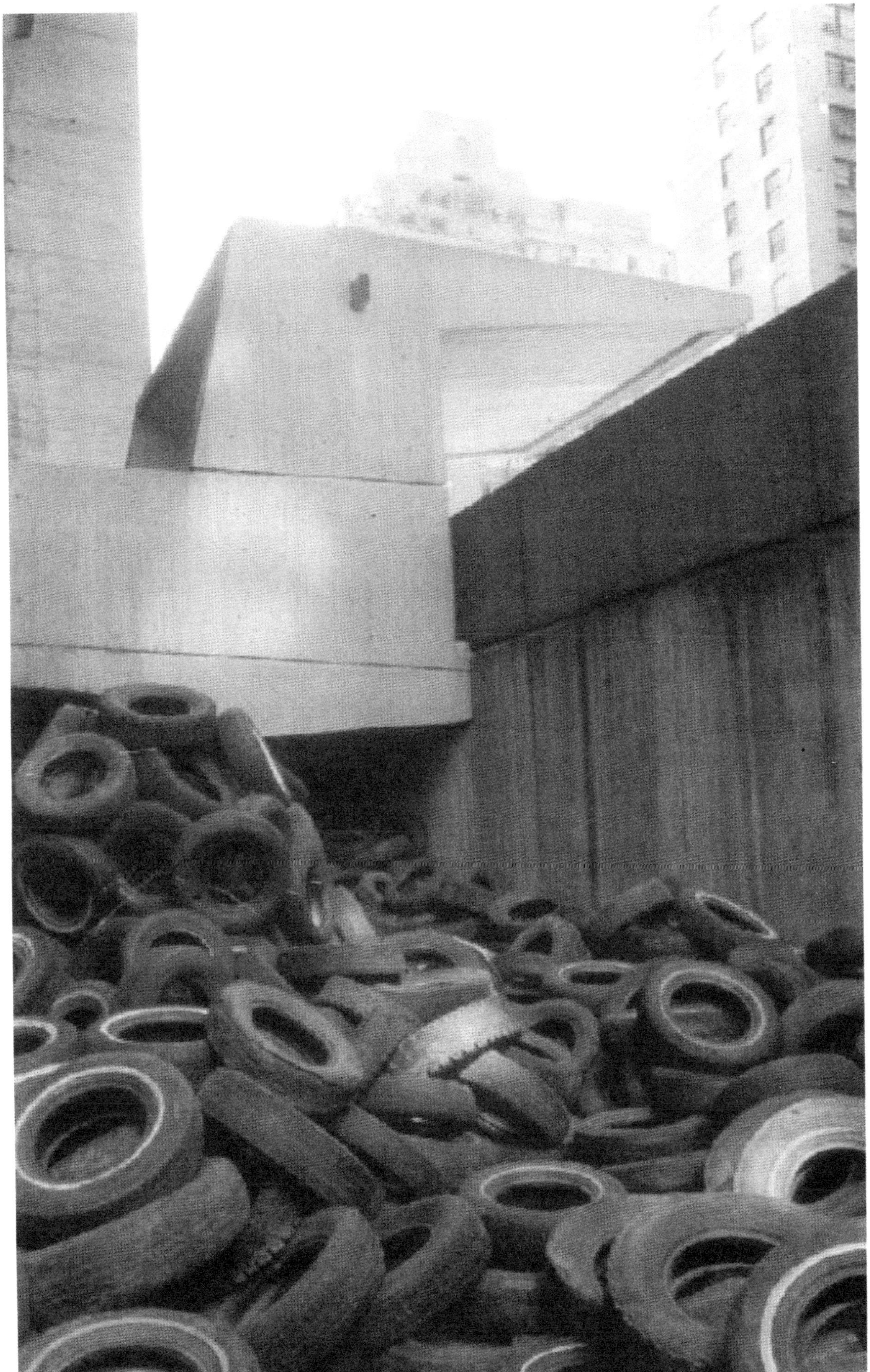

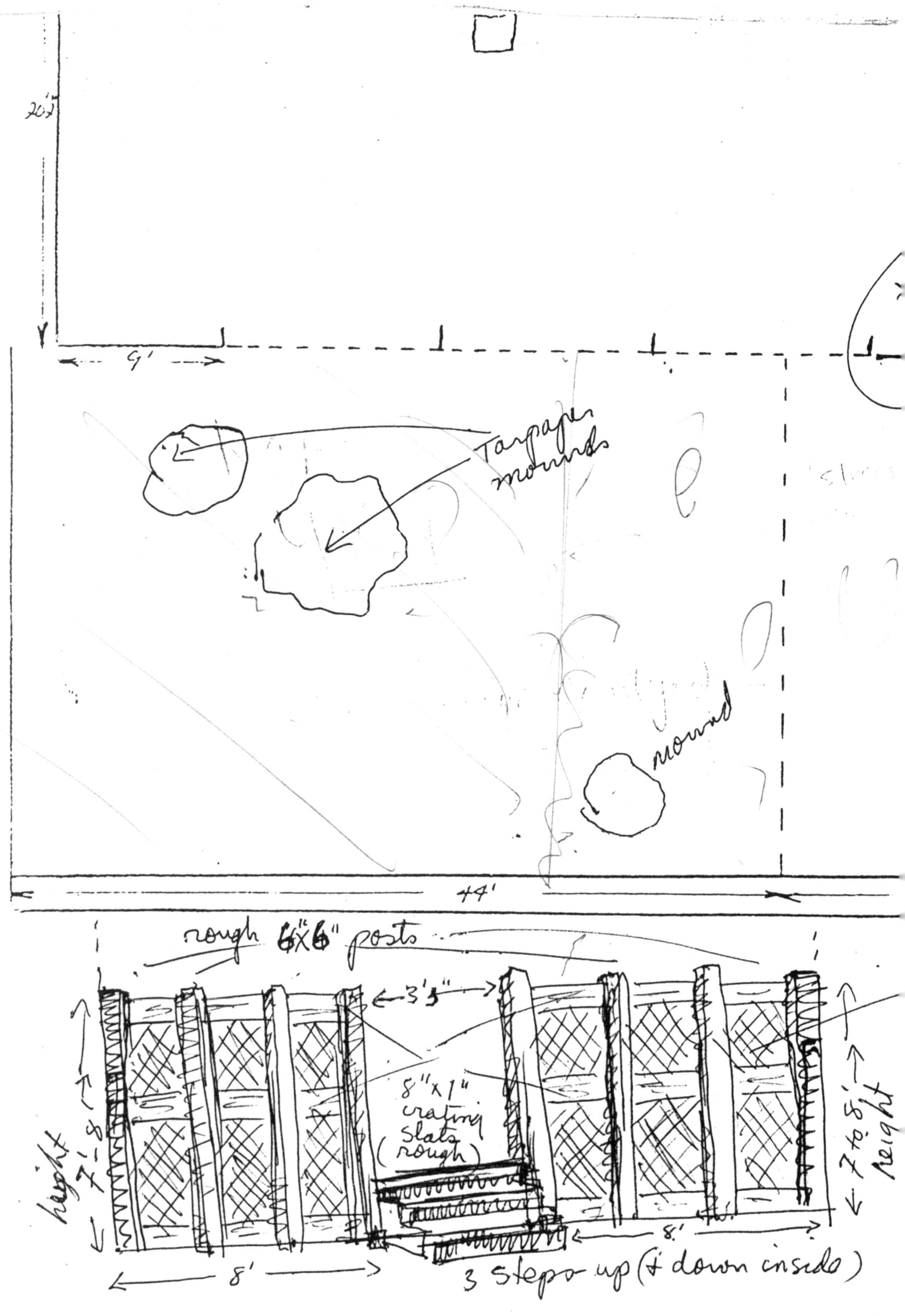

20'
9'
Tarpaper mounds
mound
44'
rough 6"x6" posts
3'3"
8"x1" crating slats (rough)
height 7'-8'
7' to 8' height
8'
8'
3 steps up (& down inside)

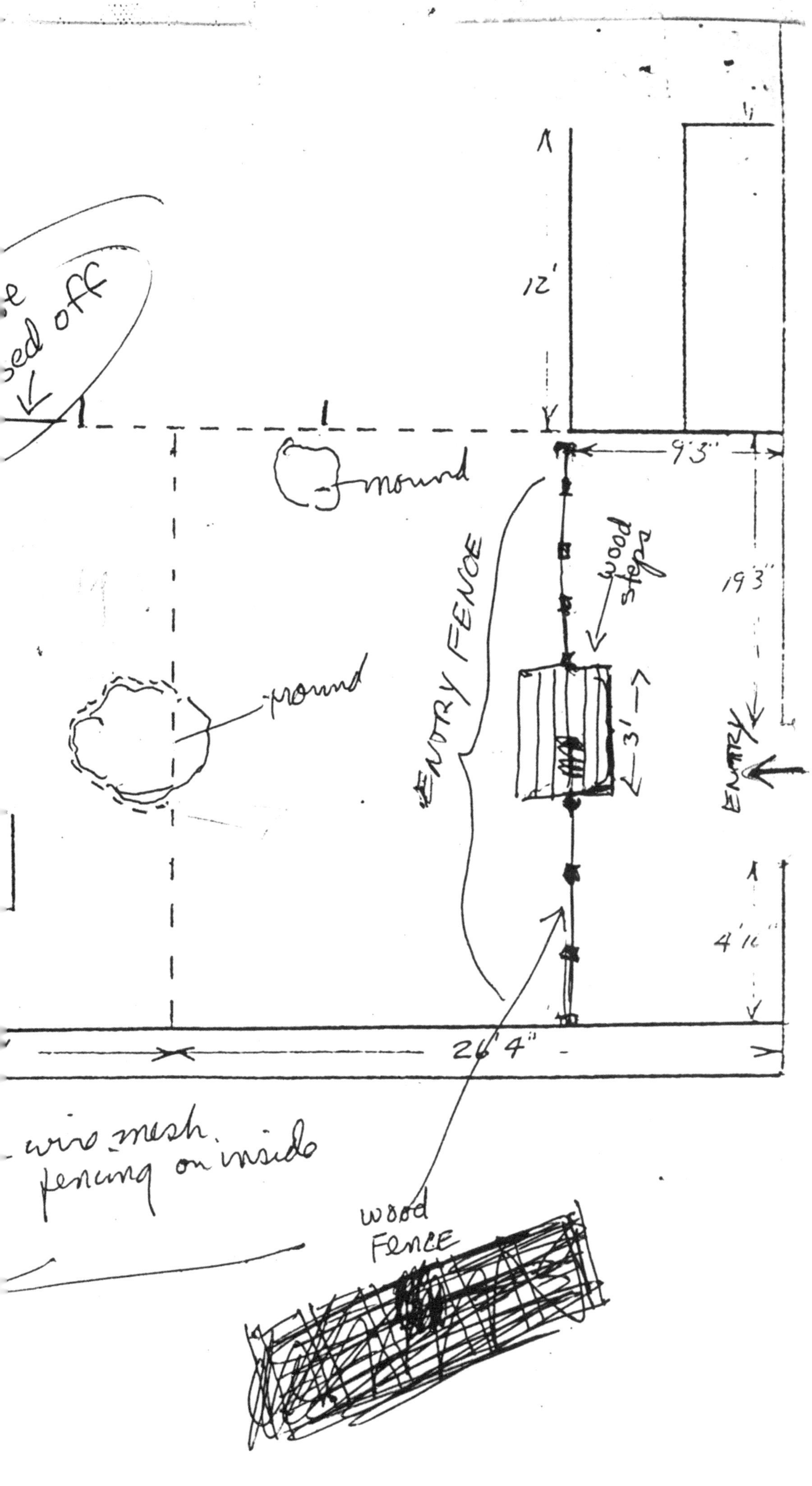
12'
mound
ENTRY FENCE
wood steps
9'3"
19'3"
3'
mound
ENTRY
4'11"
26'4"
wire mesh fencing on inside
wood Fence

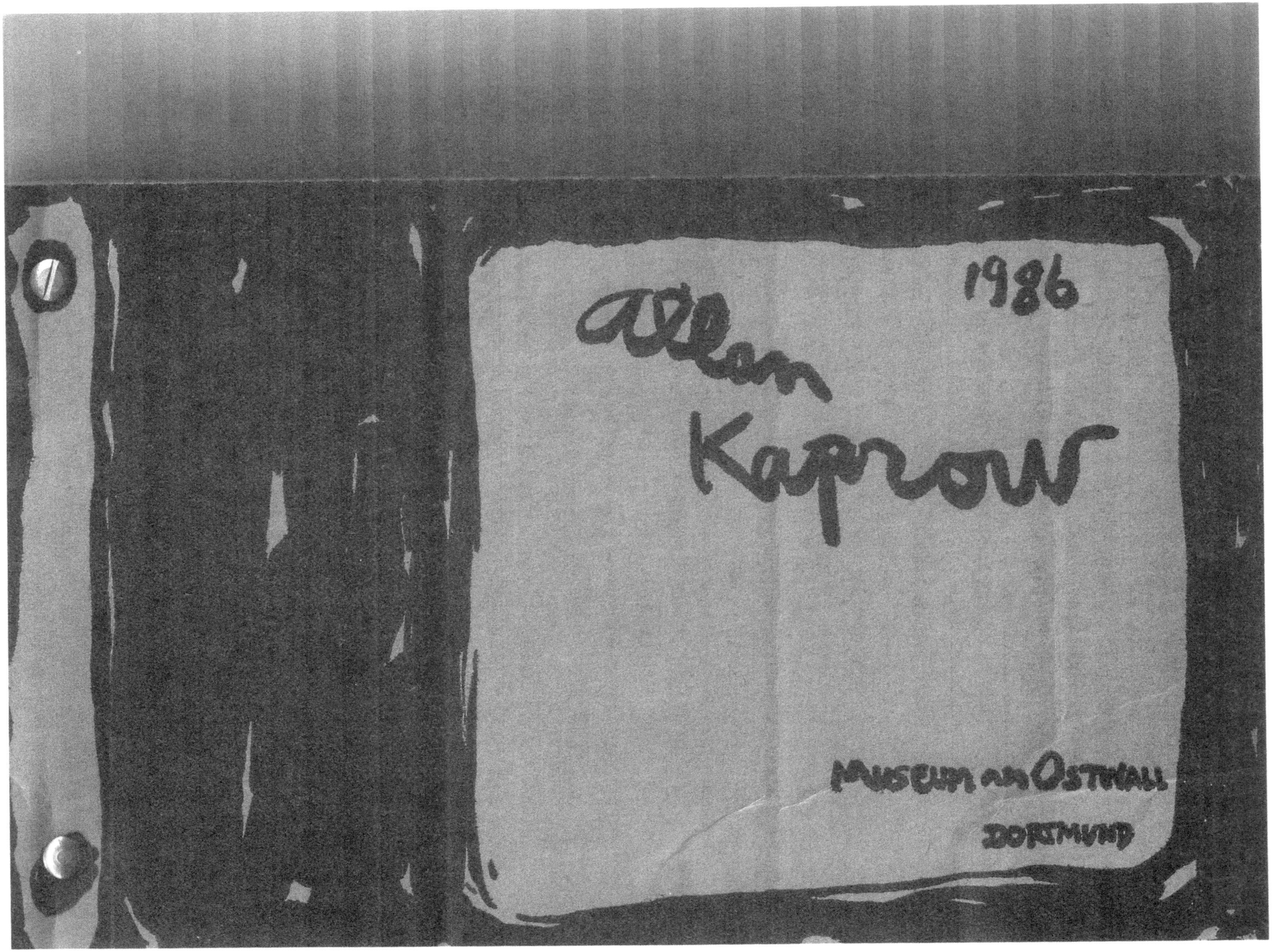
1986
Allan Kaprow
MUSEUM AM OSTWALL
DORTMUND

COLLAGEN, ENVIRONMENTS, VIDEOS, BROSCHüREN, GESCHI CHTEN, HAPPENING- UND ACTI VITY-DOKUMENTE 1956-1986

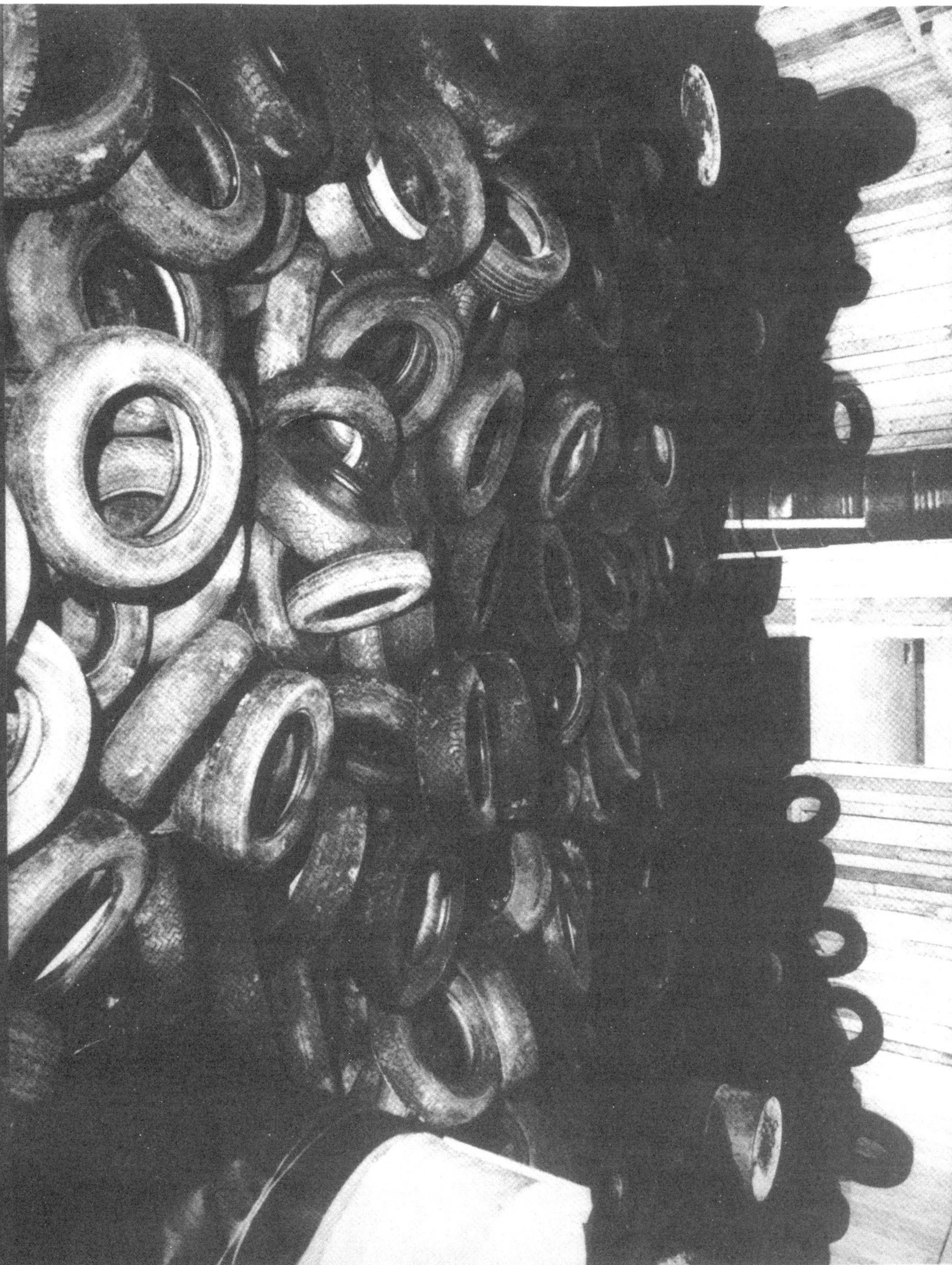

Yard. 1986 (1961). Environment, Dortmund

Sawdust. 1986 (1970). Environment, Dortmund

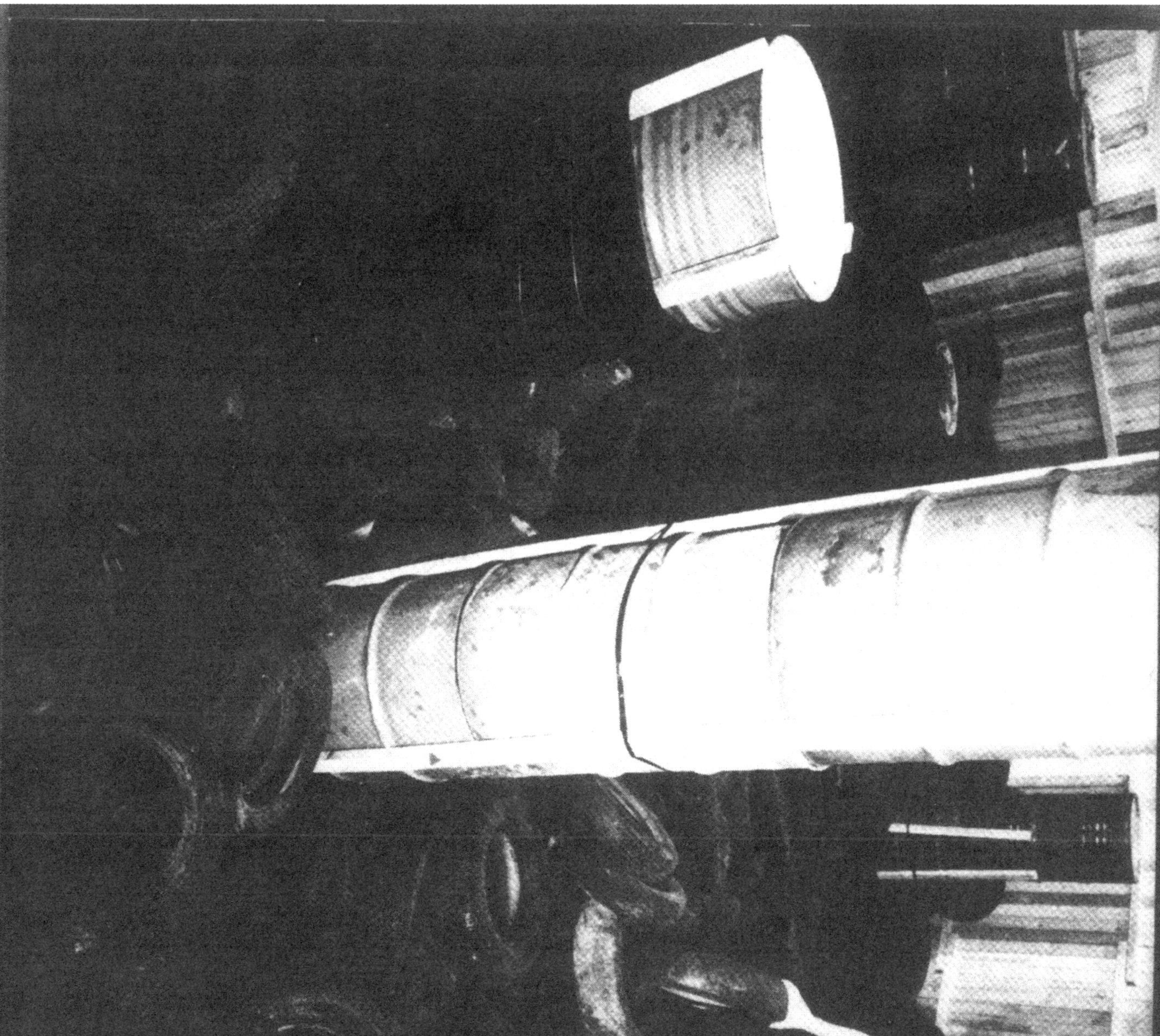

Yard. 1986 (1961). Environment, Dortmund

Yard. 1986 (1961). Environment, Dortmund

The Readymade Boomerang

Certain Relations in 20th Century Art

Art Gallery of New South Wales
Bond Stores 3/4, Millers Point

11 April – 3 June 1990

The Eighth Biennale of Sydney

Dear Judy Thanks for the plan. It required an entire revamping of the concept. Here [is]
one that should work out well; the bottleneck is its main feature of exchange betw[een]
black and white. As I said on the phone, visitors will be encouraged to continuously
exchange tires from one to the other. If you can have all the construction in place when
[I] arrive [and] also 400 tires, I can finish the spraying of the tires, and mount the display info
myself on the day of the opening. (I will need a bit of help though....
URGENT! I've heard nothing from Quantas! I must leave from L[illegible]
on Saturday April 7? at either 9:30PM or 10:30PM since my flight f[rom]
Frankfurt arrives at [illegible]:00PM that night. I'm concerned that there may be no [illegible]

— Best wishes
Allan K

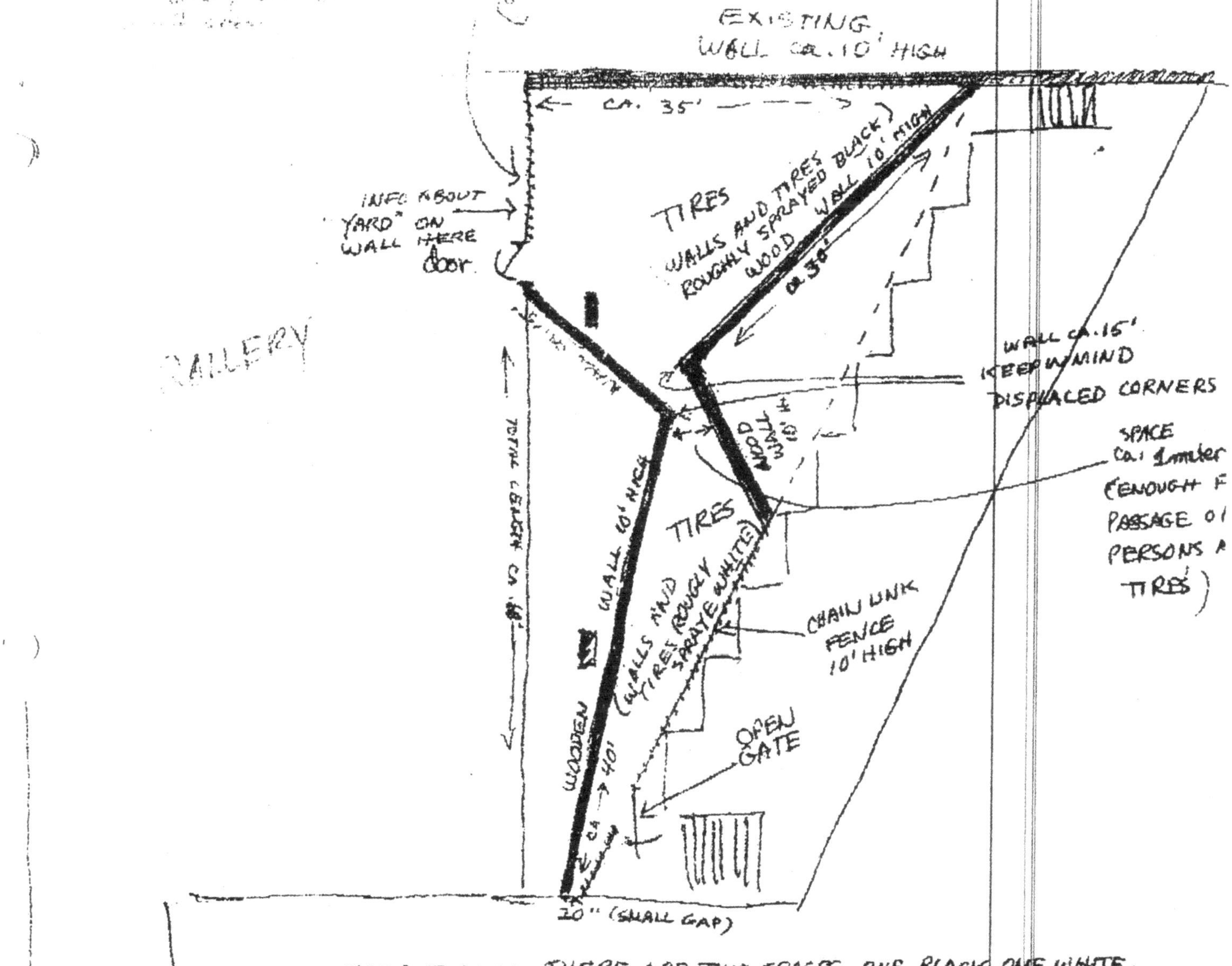

ESSENTIALLY, THERE ARE TWO SPACES, ONE BLACK, ONE WHITE.
WOOD WALLS TO BE ROUGH, STANDARD, CONSTRUCTION, 16" CENTE[RS]
OF 2"X4" STUDS, ANCHORED, WITH ONE SIDE SHEATHED
WITH CHEAPEST PLYWOOD PANEL. CHAIN LINK FENCE TO BE RENTED FROM BUILDING COMPANY. PAINT TO BE CHEAPEST POSSIBLE AS WELL.
(INSIDE SURFACE ONL[Y])

CATALOGUE PRODUCTION

René Block
Catalogue concept and realisation

Jennifer Cooke
Production editor

Helen Adkins (Berlin)
Gerlinde Gabriel (Berlin)
Ingrid Mössinger (Berlin)
Louise Neri (Sydney)
Christine Wagner (Berlin)
Preparation and compilation of catalogue material

Peter Thorn MCA
Production Manager

Antoinette Cassar
Production Assistant

Bloxham & Chambers Pty Ltd
Typesetting and Printing

Graham Ramsay & Associates
Platemaking

Critical and/or artist's statements were received from each artist or artist's representative. In instances where information was not received in time for printing, other publications were consulted. Wherever possible, the Biennale of Sydney has ensured that copyright clearance has been obtained.

National Library of Australia
Cataloguing-in-Publication entry

Biennale of Sydney (8th: 1990).
The Readymade Boomerang: Certain Relations in 20th Century Art.

Bibliography.
ISBN 0 959 661964

1. Art, Modern - 20th century - Exhibitions. I. Title.

709.040749441

MCA

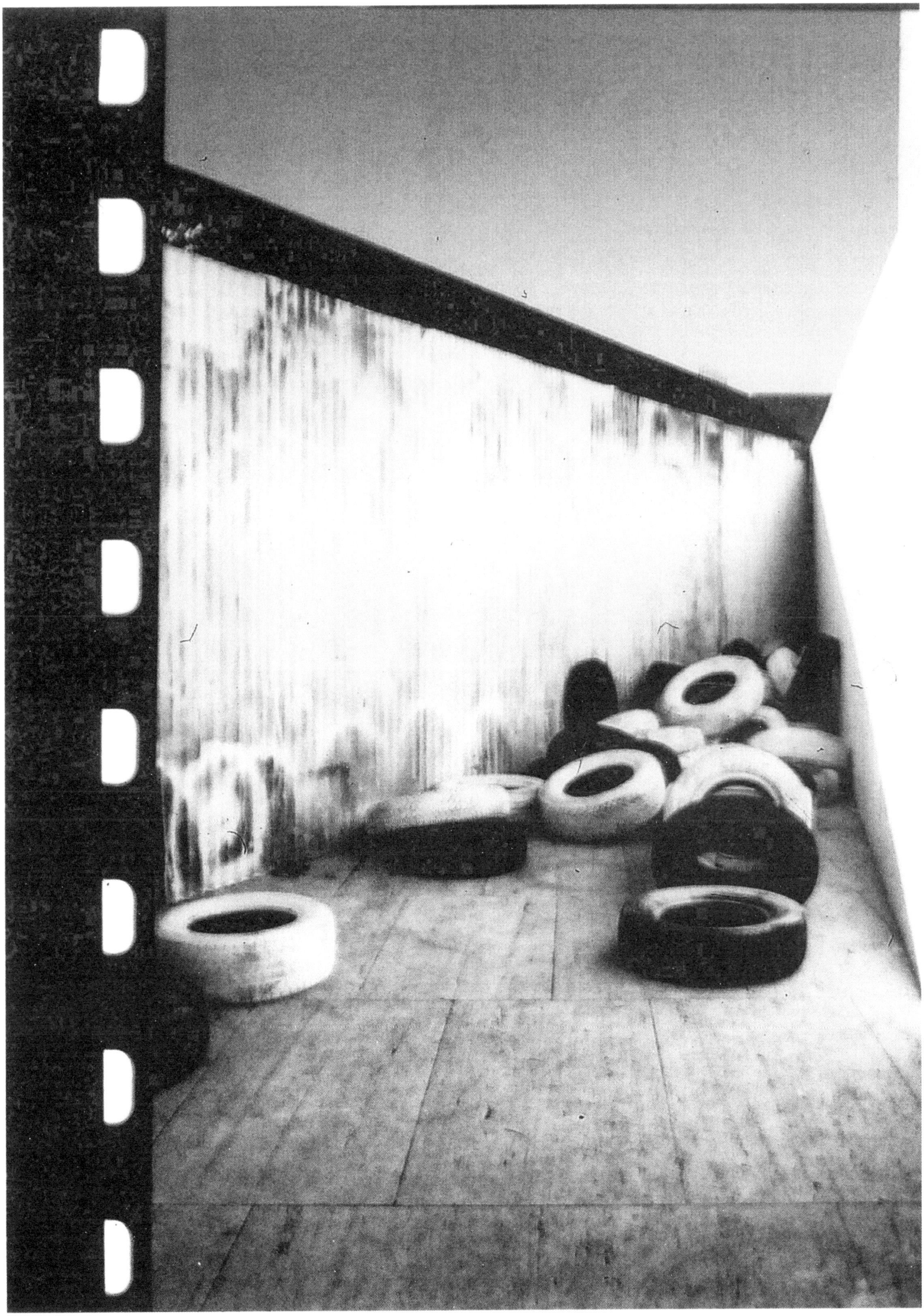

2) WHITE PAINT

for the back walls = to be sprayed roughly white (may need several coats) + corrugated iron also to be sprayed white.

Tyres to [illegible] sprayed in this section at both sides white.

[illegible]) ALLAN Days - check on tyre delivery [illegible]prox density should be 3 tyres [illegible]ep (I know this is not possible).

[illegible]) Guard to open door each day + close each evening.

(5) HEIDIE (photographer) to come at least once a week to document the public's relationship to the "changing" work. Advise her to shoot from both sides.

Enquire if she could shoot from above (eg library level)

8:00 64/66 oxford st.

I gave Judy the no of the place where we can hire an air gun $25/day BUDJET HIRE in Woollahra. 32 9146.

~~I don't have~~

I'll give you a call tomorrow

Hope this is clear enough.

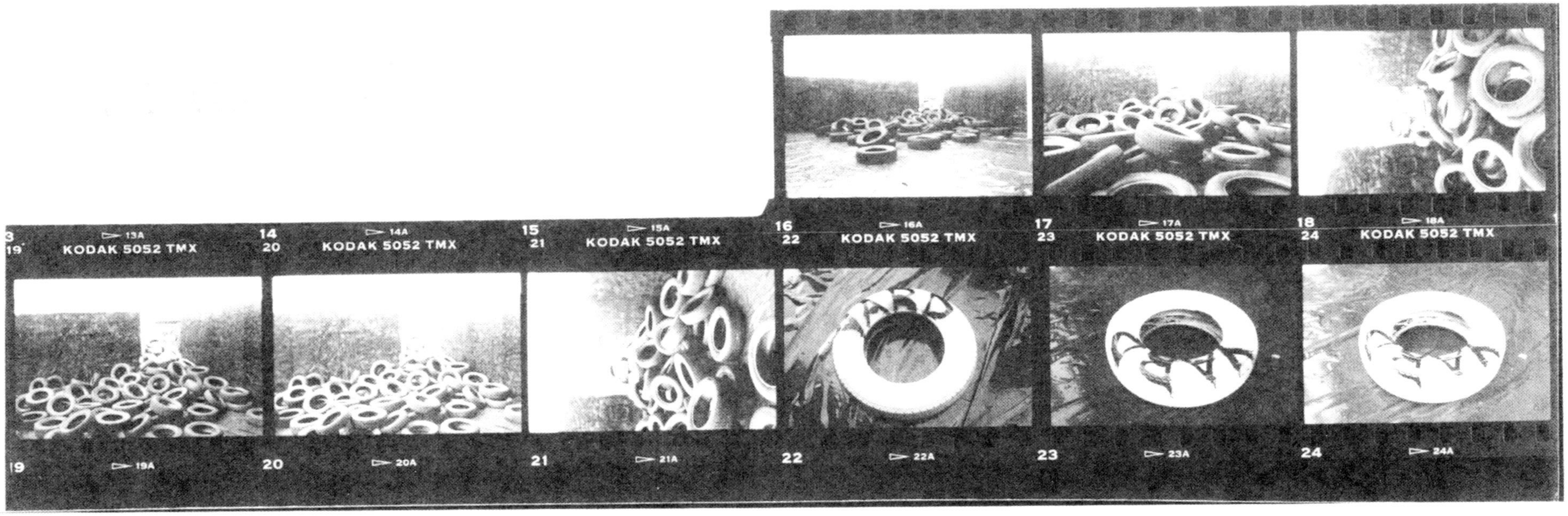
KODAK 5052 TMX
KODAK 5052 TMX
KODAK 5052 TMX
KODAK 5052 TMX
KODAK 5052 TMX
KODAK 5052 TMX

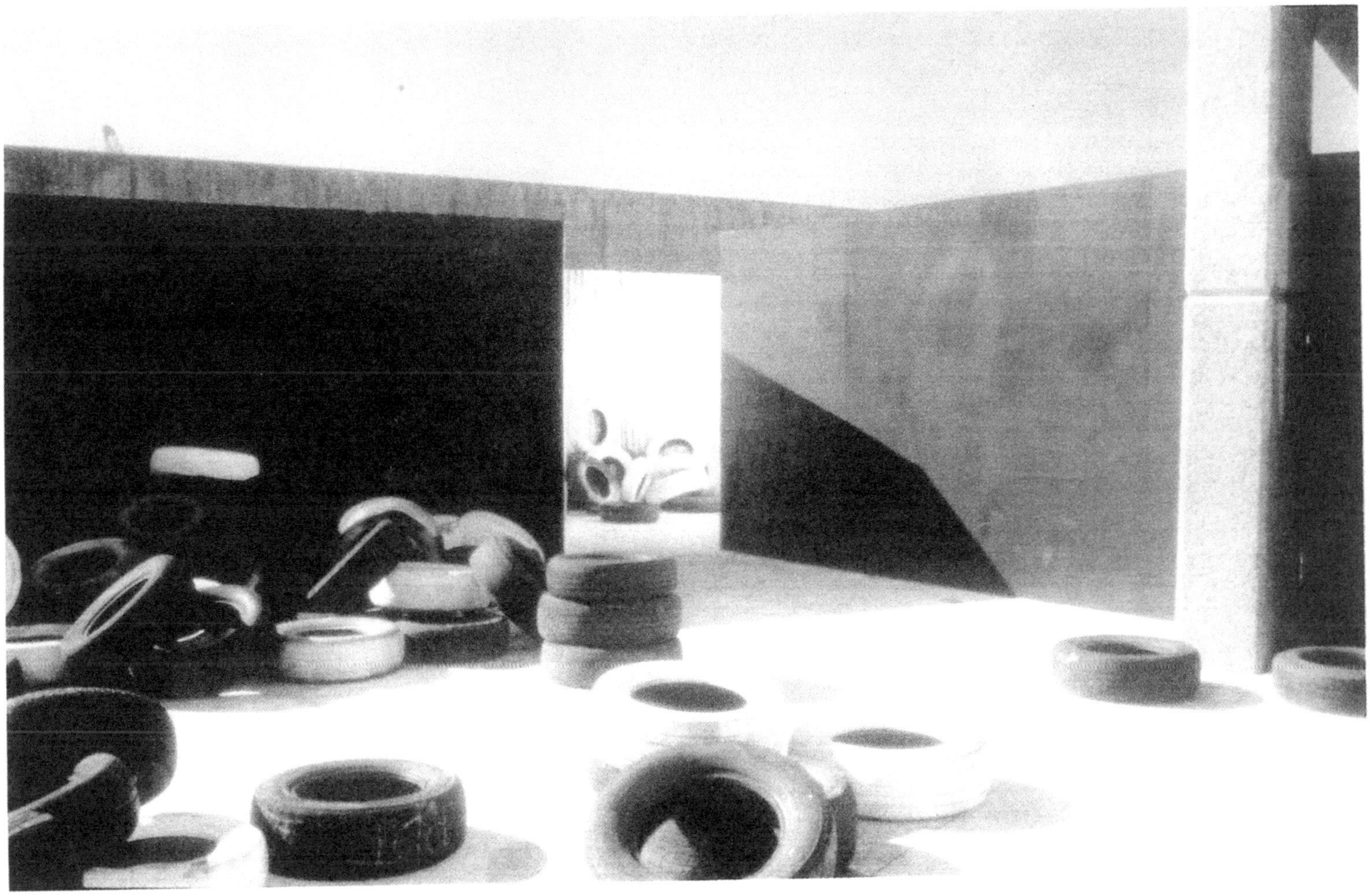

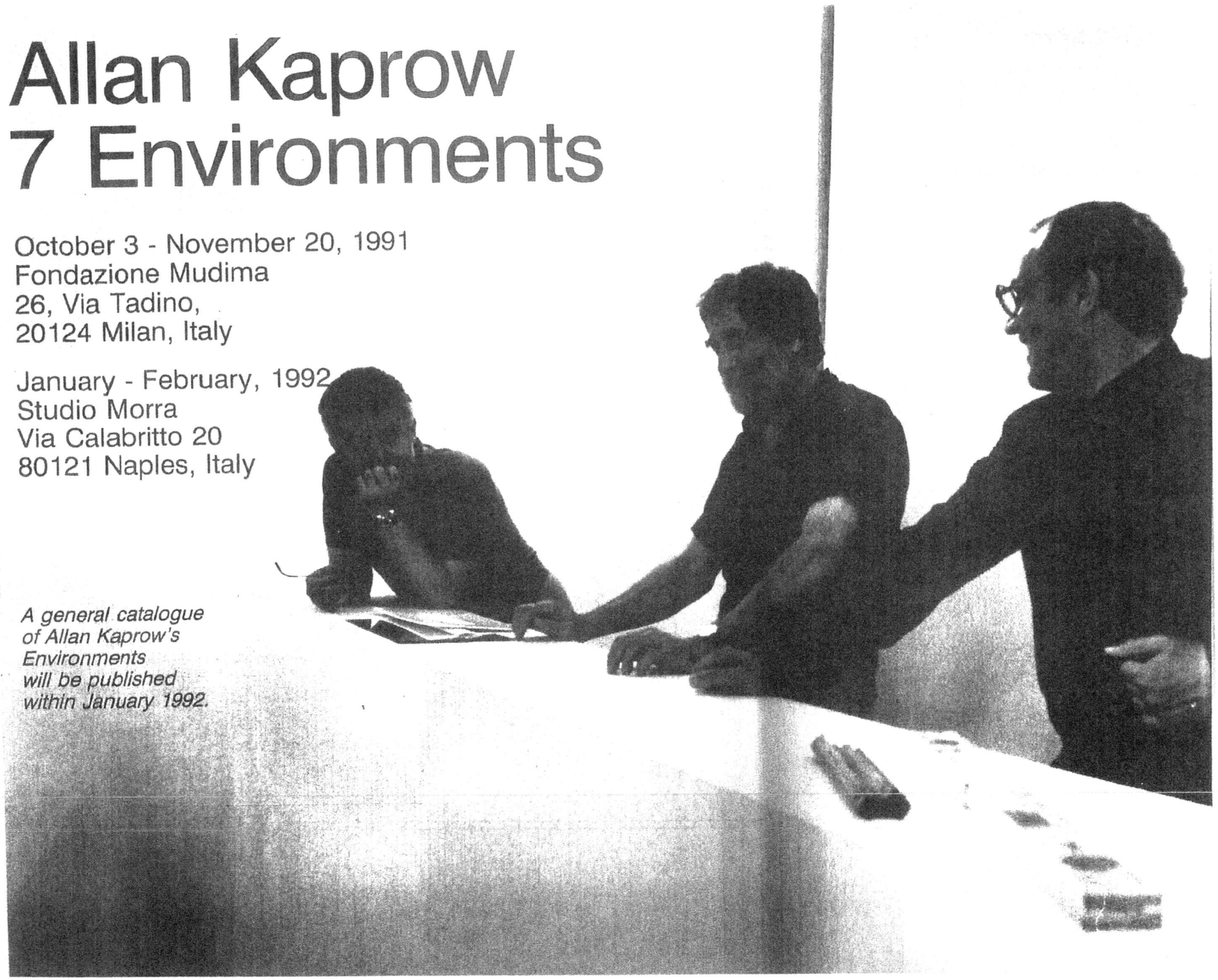
Allan Kaprow
7 Environments
October 3 - November 20, 1991
Fondazione Mudima
26, Via Tadino,
20124 Milan, Italy
January - February, 1992
Studio Morra
Via Calabritto 20
80121 Naples, Italy
A general catalogue
of Allan Kaprow's
Environments
will be published
within January 1992.

7 ENVIRONMENTS

ALLAN KAPROW

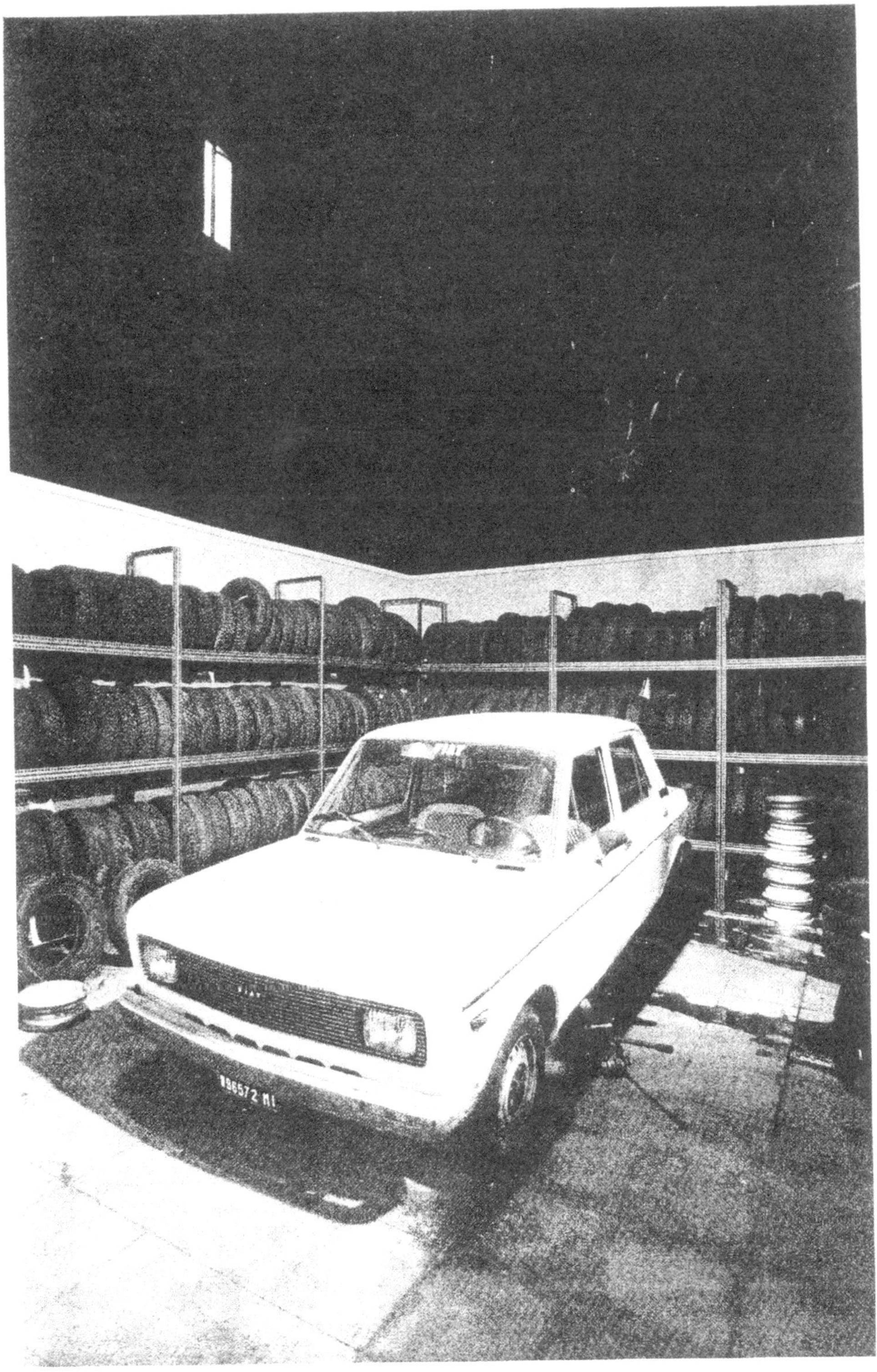

Yard, 1991 (before opening to participants)

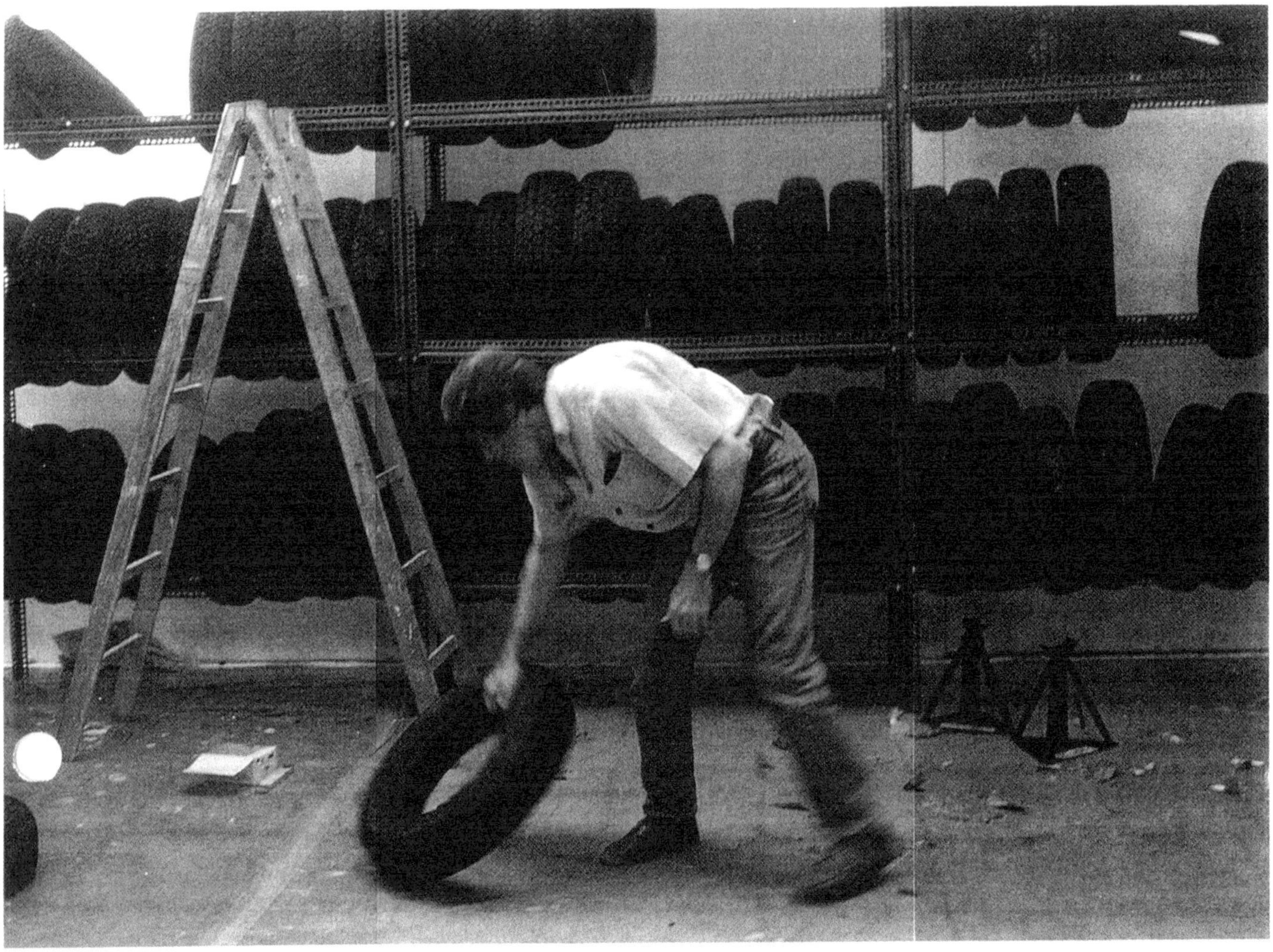

(in process), left and right.

YORK TIMES, SUNDAY, APRIL 23, 1961.
presents
OPENING MAY 25
THROUGH JUNE 23
ADMISSION . . . 75c.
Artists and Students . 25
FOREIGN POLICY TA
Skin P

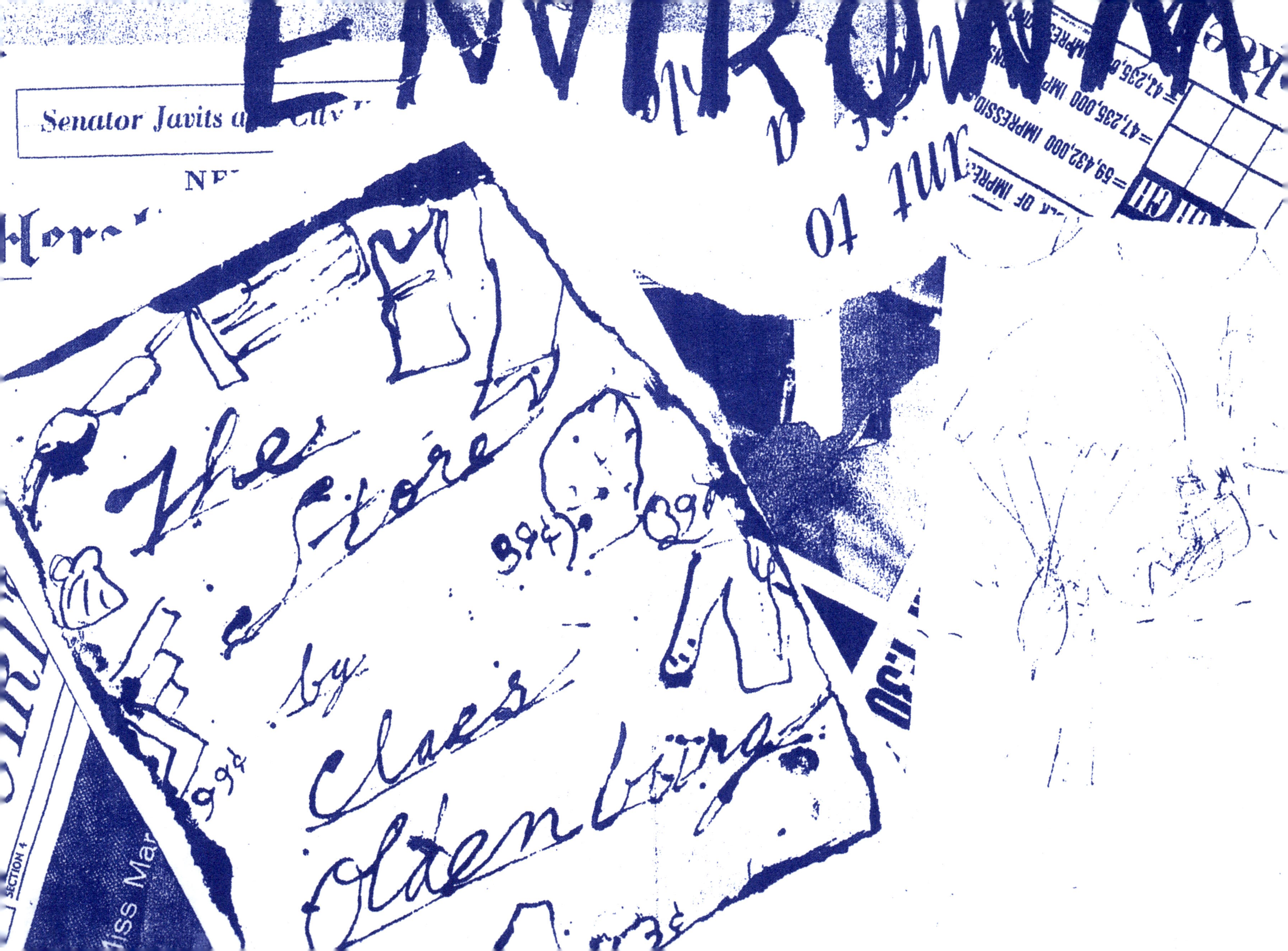
ENVIRONM
Senator Javits
The Store by Claes Oldenburg
=59,432,000 IMPRESSIONS
=47,235,000 IMPRESSIONS
SECTION 4

Index

Exhibition History for *Yard*, 1961

1961 May 25–June 23. "Environments, Situations, Spaces," Sculpture garden at Martha Jackson Gallery, New York.

1967 September 15–October 22. "Allan Kaprow," Pasadena Art Museum, Pasadena, California.

1970 November 6–January 6. "Happening and Fluxus," Neuer Kölnischer Kunstverein, Cologne, Germany.

1981 October 16–November 29. "Schwarz," Kunsthalle Düsseldorf, Düsseldorf, Germany.

1982 October 7–December 5. "Kunst wird Material," Neue Nationalgalerie, Berlin, Germany.

1984 September 20–December 2. "BLAM!: The Explosion of Pop, Minimalism, and Performance 1958–1964," Sculpture Court, Whitney Museum of American Art, New York.

1986 August 24–October 5. "Allan Kaprow: Collagen, Environments, Videos, Brochüren, Geschichten, Happening–Und Activity–Dokumente 1956–1986," Museum am Ostwall, Dortmund, Germany.

1990 April 11–June 3. "The Readymade Boomerang: Certain Relations in 20th Century Art," Art Gallery of New South Wales in conjunction with the Eighth Biennale of Sydney, Sydney, Australia.

1991 October 3–November 20. "7 Environments," Fondazione Mudima, Milan, Italy.

1998 February 8–May 10. "Out of Actions: Between Performance and the Object, 1949–1979," Geffen Contemporary at the Museum of Contemporary Art, Los Angeles, California; Traveled to and installed at MAK—Austrian Museum of Applied Arts, Vienna, Austria, June 17–September 6.

2003 July 3–September 28. "Living Theatre/Labyrinths of the Imaginary," Castel Sant'Elmo, Naples, Italy.

2003 September 29–November 5. "Critical Mass: Happenings, Fluxus, Performance, Intermedia and Rutgers University 1958–1972" Mason Gross Art Galleries, Rutgers, The State University, New Brunswick, New Jersey. Version by Geoffrey Hendricks.

2006 September 29–November 5. "Art, Life & Confusion/47th October Salon," A former Turkish bath in conjunction with the Belgrade Cultural Center, Belgrade, Serbia.

2007 February 10–April 22. "Allan Kaprow—Art As Life," Van Abbemuseum, Eindhoven, The Netherlands. Version by Eva Meyer-Hermann.

2008 January 19–February 10. "Allan Kaprow—Art as Life," Loggia della Mercanzia di Piazza Banchi, Museo d'Arte Contemporanea di Villa Croce, Genoa, Italy. Version by Geoffrey Hendricks and Pietro Millefiore.

2009 September 23–October 24. "Allan Kaprow Yard," Hauser & Wirth New York, New York. Versions by Sharon Hayes, William Pope.L and Josiah McElheny.

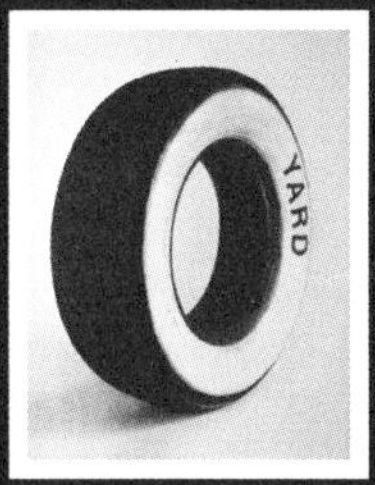

R Allan Kaprow
Yard, 1990
Offset lithograph
From portfolio of prints made by 21 artists participating in "The Readymade Boomerang," Sydney Biennale, Australia, 1990
Edition of XLV
Printed by Sinnott Brothers, Sydney, Australia
© Allan Kaprow Estate
Courtesy Hauser & Wirth

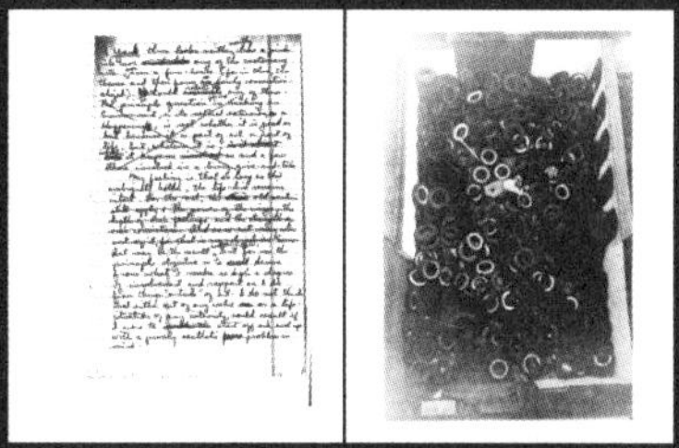

L Artist's notes on *Yard*, 1961
Research Library, The Getty Research Institute (G.R.I), Los Angeles, California (980063)

R Overhead view of Kaprow in *Yard*, 1961
"Environments, Situations, Spaces"
Martha Jackson Gallery, New York
G.R.I.
Photo: © Robert R. McElroy/ Licensed by VAGA, New York, NY

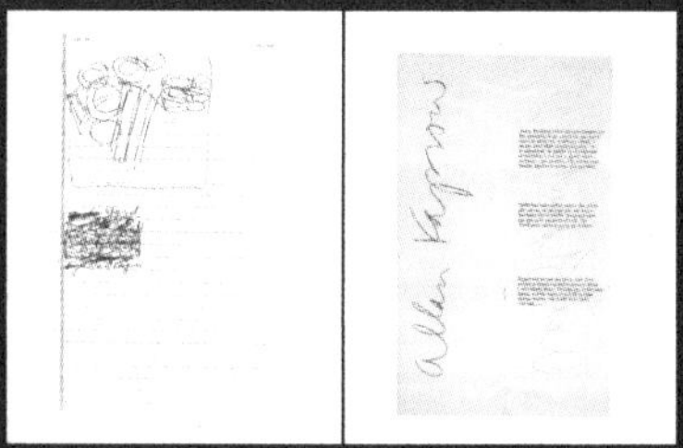

L Allan Kaprow
Sketch for *Yard*, 1961
G.R.I.

R Artist's statement in brochure for "Environments, Situations, Spaces," 1961
G.R.I.

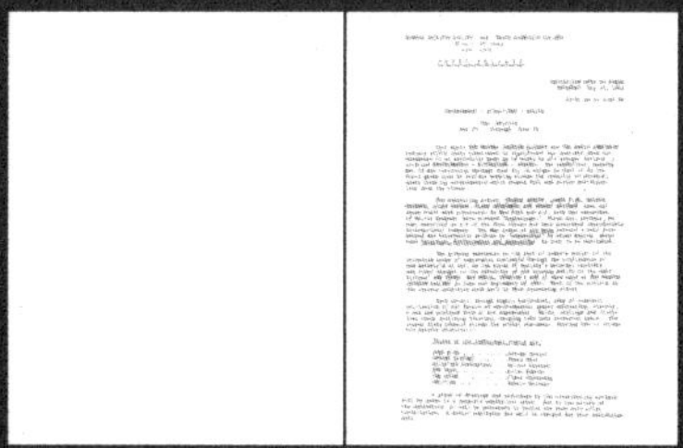

R Press Release, 1961
G.R.I.

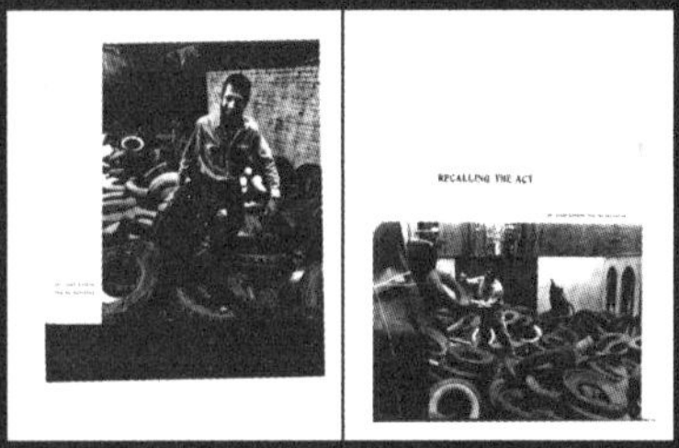

L Kaprow in *Yard*, 1961
Martha Jackson Gallery
G.R.I.
Photo: © Ken Heyman-Woodfin Camp

R The artist in *Yard*, 1961
Martha Jackson Gallery
G.R.I.
Photo: © Ken Heyman-Woodfin Camp

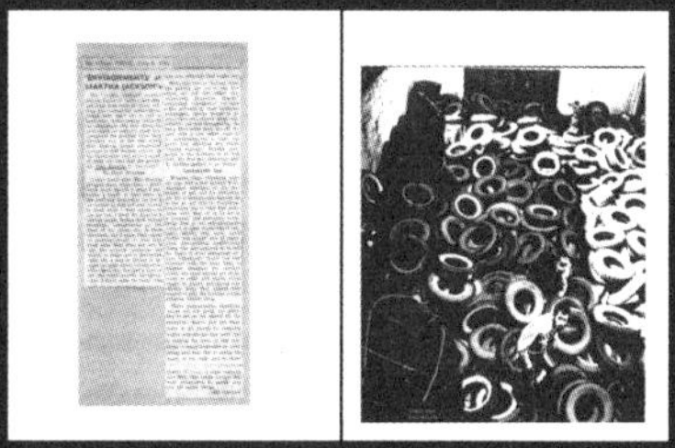

L Review of the exhibition
Jill Johnston, *the village VOICE*, July 6, 1961
G.R.I.
© Jill Johnston

R Kaprow and son in *Yard*, 1961
G.R.I.
Photo: © Ken Heyman-Woodfin Camp

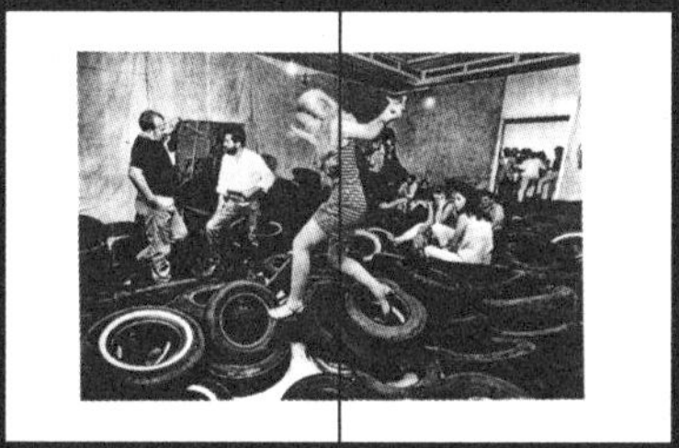

L – R *Yard* with participants, 1967
"Allan Kaprow"
Pasadena Art Museum, Pasadena, California
G.R.I.
Photo: © Julian Wasser

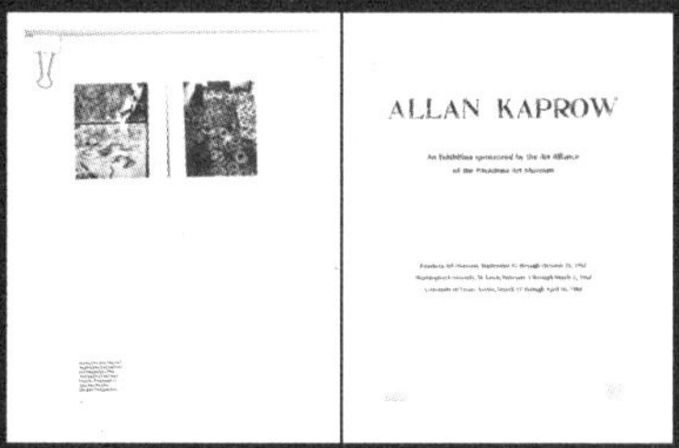

L Spread from Allan Kaprow's *Assemblage, Environments and Happenings*
Harry N. Abrams, New York, 1966
Photo on left: © Hans Namuth
Photo on right: © Ken Heyman-Woodfin Camp

R Title page of "Allan Kaprow," 1967
Pasadena Art Museum

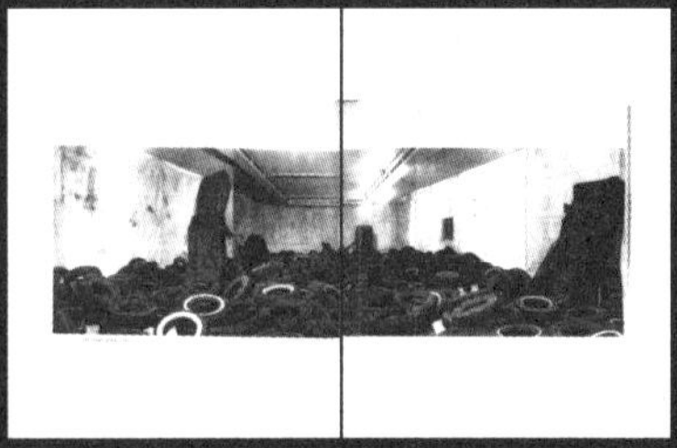

L – R *Yard*, 1967
Pasadena Art Museum
G.R.I.
Photo: © Julian Wasser

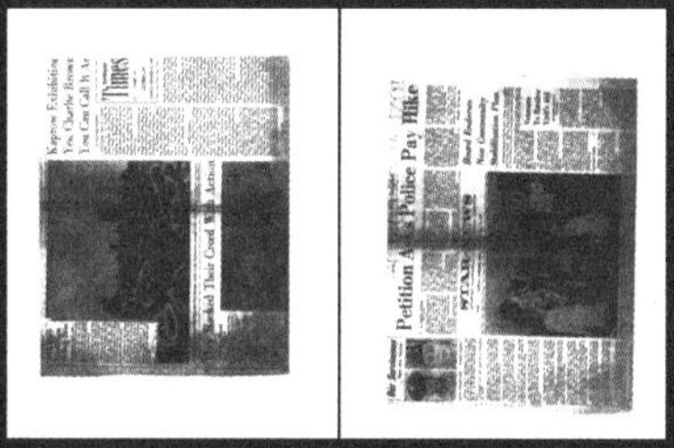

L Review of solo exhibition at Pasadena Art Museum
William Wilson, *Los Angeles Times*, September 16, 1967
G.R.I.
© *Los Angeles Times*

R Image of artist with docents at the Pasadena Art Museum
Star-News, Pasadena, September 13, 1967
G.R.I.
© *Star-News, Pasadena*

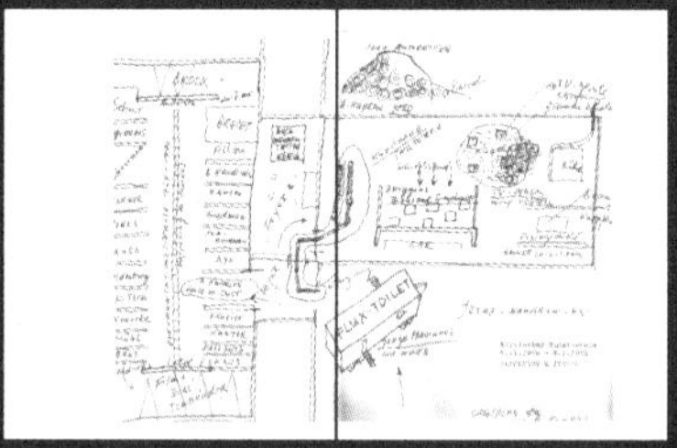

L – R Cover of brochure for "Happening and Fluxus," 1970
Neuer Kölnischer Kunstverein, Cologne, Germany

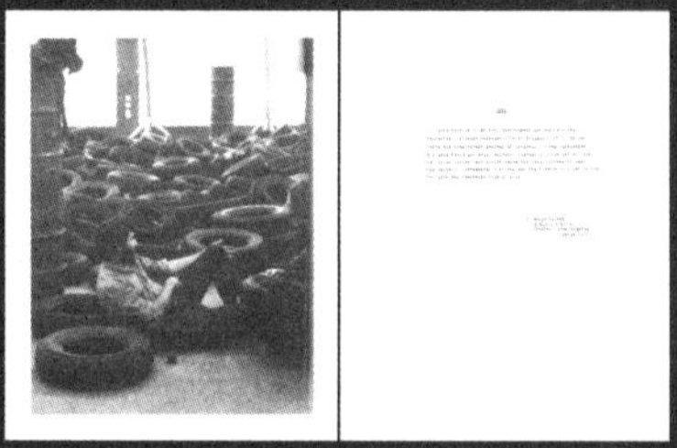

L Kaprow in *Yard*, 1970
"Happening and Fluxus"
Neuer Kölnischer Kunstverein
G.R.I.
Photo: © Geoffrey Hendricks

R Note by the artist, 1971
G.R.I.

2

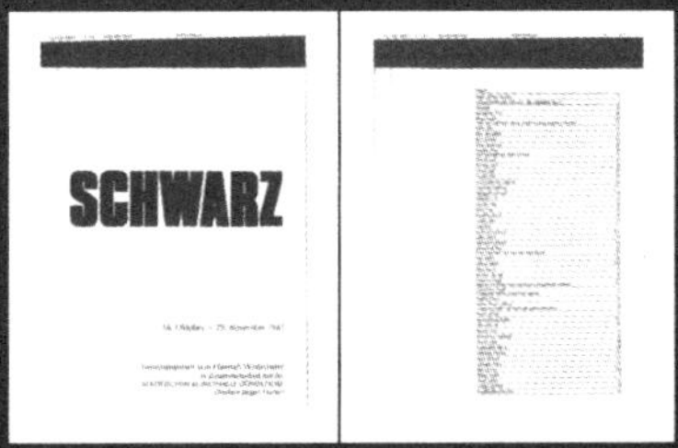

L Title page of “Schwarz,” 1981
Kunsthalle Düsseldorf,
Düsseldorf, Germany

R Content page of “Schwarz,” 1981
Kunsthalle Düsseldorf

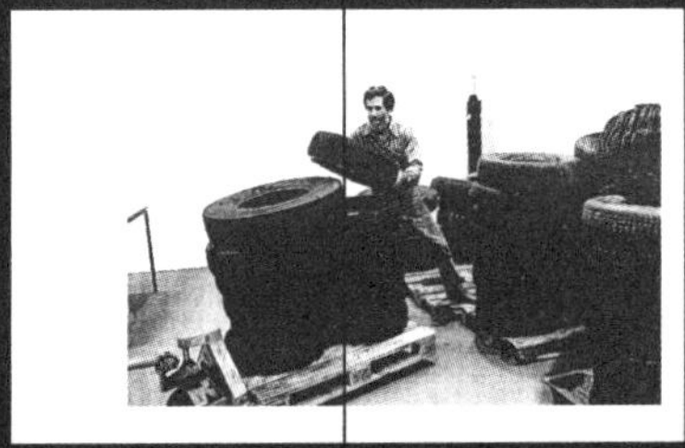

L Kaprow installing *Yard*, 1981
– “Schwarz”
R Kunsthalle Düsseldorf
Photographer unknown

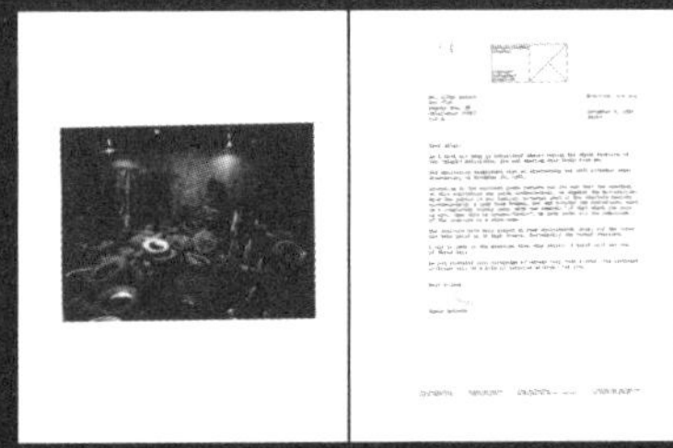

L *Yard*, 1981
Kunsthalle Düsseldorf
G.R.I.
Photo: © Walter Klein

R Letter from Klaus Schrenk, 1981
G.R.I.

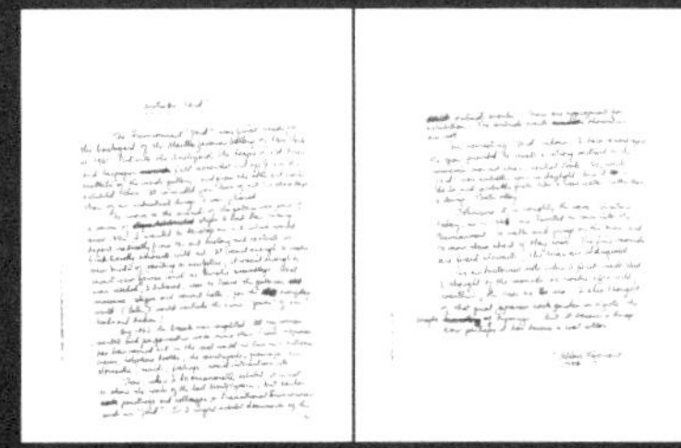

L Artist’s notation on *Yard*, 1982
– G.R.I.
R

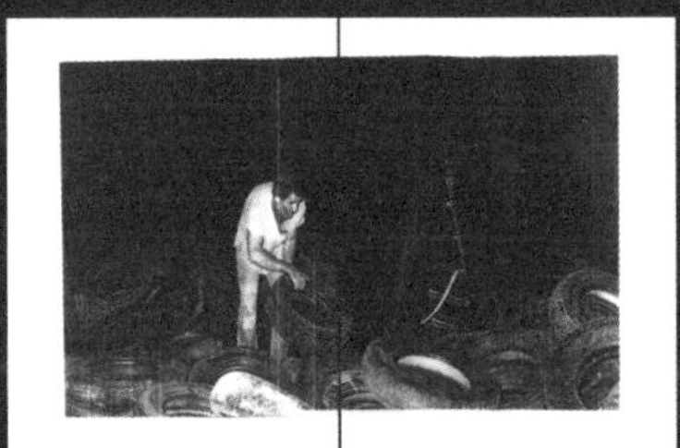

L Kaprow installing *Yard*, 1982
– “Kunst wird Material”
R Neue Nationalgalerie, Berlin,
Germany
G.R.I.
Photographer unknown

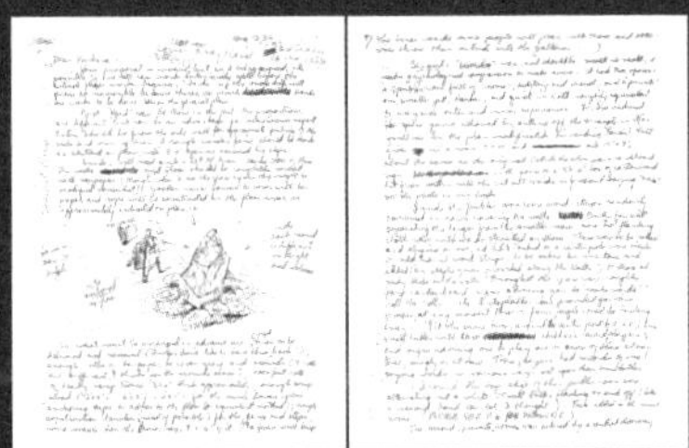

L Artist’s letter to Barbara Haskell,
– 1984
R G.R.I.

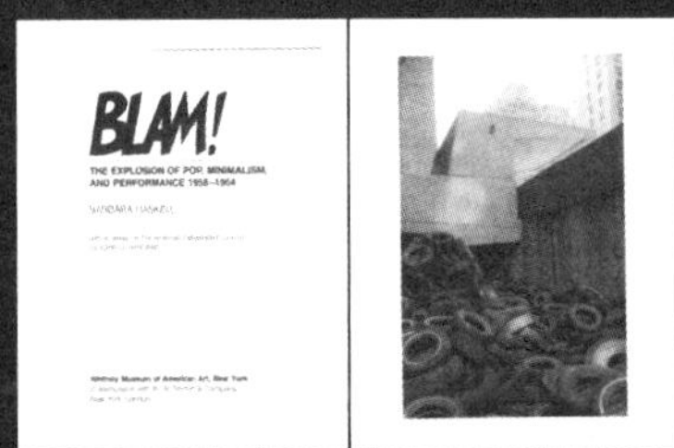

L Title page of “BLAM! The
Explosion of Pop, Minimalism
and Performance 1958–1964,”
1984
Whitney Museum of American
Art, New York

R *Yard*, 1984
“BLAM!”
Whitney Museum of American Art
Photo: Geoffrey Clemens
© Whitney Museum of American
Art, New York

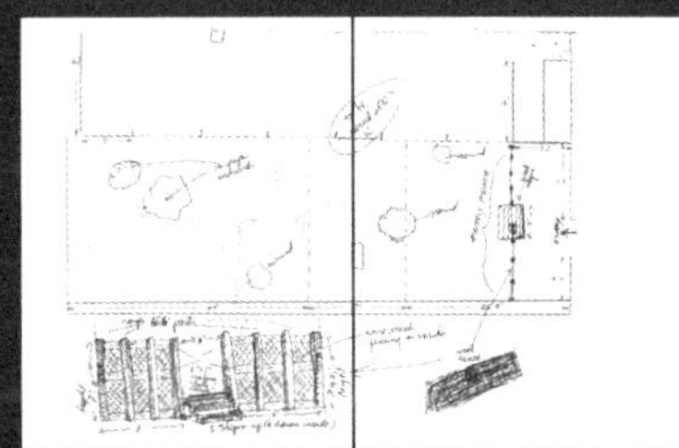

L Sketch for installation of *Yard*
– at Whitney Museum of American
R Art, 1986
G.R.I.

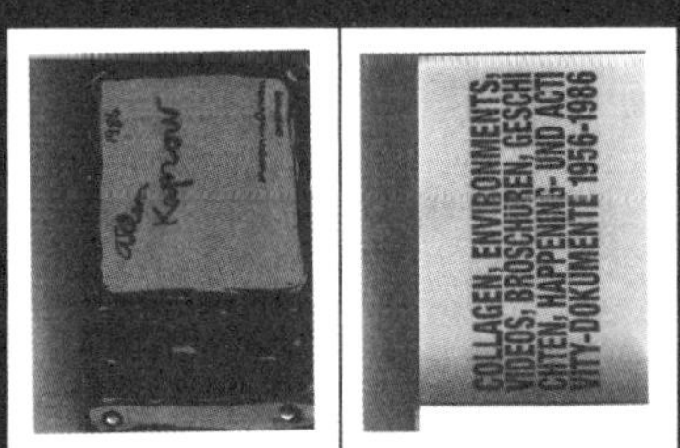

L Cover of “Allan Kaprow:
Collagen, Environments, Videos,
Broschüren, Geschichten,
Happening–und Activity–
Dokumente 1956–1986,” 1986
Museum am Ostwall, Dortmund,
Germany

R Title page, 1986
Museum am Ostwall

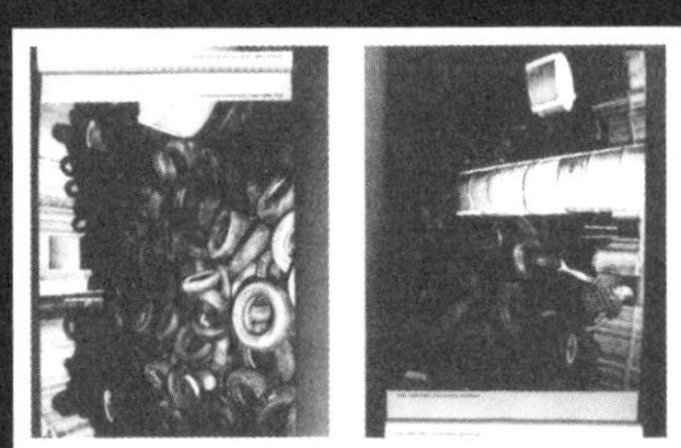

L *Yard*, 1986
“Allan Kaprow”
Museum am Ostwall
Photo: Hans Müller © Wolfgang
Feelisch, Remscheid, Germany

R Museum am Ostwall
Photo: Hans Müller © Wolfgang
Feelisch, Remscheid, Germany

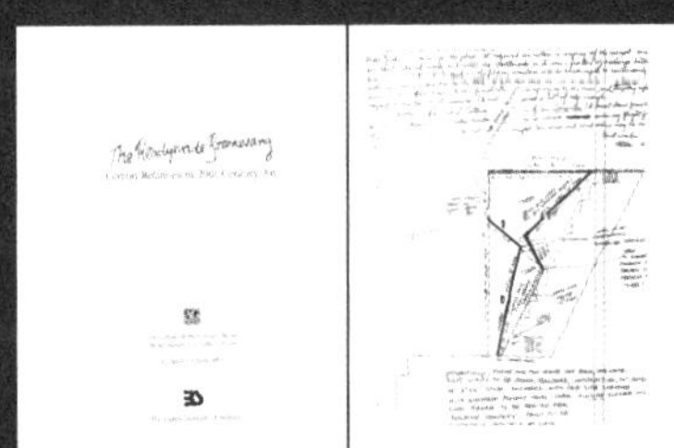

L Title page of “The Readymade
Boomerang: Certain Relations in
20th Century Art,” 1990
Eighth Biennale of Sydney,
Australia

R Installation plan for *Yard*, 1990
Eighth Biennale of Sydney

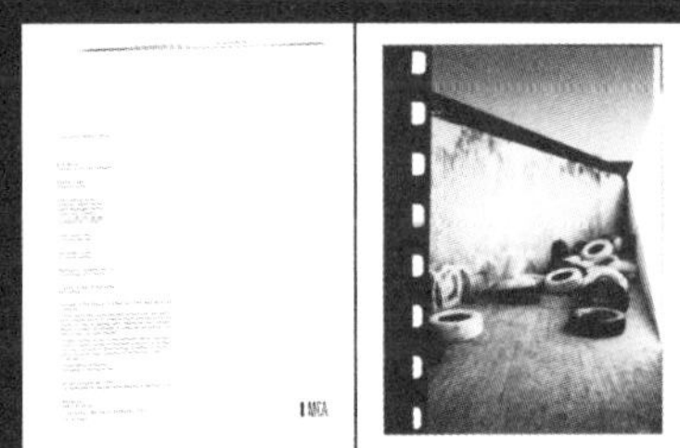

L Colophon of “The Readymade
Boomerang,” 1990
Eighth Biennale of Sydney

R *Yard*, 1990
“The Readymade Boomerang”
Art Gallery of New South Wales,
Eighth Biennale of Sydney
Photo: © Heidrun Lohr

3

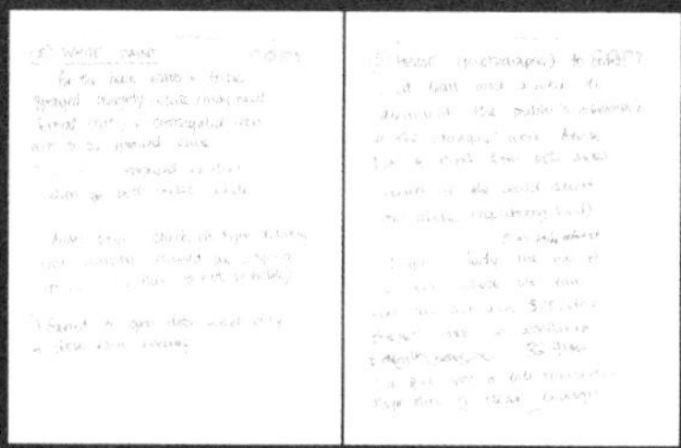

L – R Installation notes, 1990
Eighth Biennale of Sydney

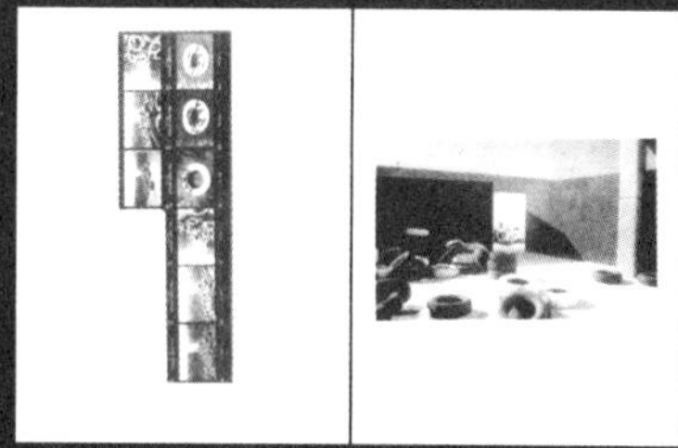

L Contact prints of *Yard*, 1990
Art Gallery of New South Wales,
Eighth Biennale of Sydney
Photos: © Heidrun Lohr

R *Yard*, 1990
Art Gallery of New South Wales,
Eighth Biennale of Sydney
Photo: © Heidrun Lohr

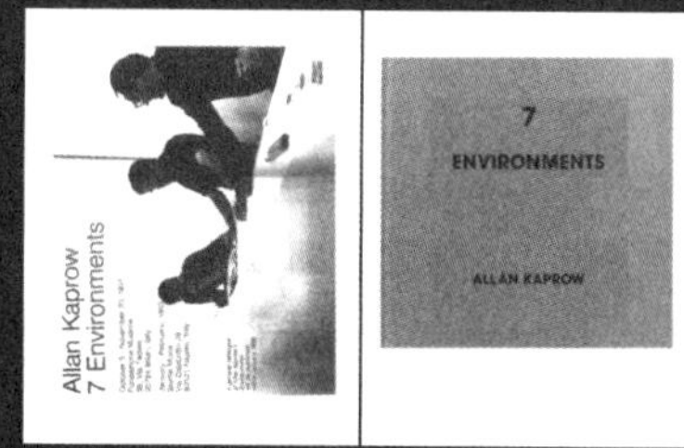

L *BULL SHIT 01*, 1991
News bulletin for "Allan Kaprow:
7 Environments"
Fondazione Mudima, Milan, Italy

R Cover of "7 Environments: Allan
Kaprow," 1992
Fondazione Mudima and Studio
Morra, Naples, Italy

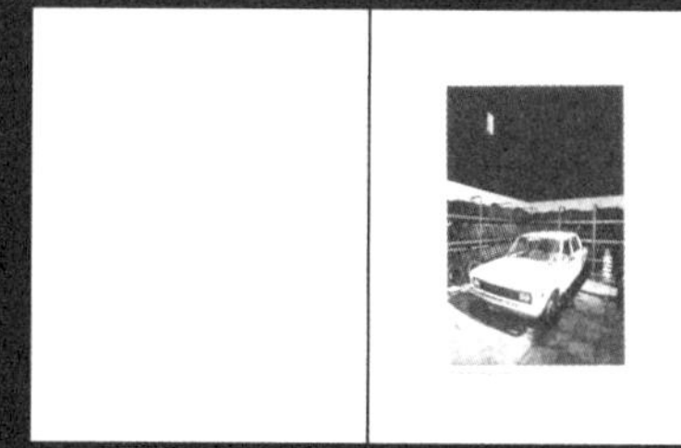

R *Yard*, 1991
"7 Environments: Allan Kaprow"
Fondazione Mudima
Photo: © Enrico Cattaneo

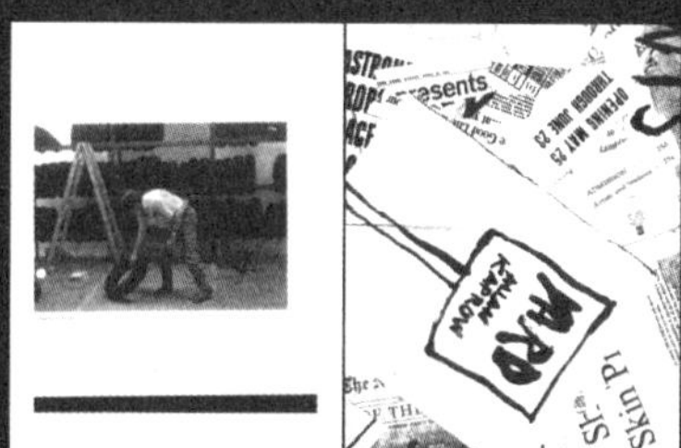

L Kaprow installing *Yard*, 1991
Fondazione Mudima
Photo: © Fabrizio Garghetti

R Detail of poster for "Environ-
ments, Situations, Spaces"
Martha Jackson Gallery,
New York, 1961

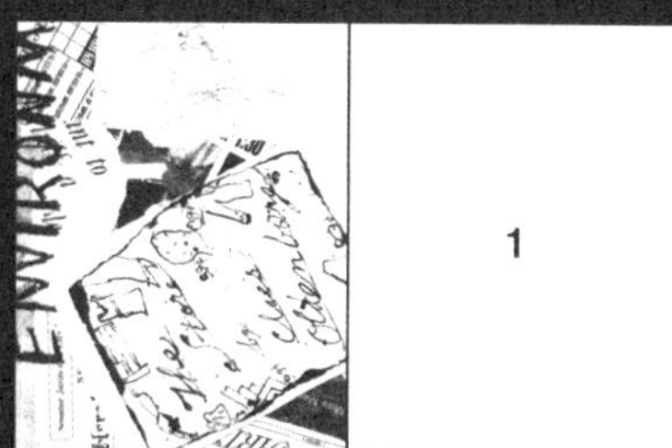

L Detail of poster for "Environ-
ments, Situations, Spaces"
Martha Jackson Gallery,
New York, 1961

2 3

4 5

6 7

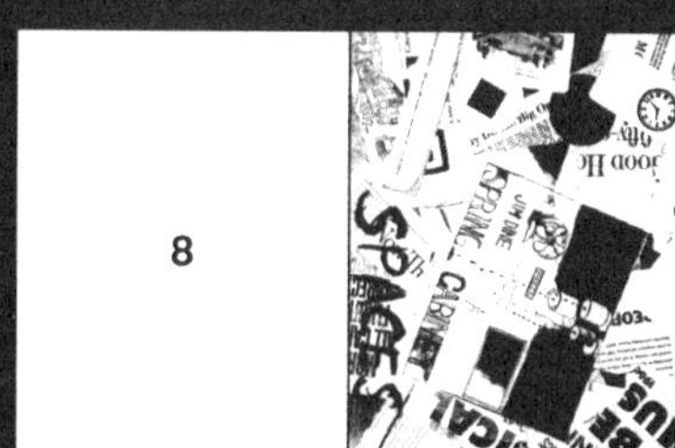

R Detail of poster for "Environ-
ments, Situations, Spaces"
Martha Jackson Gallery,
New York, 1961

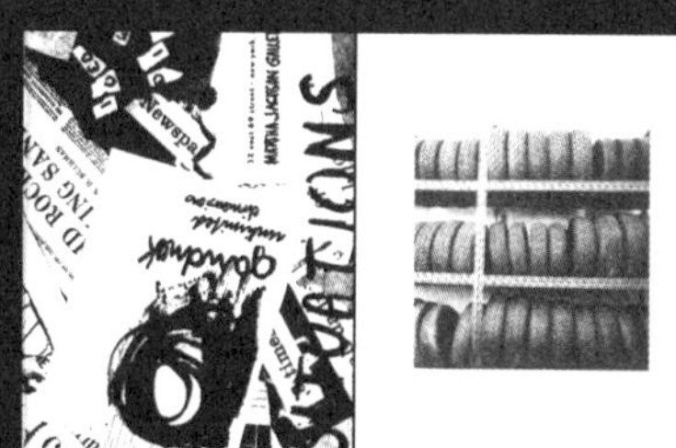

L Detail of poster for "Environ-
ments, Situations, Spaces"
Martha Jackson Gallery,
New York, 1961

R Detail of *Yard*, 1991
Fondazione Mudima
Photo: © Giovanni Ricci

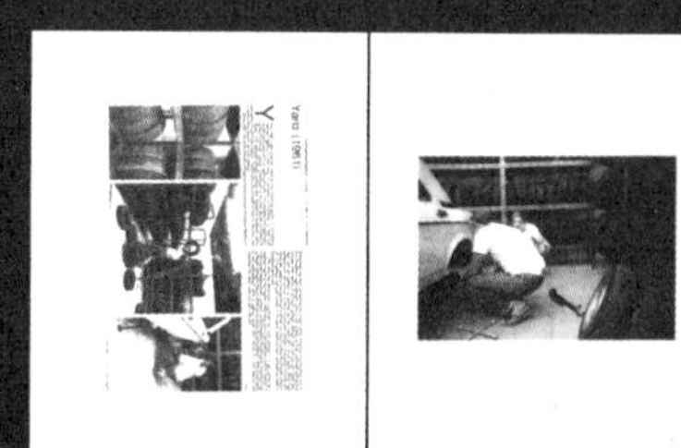

L Kaprow statement on *Yard*, 1991,
from news bulletin for "Allan
Kaprow: 7 Environments"
Fondazione Mudima

R *Yard* being installed, 1991
Fondazione Mudima
Photo: © Fabrizio Garghetti

4

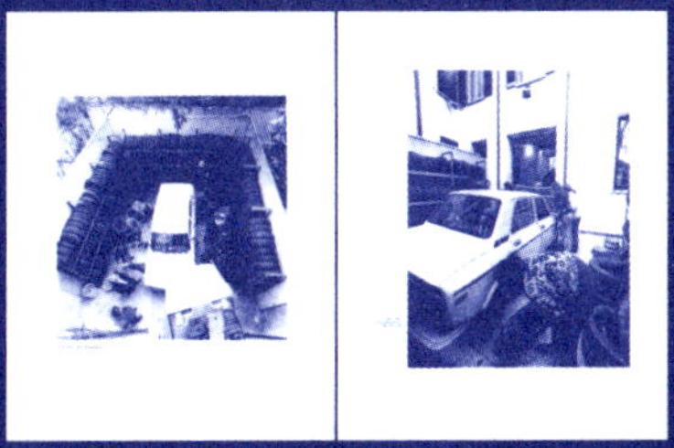

L *Yard* with participants, 1991
Fondazione Mudima
Photo: © Giovanni Ricci

R *Yard* with participants, 1991
Fondazione Mudima
Photo: © Giovanni Ricci

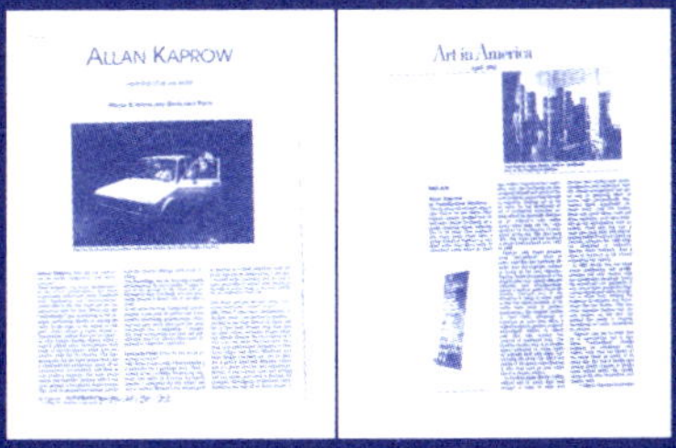

L Interview with the artist
Helena Kontova and Giancarlo Politi, *Flash Art International* 25, no. 162 (January–February) 1992, pp. 92–95.
© *Flash Art International Edition*

R Review of exhibition
Meyer Raphael Rubenstein, *Art in America* 80, no. 4 (April) 1992, p. 171
© *Art in America Magazine*
Courtesy of Brant Art Media, LLC.

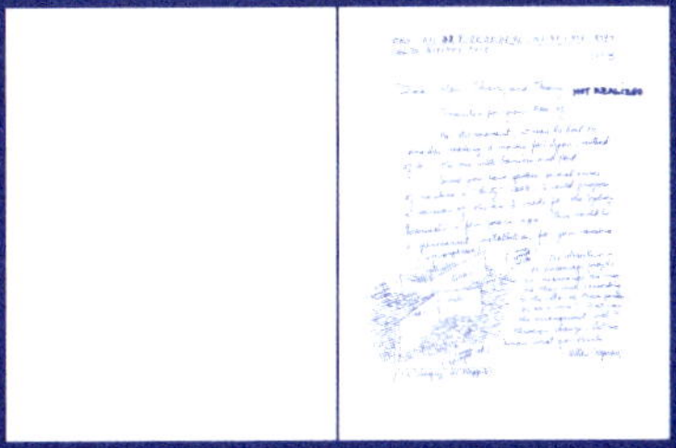

R Letter proposing new version of *Yard* for "2ème biennale d'art contemporain: Et tous ils changent le monde"
Musée d'art contemporain Lyon, Lyon, France, 1993
Not realized
G.R.I.

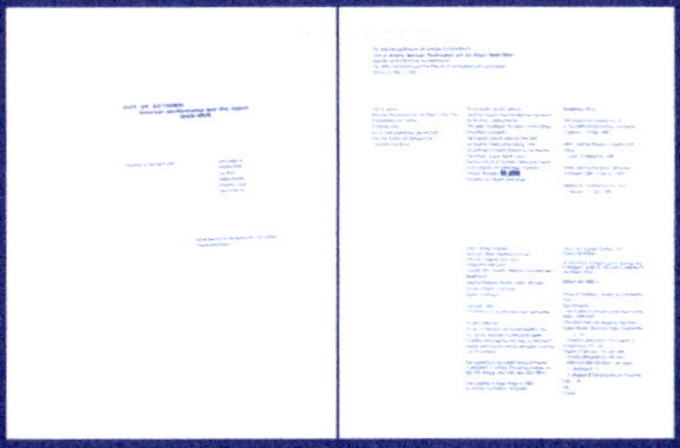

L Title page of "Out of Actions: between performance and the object, 1949–1979," 1998
Museum of Contemporary Art, Los Angeles, California

R Colophon of "Out of Actions," 1998
Museum of Contemporary Art, Los Angeles

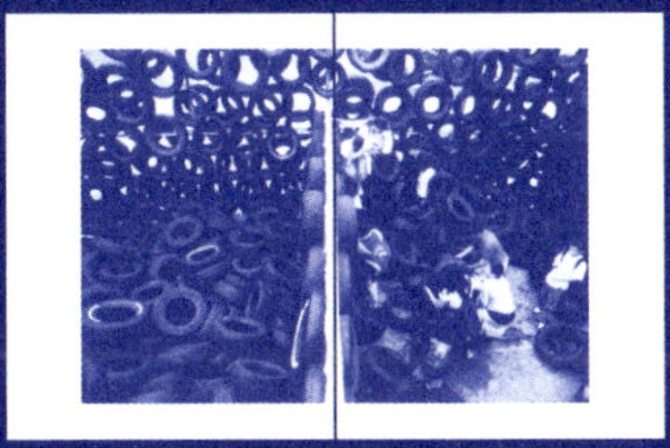

L – R *Yard* with participants, 1998
"Out of Actions"
The Geffen Contemporary at the Museum of Contemporary Art, Los Angeles
Photo: © Alex Slade

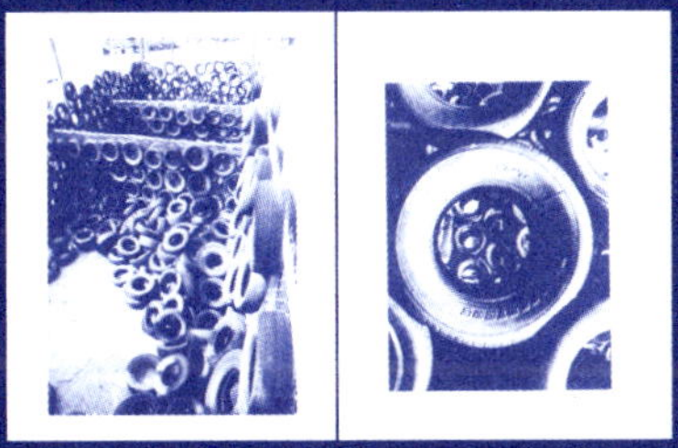

L *Yard*, 1998
Museum of Contemporary Art, Los Angeles
Photo: © Alex Slade

R *Yard*, 1998
Museum of Contemporary Art, Los Angeles
Photographer unknown

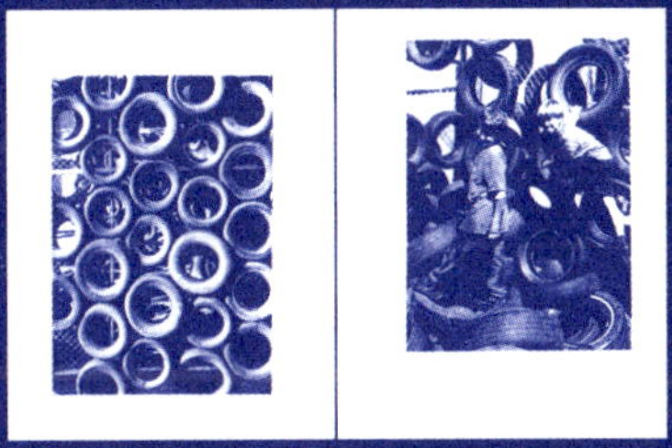

L *Yard*, 1998
Museum of Contemporary Art, Los Angeles
Photographer unknown

R *Yard* with participants, 1998
Museum of Contemporary Art, Los Angeles
Photographer unknown

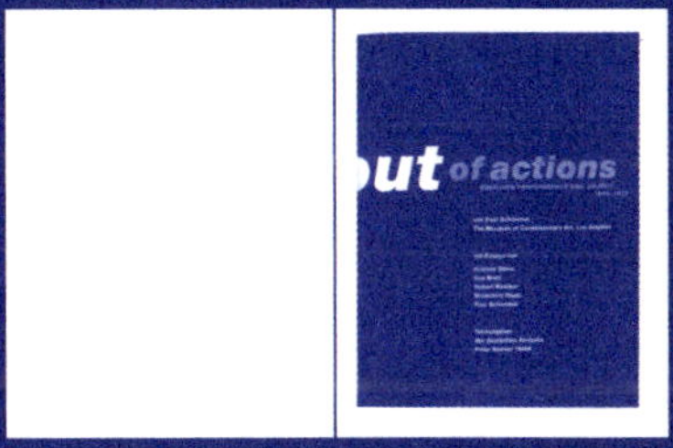

R Title page of "Out of Actions: zwischen performance und object 1949–1979," 1998
MAK—Österreichisches Museum für angewandte Kunst, Vienna, Austria

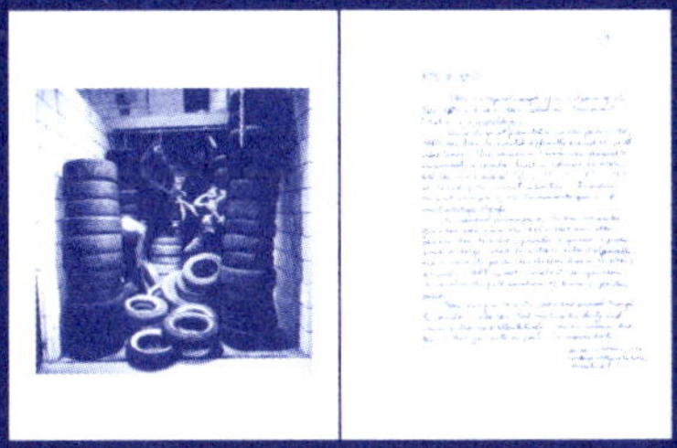

L *Yard* with participants, 1998
MAK
Photo: © Gerald Zugman/MAK

R Artist's note on *Yard*, 1998
G.R.I.

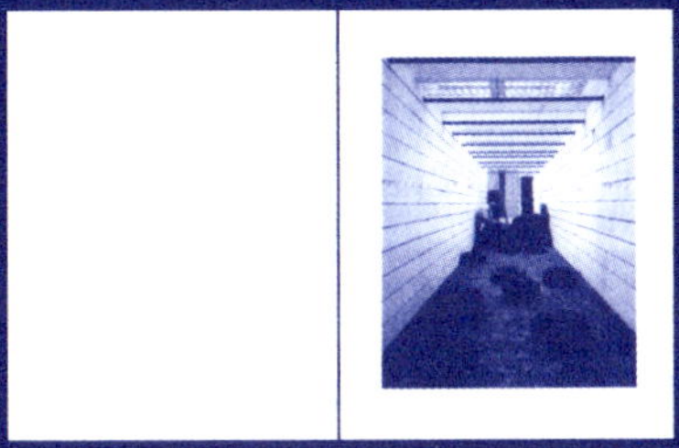

R The artist installing *Yard*, 1998
MAK
Photo: © Gerald Zugman/MAK

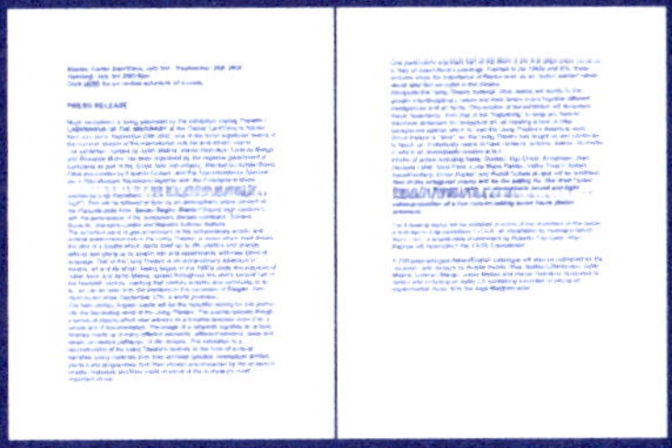

L – R Press release for "Living Theatre/ Labyrinths of the Imaginary," 2003
Castel Sant'Elmo, Naples, Italy

L Plan of *Yard* for Giuseppe Morra, 2003
G.R.I.

R Notes to Giuseppe Morra on *Yard*, 2003
G.R.I.

5

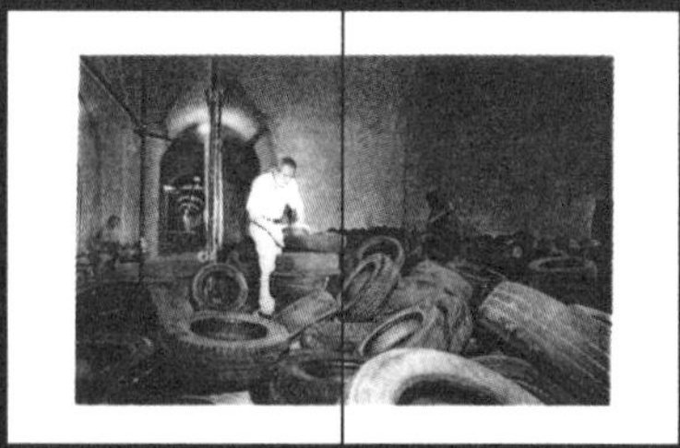

L Kaprow installing Yard, 2003
– "Living Theatre/Labyrinths of the
R Imaginary"
Castel Sant'Elmo
Photographer unknown

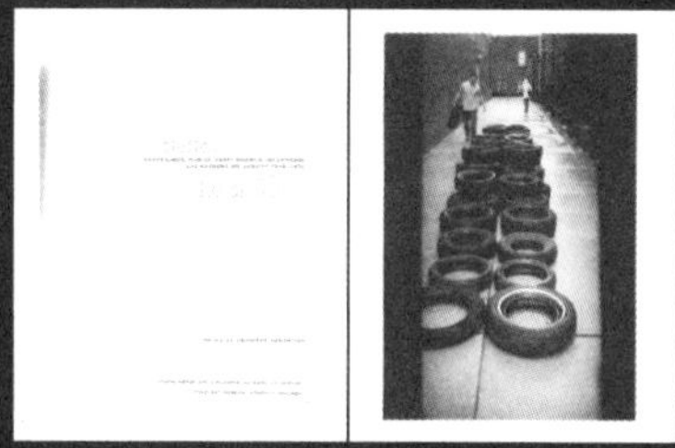

L Title page of "Critical Mass: Happenings, Fluxus, Performance, Intermedia and Rutgers University 1958–1972," 2003
Rutgers, The State University, New Brunswick, New Jersey

R *Yard (Carpets)*, with participant, 2003
"Critical Mass"
Mason Gross Art Galleries, Rutgers
Version by Geoffrey Hendricks
Photo: © Geoffrey Hendricks

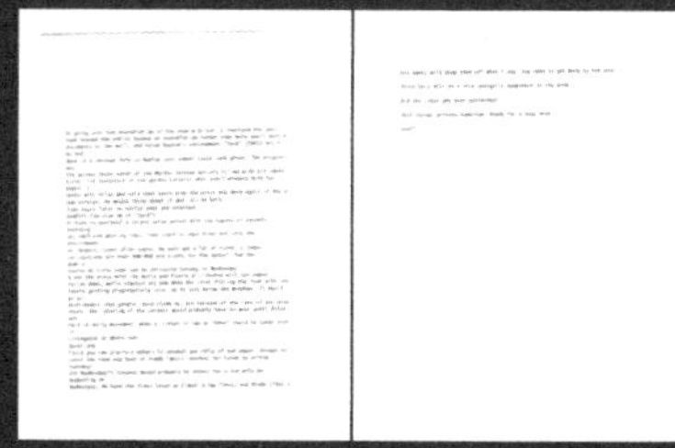

L Note regarding *Yard* written by
– Geoffrey Hendricks, 2003
R Courtesy Geoffrey Hendricks

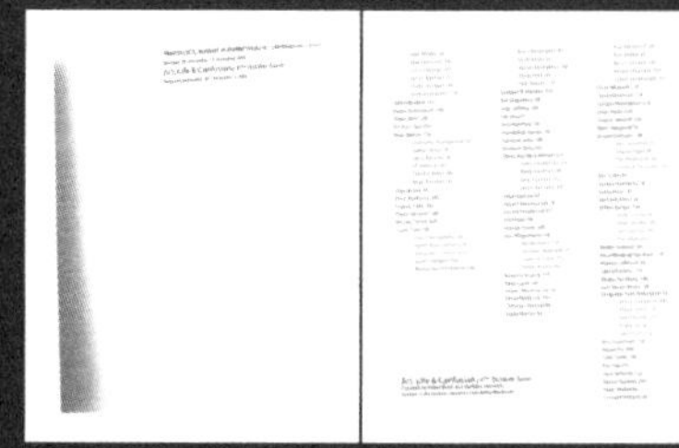

L Title page of "Art, Life & Confusion/47th October Salon," 2006
Belgrade, Serbia

R Artists in "47th October Salon"

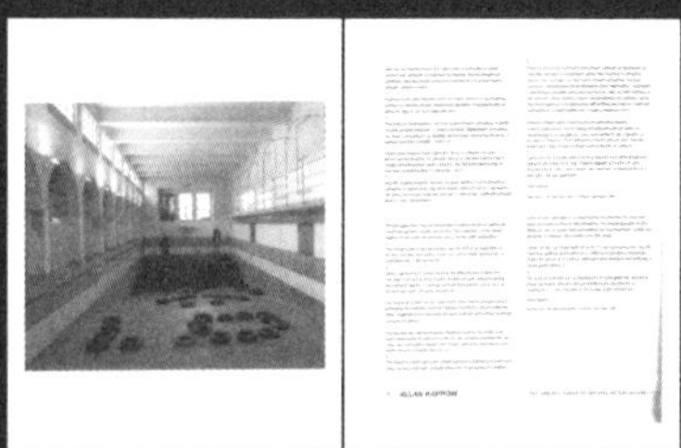

L *Yard*, 2006
"47th October Salon"
Photo: © Daniel and Gabriel Glid

R Catalog entry and quotes from "Art, Life & Confusion/47th October Salon," 2006
Excerpted from Kaprow essay "The Real Experiment"
Artforum 22, no. 4 (December) 1983, pp. 37–43

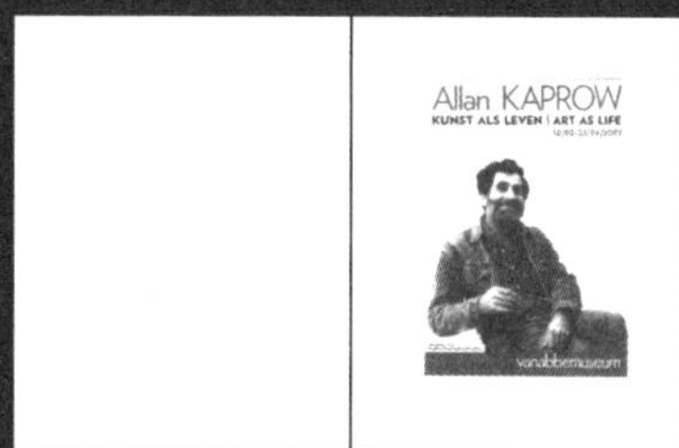

R Announcement for "Allan Kaprow—Kunst Als Leven/Art as Life," 2007
Van Abbemuseum, Eindhoven, The Netherlands

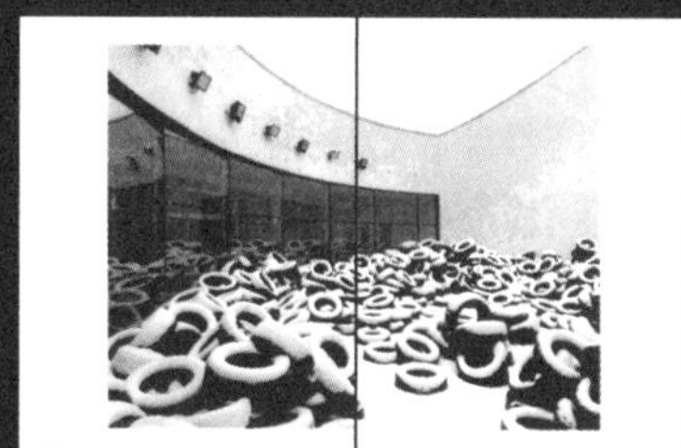

L *Yard*, 2007
– "Allan Kaprow—Art as Life,"
R Van Abbemuseum
Version by Eva Meyer-Hermann
Photo: © Peter Cox

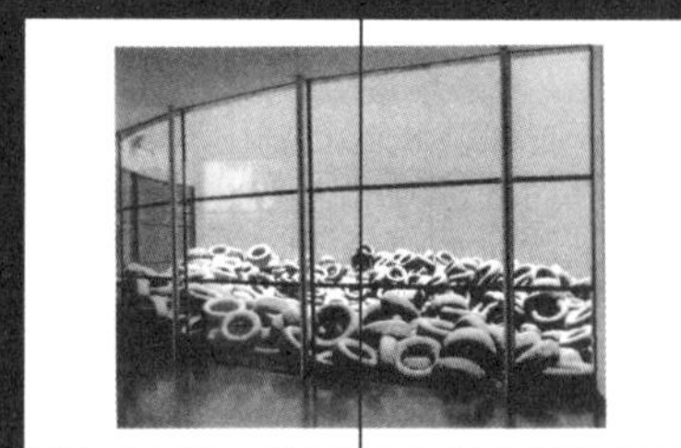

L Van Abbemuseum
– Photo: © Peter Cox
R

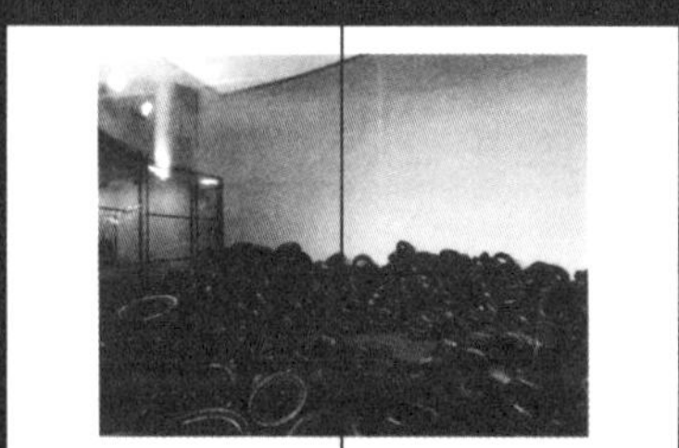

L Van Abbemuseum
– Photo: © Peter Cox
R

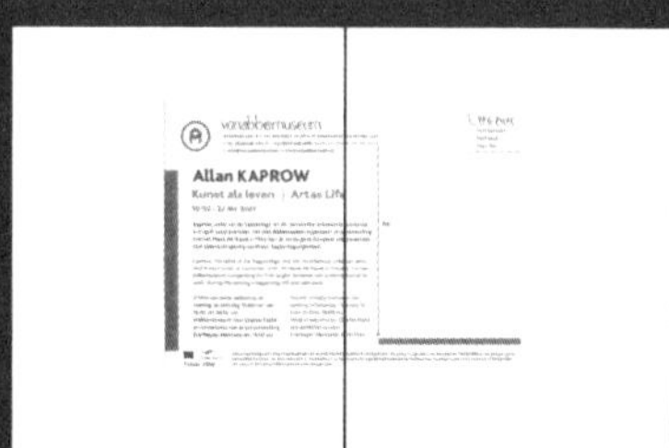

L Invitation to Kaprow exhibition,
– 2007
R Van Abbemuseum

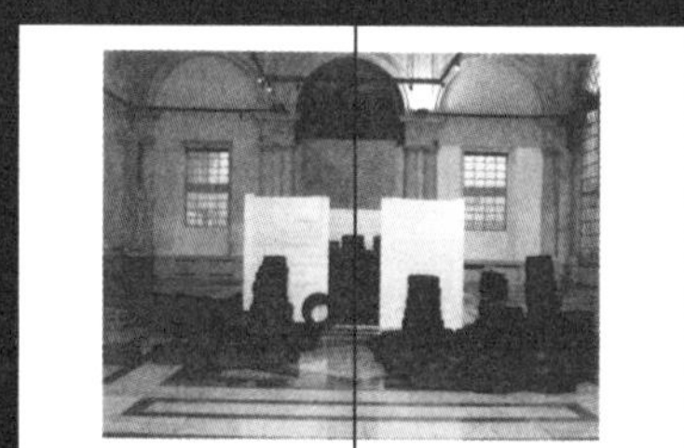

L *Yard (Carpets)*, 2008
– "Allan Kaprow—Art as Life"
R Museo d'Arte contemporanea di Villa Croce, Genoa, Italy
Version by Geoffrey Hendricks and Pietro Millefiore
Photo: © Mario Parodi

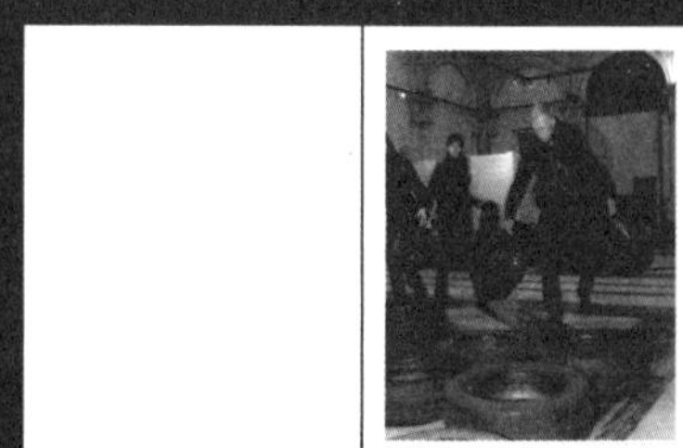

R *Yard (Carpets)* with participants, 2008
Museo d'Art contemporanea di Villa Croce
Photo: © Mario Parodi

6

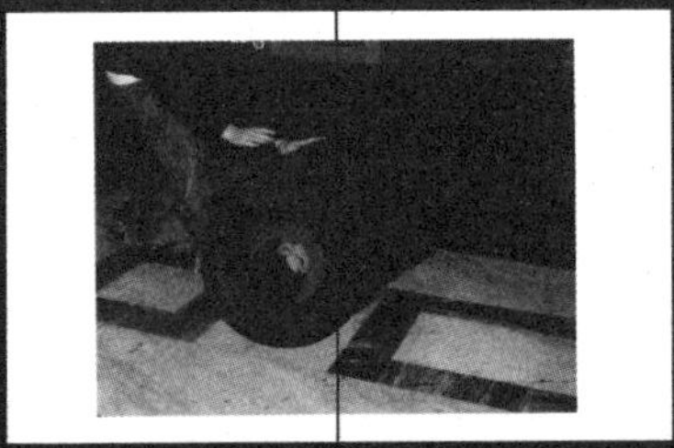

L Museo d'Art contemporanea di
– Villa Croce
R Version by Geoffrey Hendricks and Pietro Millefiore
Photo: © Mario Parodi

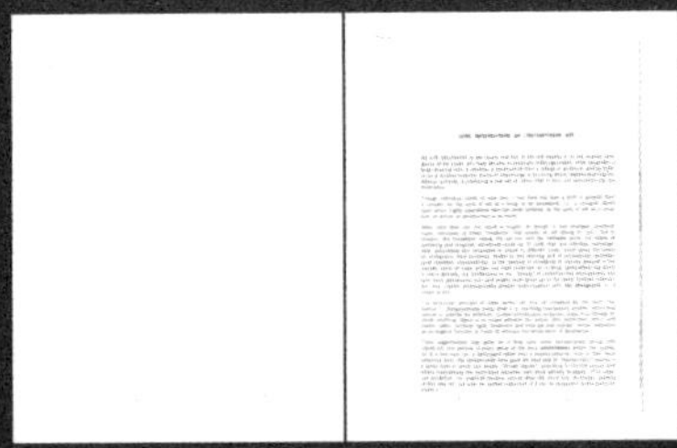

R *Some Observations on Contemporary Art*
Kaprow essay published in "New Forms—New Media," 1960
Martha Jackson Gallery, New York, 1960
(Condensed from a book to be published soon entitled "Paintings, Environments and Happenings")

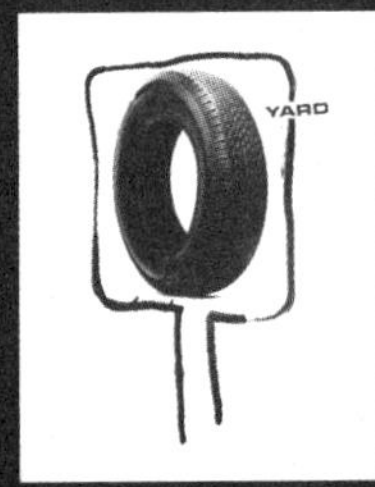

L *Yard*, 1970
Lithograph
88.3 × 61.9 cm
(34¾ × 24⅜ inches)
Artist Proof
© Allan Kaprow Estate
Courtesy Hauser & Wirth

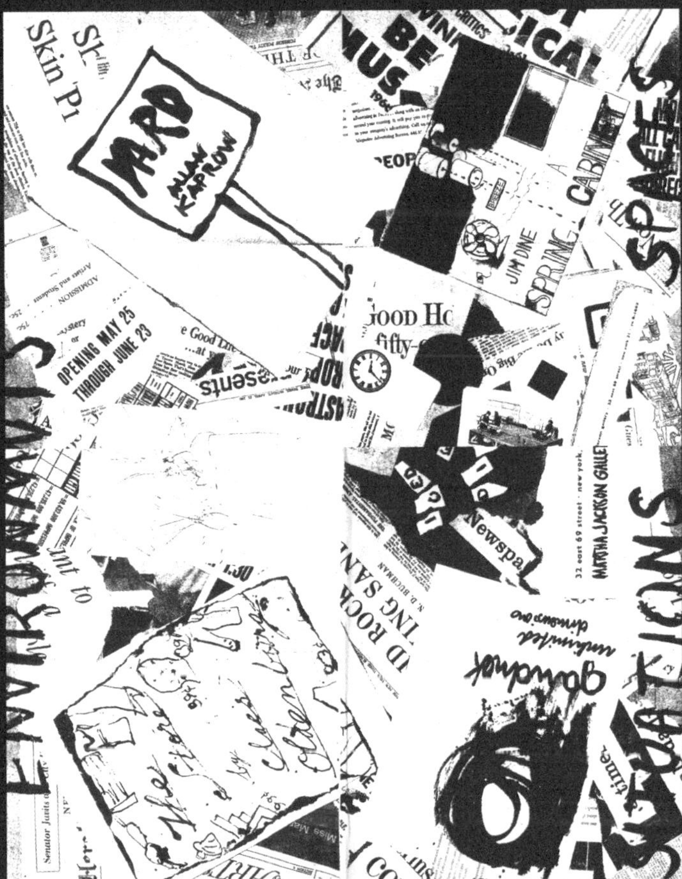

Poster for "Environments, Situations, Spaces," 1961
Martha Jackson Gallery, New York
© Allan Kaprow Estate
Courtesy Hauser & Wirth

A selected facsimile from the Allan Kaprow Estate workfile on *Yard* published on the occasion of

Allan Kaprow Yard
Hauser & Wirth New York
September 23–October 31, 2009

Design by An Art Service

Coordinated by Tamara Bloomberg and Sylvia Bandi
Special thanks to Mirella Roma and Blair Taylor

Cover image based on
Yard for exhibition "Environments, Situations, Spaces," 1961
Ink on paper
34.3 × 26.7 cm
(13½ × 10½ inches)

ISBN: 978–3–033–02112–9
Printed by Magnum Offset, Hong Kong

www.hauserwirth.com

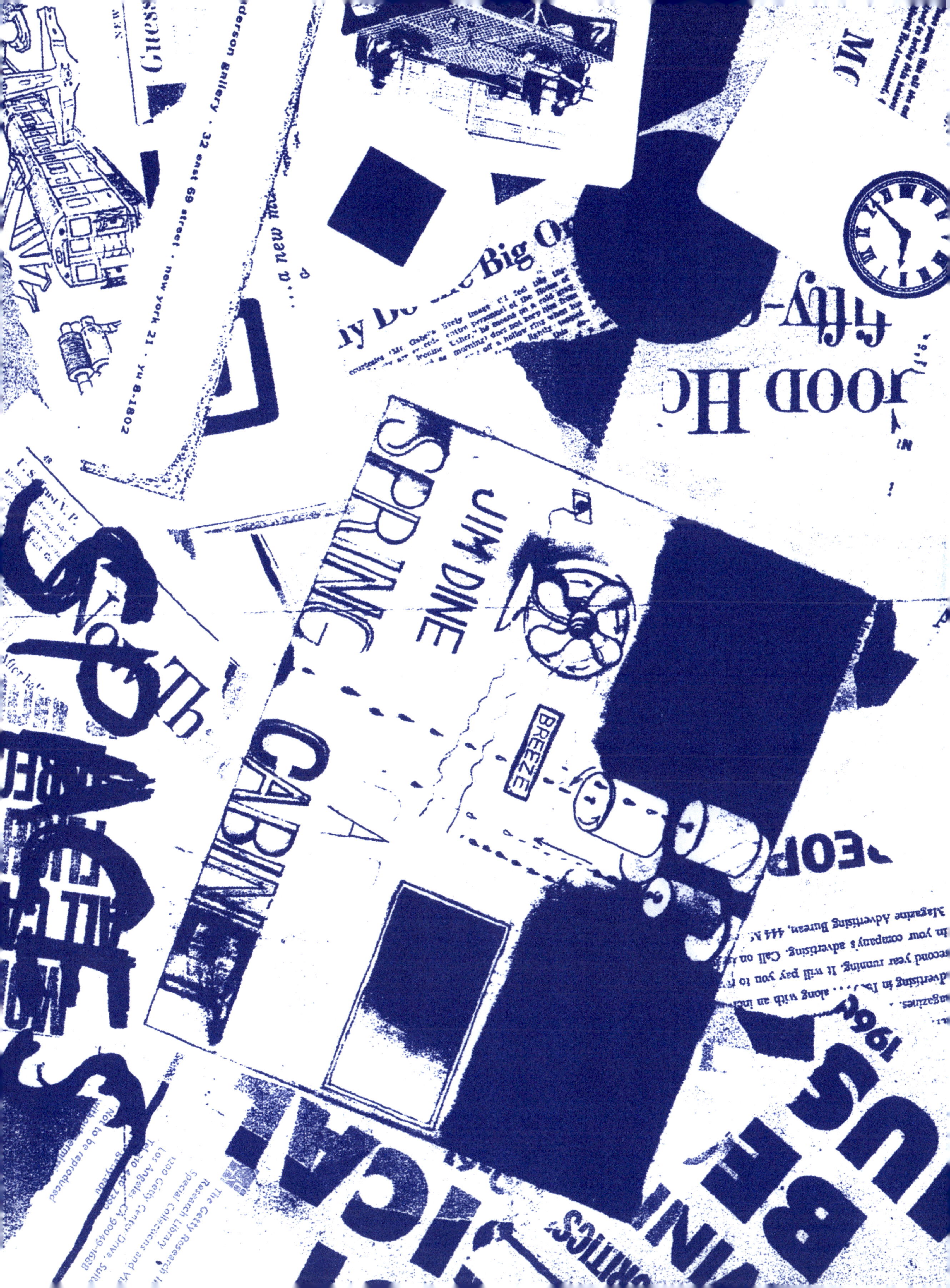
JIM DINE
SPRING
CABIN
BREEZE
32 east 69 street . new york 21 . yu 8-1802

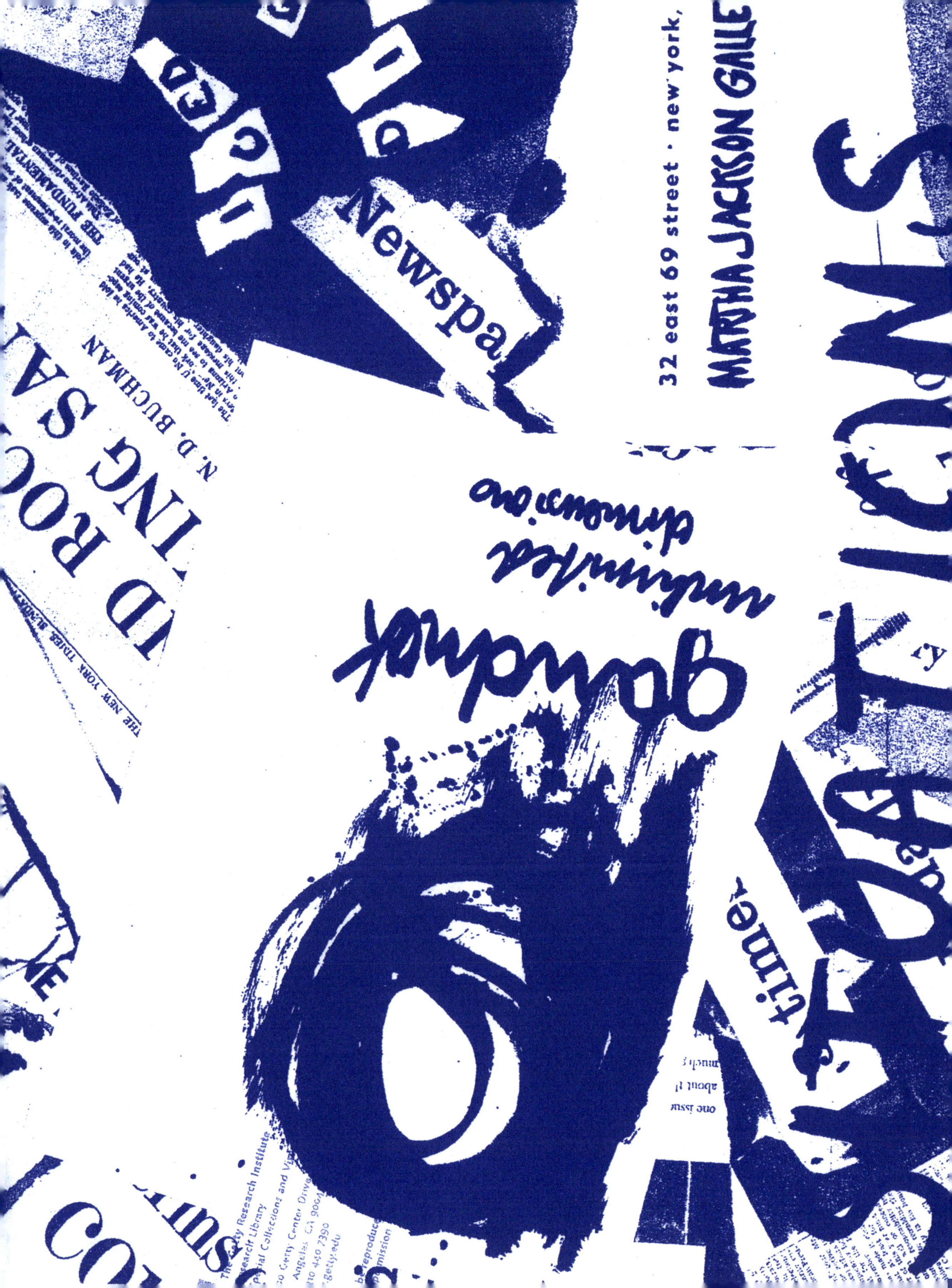
goodnough
unlimited dimensions
32 east 69 street · new york,
MARTHA JACKSON GALLE
Newspa
N. D. BUCHMAN
THE NEW YORK TIMES
THE FUNDAMENTAL
times

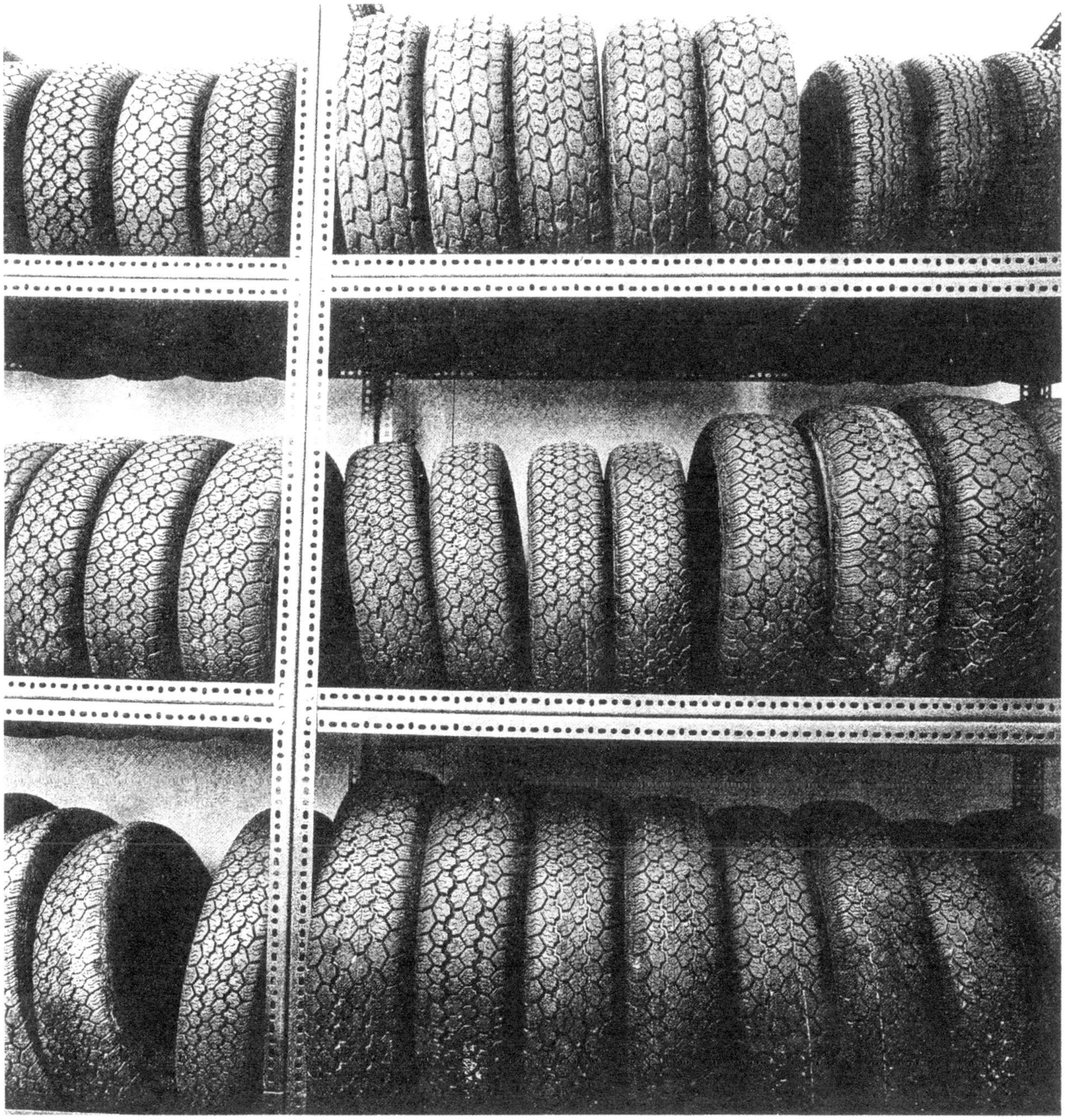

Yard (1961)

Yard (1961) was originally made in the sculpture garden of the Martha Jackson Gallery in New York. It consisted of hundreds of used tires covering the ground in no particular order. Five tarpaper mounds emerged from the tires, vaguely reminiscent of the rock garden of Ryoanji in Kyoto. (The tarpaper actually covered Mrs. Jackson's sculpture collection, which couldn't be moved!). Visitors were encouraged to walk on the tires, and to throw them around as they pleased.

Since 1961, the work (whose conceptual rights belong to Wolfgang Feelisch in Remscheid) has been remade seven or eight times in Europe and America; and on each occasion it was changed, more or less greatly, to fit the particular spaces and contexts. This version is the most radically distinct. The tires are new rather than used; they are stacked on shelves as they would be in a tire store, rather than scattered over the ground. A car is introduced, instead of tarpaper mounds, and visitors are urged to change the car's wheels by using a pneumatic wrench or spanner. Furthermore, the gray tonality of the early version is here replaced by walls of fluorescent acid-rose.

This time, the participant is not like the child playing in a city dump, as I imagined myself in the original YARD. Now, she or he becomes a kind of "worker" in consumerist imagery which, however, is still located in the art world. Questions may be asked. Where is the art? What is one doing by participating? What is one doing by not participating? What is gained, either way? Whom is it for? Should you remember this when next you get a flat tire?

A.K.

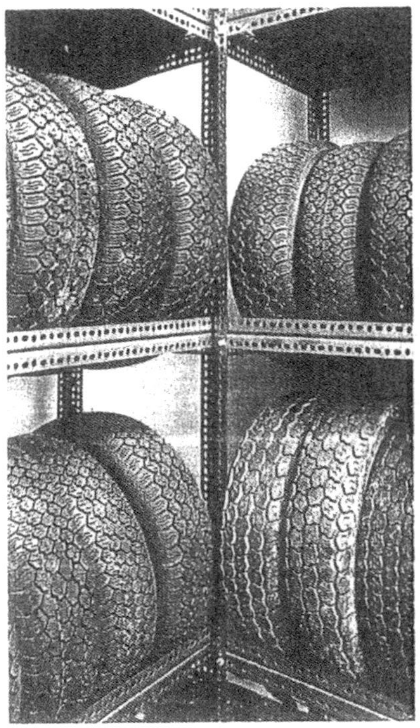

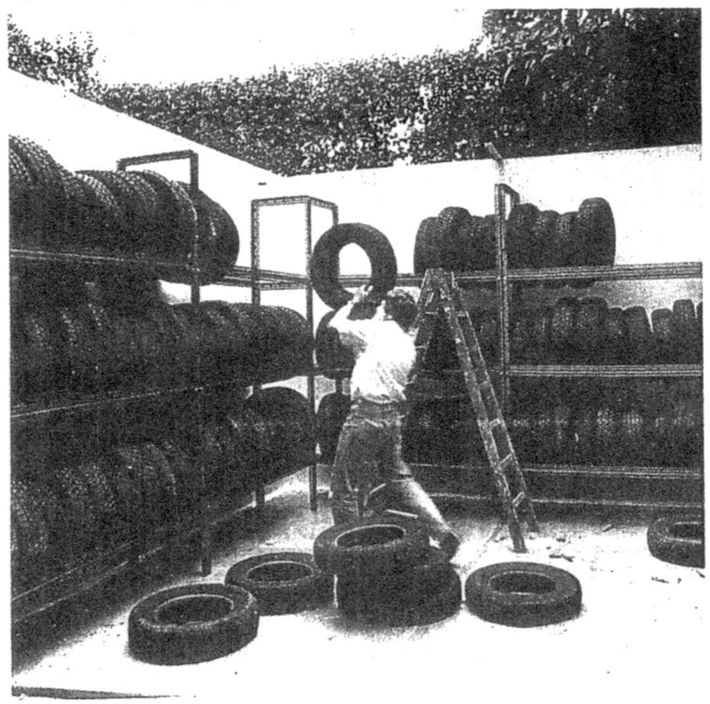

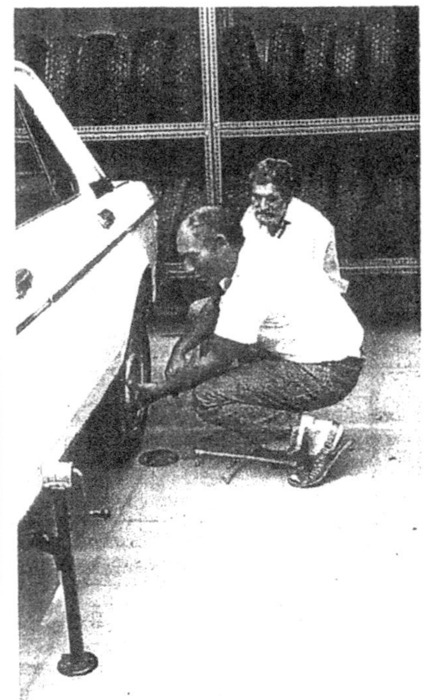

Allan Kaprow, "Yard", 1991, (details)

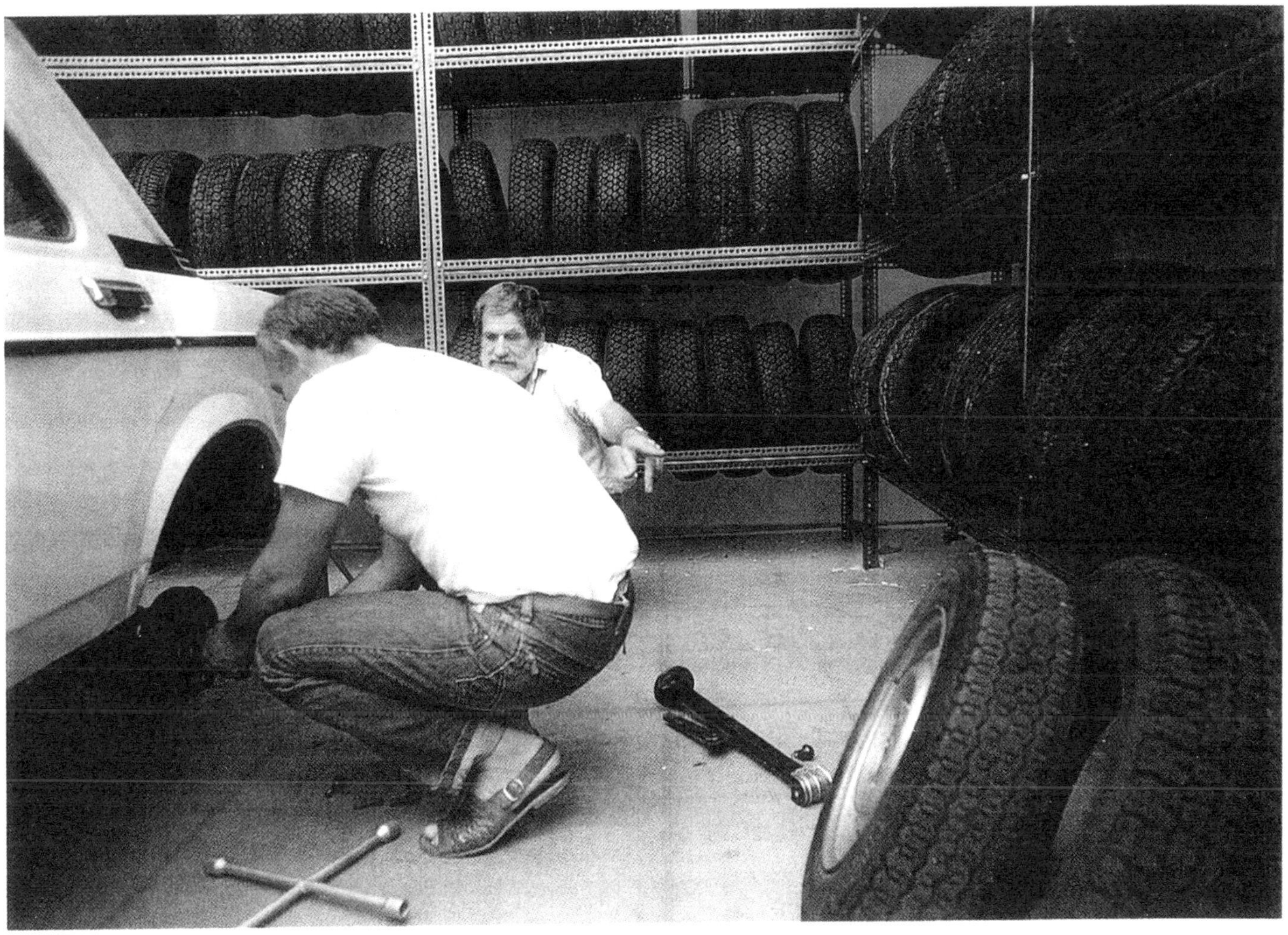

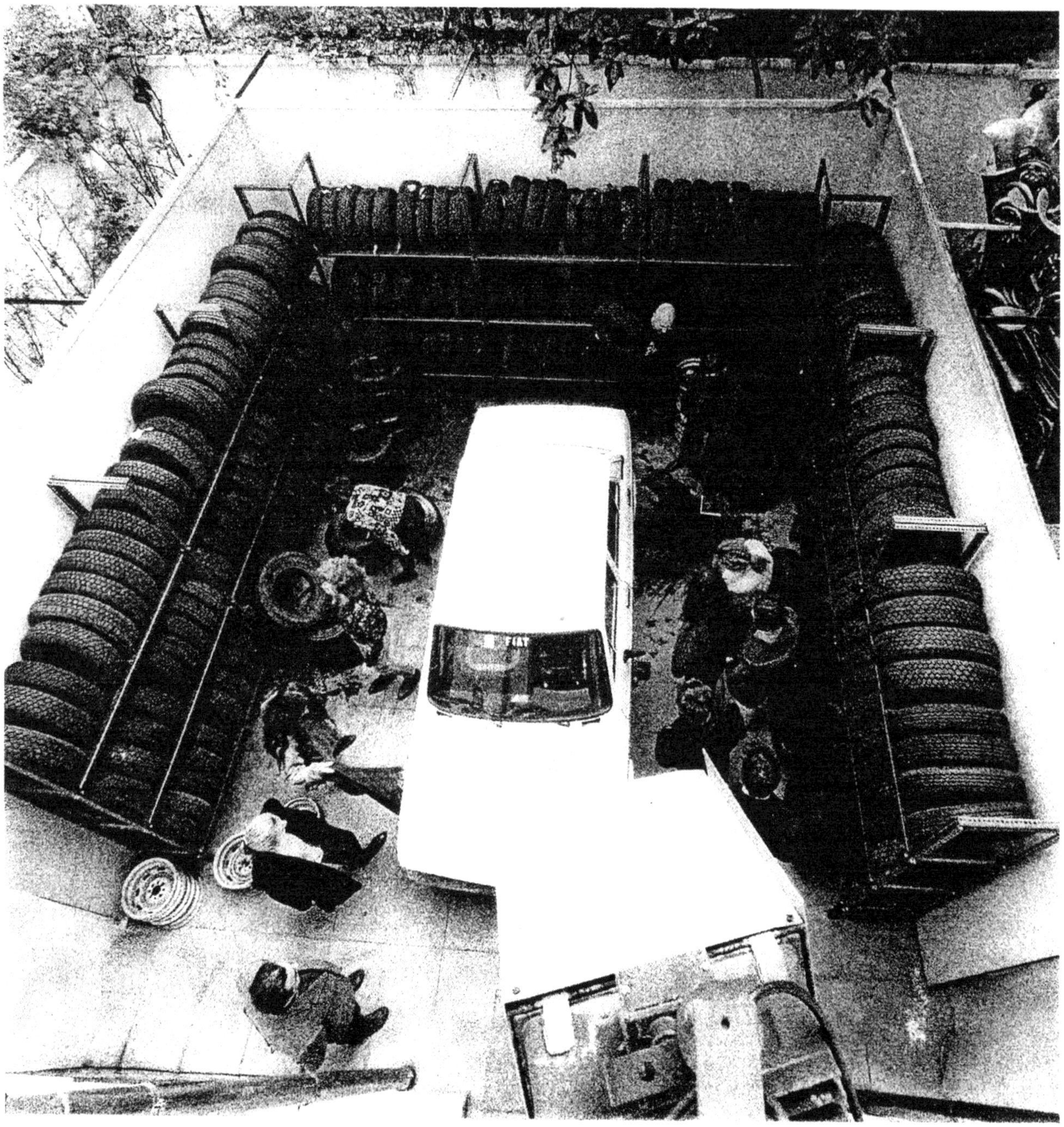

Yard, 1991, (with participants).

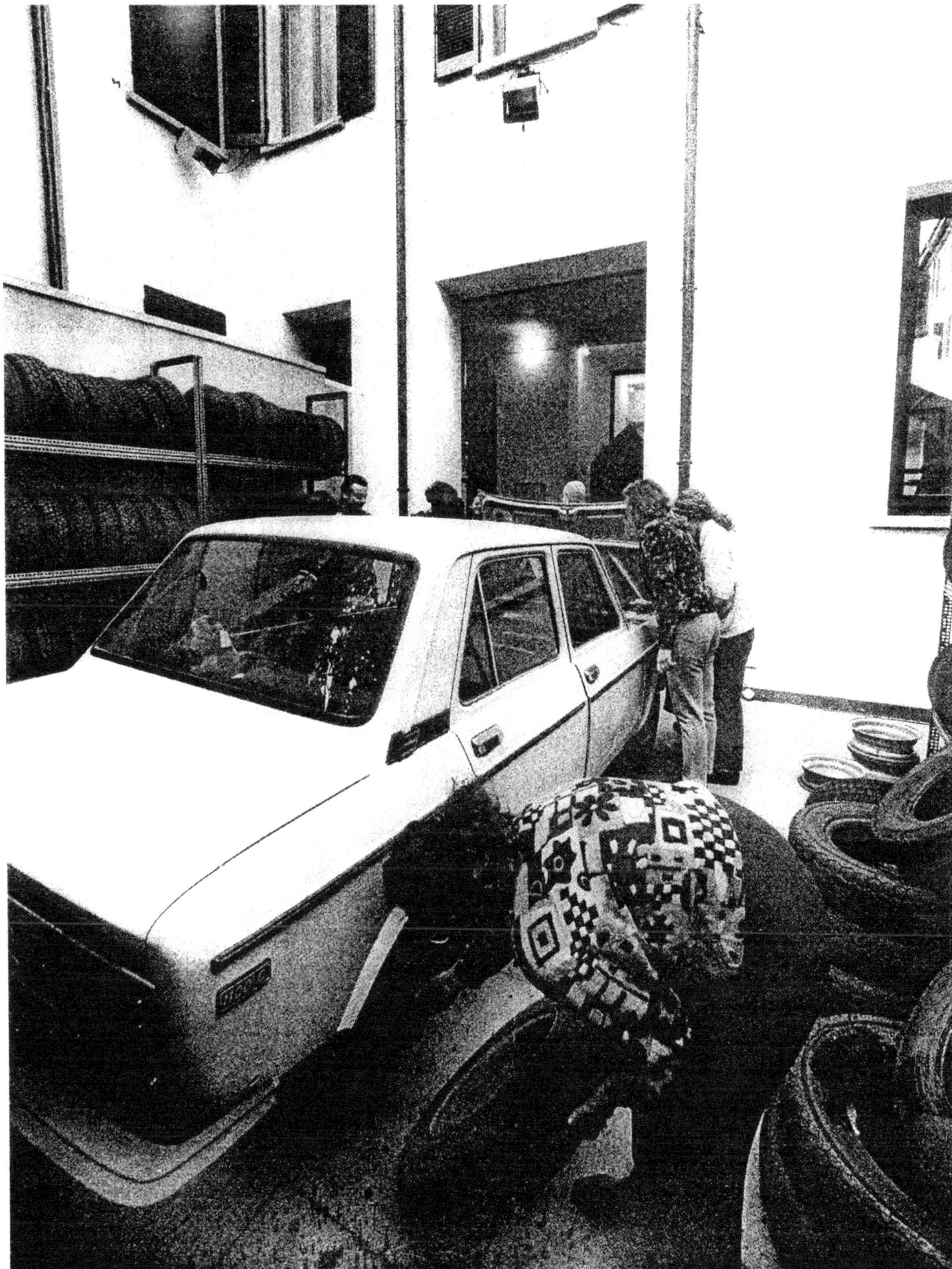

Yard, 1991,
(with participants),
left and right.

ALLAN KAPROW

HAPPENS TO BE AN ARTIST

HELENA KONTOVA AND GIANCARLO POLITI

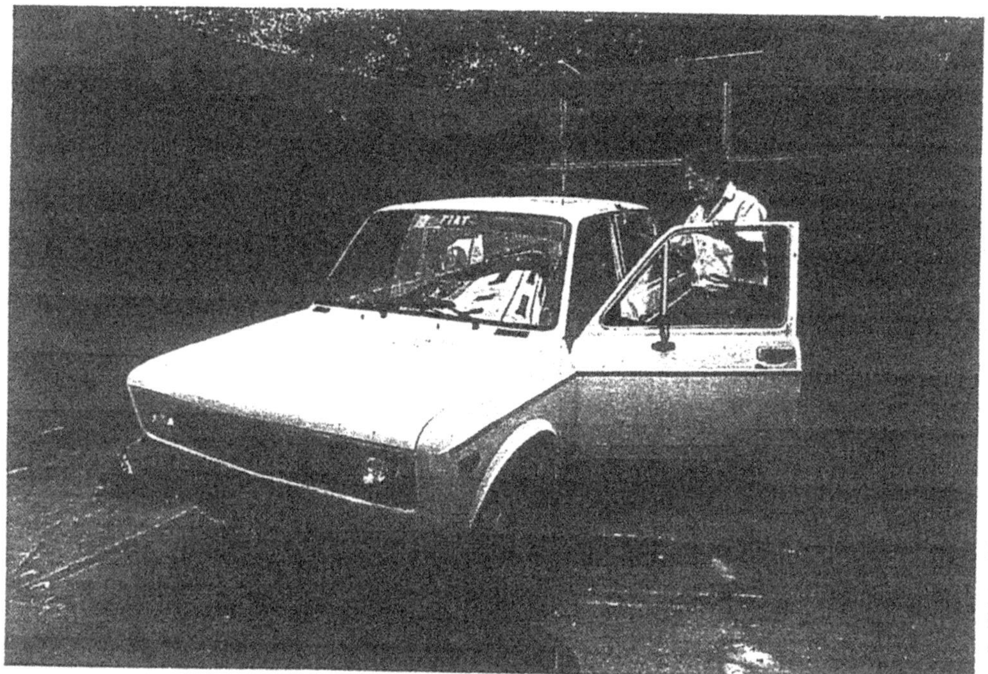

YARD, 1961/91. ENVIRONMENT. COURTESY FONDAZIONE MUDIMA, MILAN. PHOTO FABRIZIO GARGHETTI.

Helena Kontova: *How did you come to use the words "happening" and "environment"?*

Allan Kaprow: The word "performance" or the word "installation" are more traditionally understood words compared with "happening" and "environments" which refer to the real world and are not associated with the arts. When you say "performance," you're referring to, for example, performing Hamlet or playing the violin on the stage, so the history of "the arts" with a theater, a frame, around it. "Installation" implies the verb "to install": an artist installs discrete objects within a neutral gallery space. Environments were made in non-art spaces which were not neutral, they had an identity. The happening also had no frame around them, but it eliminated the exhibitional aspect of the environment: you couldn't visit them as you would a museum. The work would vanish into imperfect memory when it was over, perhaps a few photos would remain. The work is documented through gossip! And the stories change with each retelling.

The assemblage was the first step towards the happening. To put it simply, I began to pull all the garbage in the world into art. Garbage is easy, it's cheap, it's also interesting because it doesn't last, it rots after a while.

At one point the word "happening" got too popular; it was used for politics and it was used for advertising, popular music, films, and any party some joker gave for some rich people was "a happening." I thought, this word is becoming too lame and popularized, and I've always been more interested in subjective experience.

Giancarlo Politi: *When did you decide to become an artist?*

AK: When I was a child I first remember I wanted to be a garbage man. Then I wanted to be a cowboy, because my boyhood was spent in Arizona for health reasons. I remember the first artist I met was a cowboy. Because I was always good at drawing as a child, somebody took me to see him and he talked to me. I told him I wanted to be a cowboy, and he said it was a good idea to make a little money on the side as a sure thing, in his case, selling his art. And that's what I do.

GP: *When did you become more conscious about your "career" in art?*

AK: When I came back, permanently, to the East; when I was thirteen or fourteen. I enrolled in the High School of Music and Art in New York. Friends from there told me about (Hans) Hofmann. I knew about him already, because the art world in New York was very small. We knew there were these very sophisticated Europeans in New York; Léger was there, Mondrian was there, Tanguy was there, etc., etc. So there was a general sense that American culture was at a point of crisis and opportunity. Before, if you wanted some real writing and real music, you went to Europe, for example, Hemingway or Gertrude Stein. Suddenly one had all of those people in

Art in America

April 1992

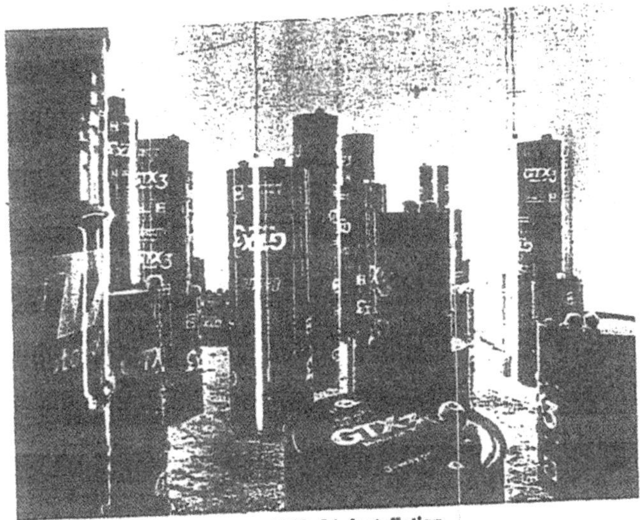

Allan Kaprow: *Apple Shrine*, 1960–91, installation view; at the Fondazione Mudima.

MILAN

Allan Kaprow at Fondazione Mudima

Talking about his student days in New York in the late 1940s, Allan Kaprow recently recalled how he had seen Marcel Duchamp as a purely historical figure, believing him to be dead. One suspects that many today might have a similar image of Kaprow—a vanished artist who did a body of innovative works about 30 years ago. In fact, Kaprow is very much alive; only, like Duchamp, he has rendered himself and much of his work invisible, supporting himself by teaching. Staying out of the art world, he has developed an art of occasional everyday actions which he privately denotes as art. Kaprow's only visible works these days are his "reinventions" of his famous Environments of the late '50s and early '60s. This show offered versions of seven Environments from 1957 to 1964.

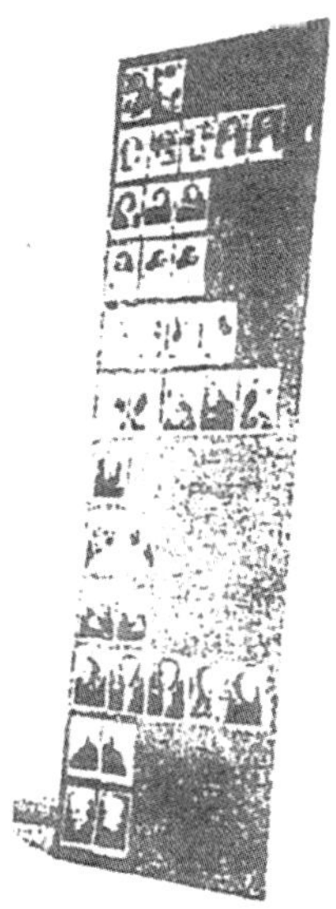

Kaprow calls these installations "reinventions" since in every case they are markedly different from the originals. Instead of acting as his own historian, Kaprow distills the essence of his original idea and, using different materials and arrangements, makes a work of great visual difference. (Perhaps one of the things he is trying to make clear is that the visual qualities of his works were never of primary importance.) The original version of *Yard* (1961) consisted of hundreds of used tires filling a walled sculpture garden. Kaprow encouraged visitors to tramp over and toss around the mounds of scattered tires. The Mudima version was in a smaller space enclosed on three sides by specially built pink walls. Surrounding the white Fiat 128 in the middle of the space were shelves of new tires such as one might see in a service station.

In the first *Apple Shrine* (1960), visitors had to wend their way through a maze of rags and chicken wire stuffed with straw, newspapers and cardboard. Now this messy arrangement has given way to gleaming black oil drums with perpendicular fluorescent lights suspended between them. Only the apples, some real, some fakes, were still there, tempting us to take them. Not all the reinventions were so orderly. *Push and Pull* was a large wire cage filled with disintegrating bales of hay and rolled-up carpets, whereas the 1963 original, dedicated to Kaprow's teacher Hans Hofmann, was a room of furniture to be moved around by the visitors.

In 1962, *Words* was two small rooms overflowing with graffiti, whereas the new version took two condensed narratives, broke the sentences into segments of one, two or three words and ingeniously distributed them throughout a whole floor, inviting the audience to decipher and reconstruct the two stories. This was tricky because Kaprow had not only broken up the text but printed the words in reverse, sometimes on cards, sometimes on mirrors.

Kaprow may like to think that he is semi-retired, but in fact these "reinventions" should properly be considered new works. True, they are based on the same ideas as works of 30 years ago, but this is hardly rare among artists: Kaprow is simply more candid about the consistency of his once innovative, now classic work.

—*Meyer Raphael Rubinstein*

FAX: 011·33·7·78·38·28·92 ; 011·33·1·4021·8384
CHG. TO: (619) 943·9418

1993

Dear Marc, Thierry and Thierry **NOT REALIZED**

Thanks for your FAX of

For the moment, it may be best to consider making 2 works for Lyon, instead of 4: the one with barriers, and Yard.

Since you have spoken several times of wanting a "dirty" YARD, I could propose a version of the one I made for the Sydney Biennale a few years ago. This could be a permanent installation for your museum.

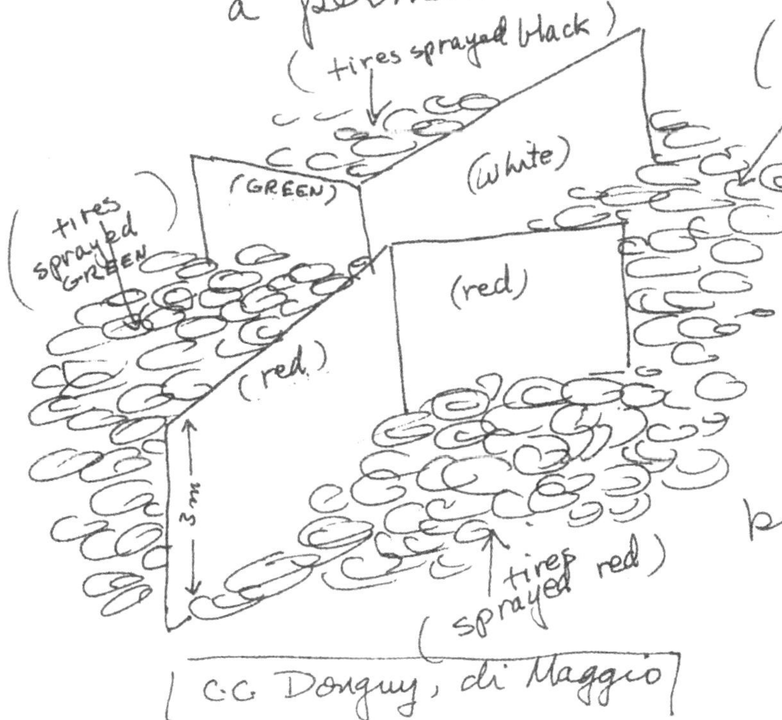

The objective is to encourage people to rearrange the tires as they wish (according to the color of their panels, or as a mix). That way the arrangement will always change. Let me know what you think.

— Allan (Kaprow)

[c.c. Donguy, di Maggio]

OUT OF ACTIONS:
between performance and the object, 1949-1979

Organized by Paul Schimmel

with essays by
Kristine Stiles
Guy Brett
Hubert Klocker
Shinichiro Osaki
Paul Schimmel

The Museum of Contemporary Art, Los Angeles
Thames and Hudson

This book was published on the occaision of the exhibition
"Out of Actions: Between Performance and the Object 1949-1979,"
organized by Paul Schimmel and presented at
The Geffen Contemporary at The Museum of Contemporary Art, Los Angeles,
February 8 - May 10,1998.

"Out of Actions:
Between Performance and the Object, 1949-1979"
is dedicated to the memory
of Sydney Irmas,
and is made possible by a generous gift
from The Audrey and Sydney Irmas
Charitable Foundation.

The exhibition has also received
significant support from the National Endowment
for the Arts, a federal agency;
The Japan Foundation; the Japan-United States
Friendship Commission;
the Austrian Cultural Institute, New York;
the Austrian Federal Chancellery - Arts;
the Austrian Consulate General in Los Angeles;
The British Council; Merrill Lynch;
Service Culturel du Consulat Général de France
à Los Angeles; and *Association Française
d'Action Artistique* A-AA
Ministère des Affaires Étrangères

Exhibition Tour

The Museum of Contemporary Art
at The Geffen Contemporary, Los Angeles
8 February - 10 May 1998

MAK - Austrian Museum of Applied Arts,
Vienna
17 June - 6 September 1998

Museu d'Art Contemporani, Barcelona
15 October 1998 - 6 January 1999

Museum of Contemporary Art, Tokyo
11 February - 11 April 1999

Editor: Russell Ferguson
Assistant Editor: Stephanie Emerson
Editorial Assistant: Jane Hyun
Design and production:
Lorraine Wild, Amanda Washburn, Yuki Nishinaka
Separations:
DeskTopProduction Bucher GmbH, Stuttgart
Printed at Cantz in Germany
Bound in Germany

First published in the United States of America
in paperback in 1998 by Thames and Hudson, Inc.
500 Fifth Avenue, New York, New York 10010.

First published in Great Britain in 1998
by Thames and Hudson Ltd, London

Library of Congress Catalog Card
Number 97-62054

British Library Cataloguing-in-Publication data
A catalogue record for this book is available from
the British Library

ISBN 0-500-28050-9

Library of Congress Cataloguing-in-Publication
Data
Paul Schimmel.
Out of actions: between performance and the
object, 1949-1979
/Paul Schimmel; with essays by Guy Brett,
Hubert Klocker, Shinichiro Osaki, Kristine Stile
p. cm.
Exhibition presented at The Museum of
Contemporary Art, Los
Angeles, 8 February - 10 June 1998.
Includes bibliographical references.
ISBN 0-914357-56-5(pbk. : alk. paper)
1. --Exhibitions. 2. . I.
. II. Museum of Contemporary Art (Los Ange
Calif.) III.
Title.
N 2000

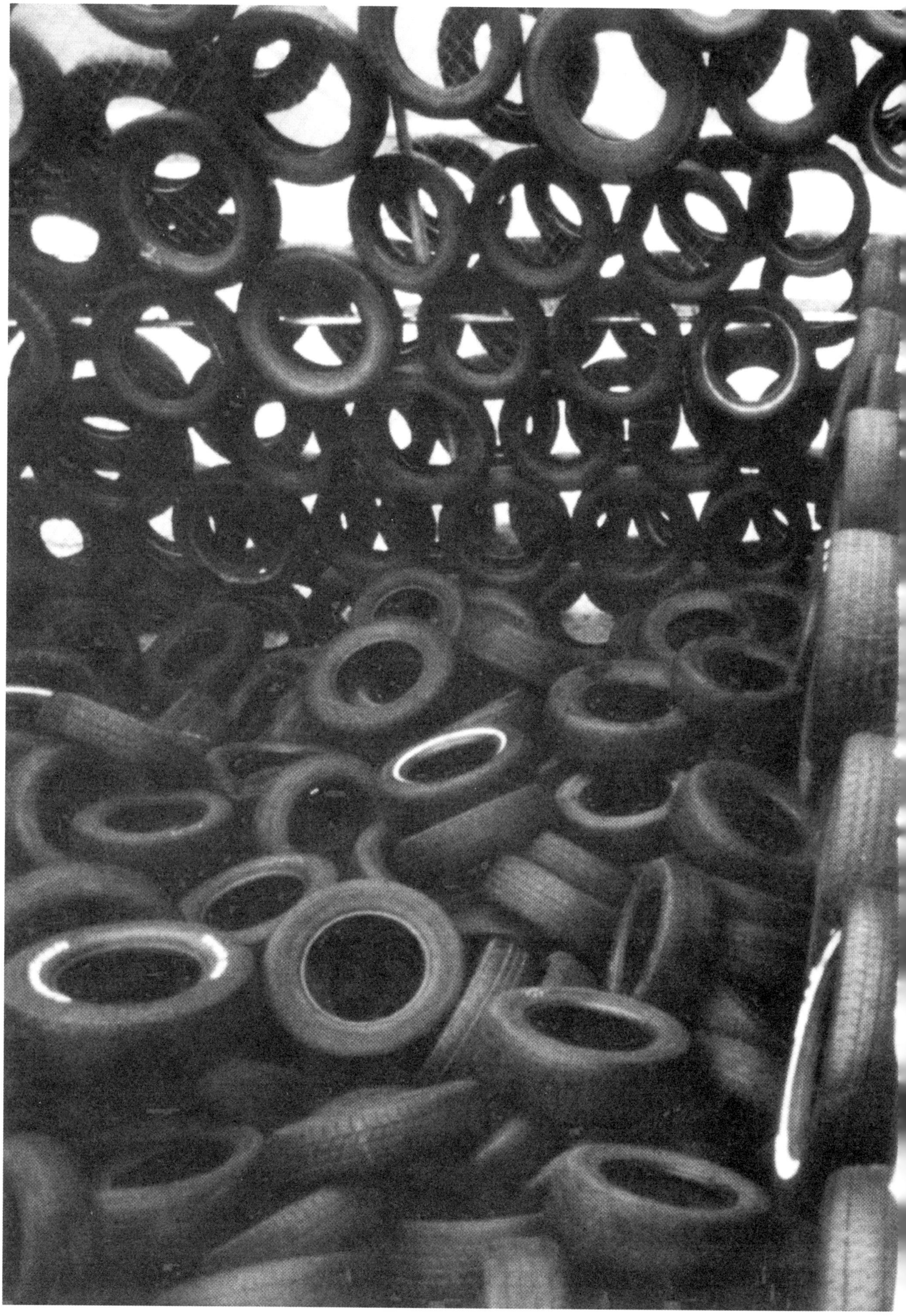

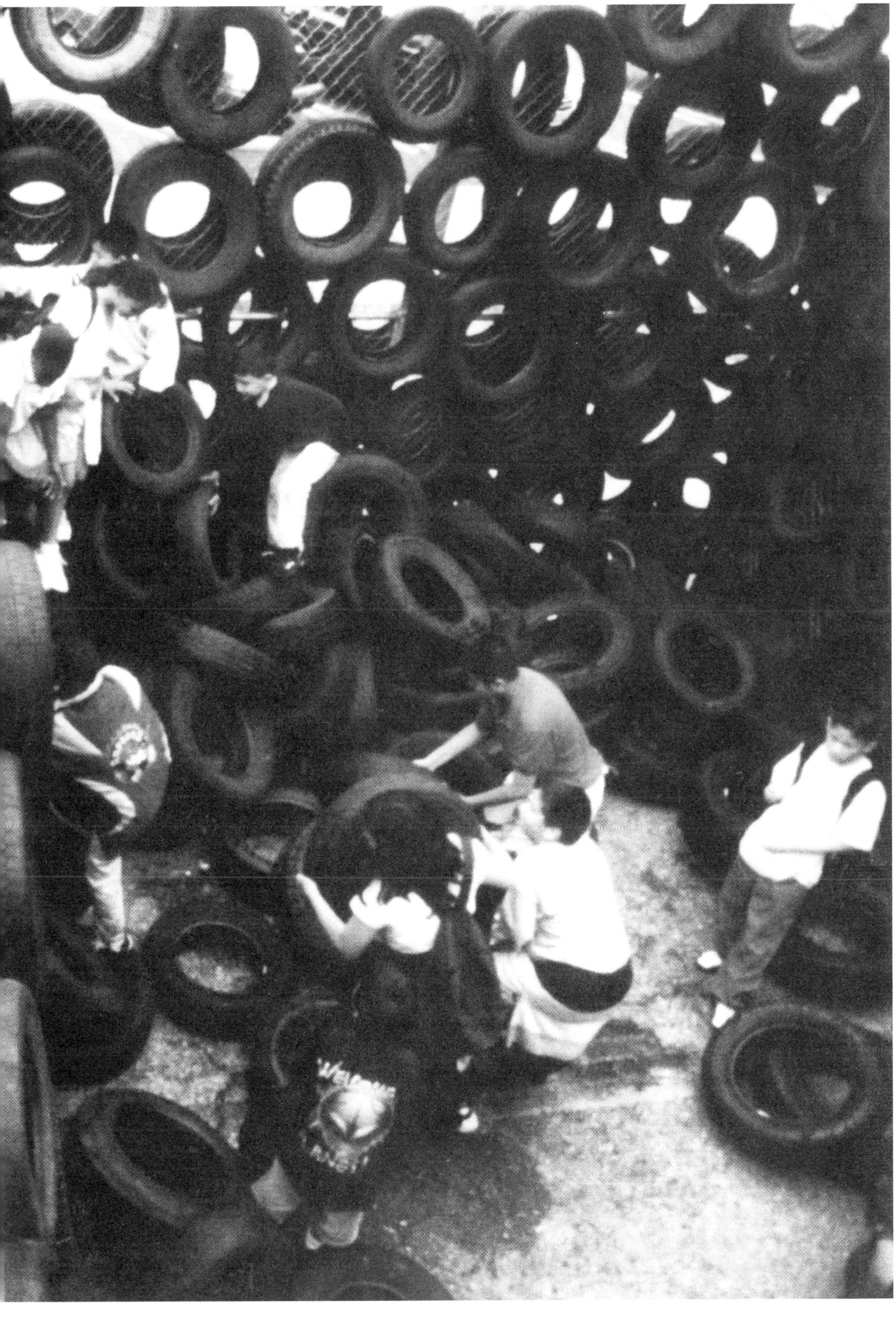

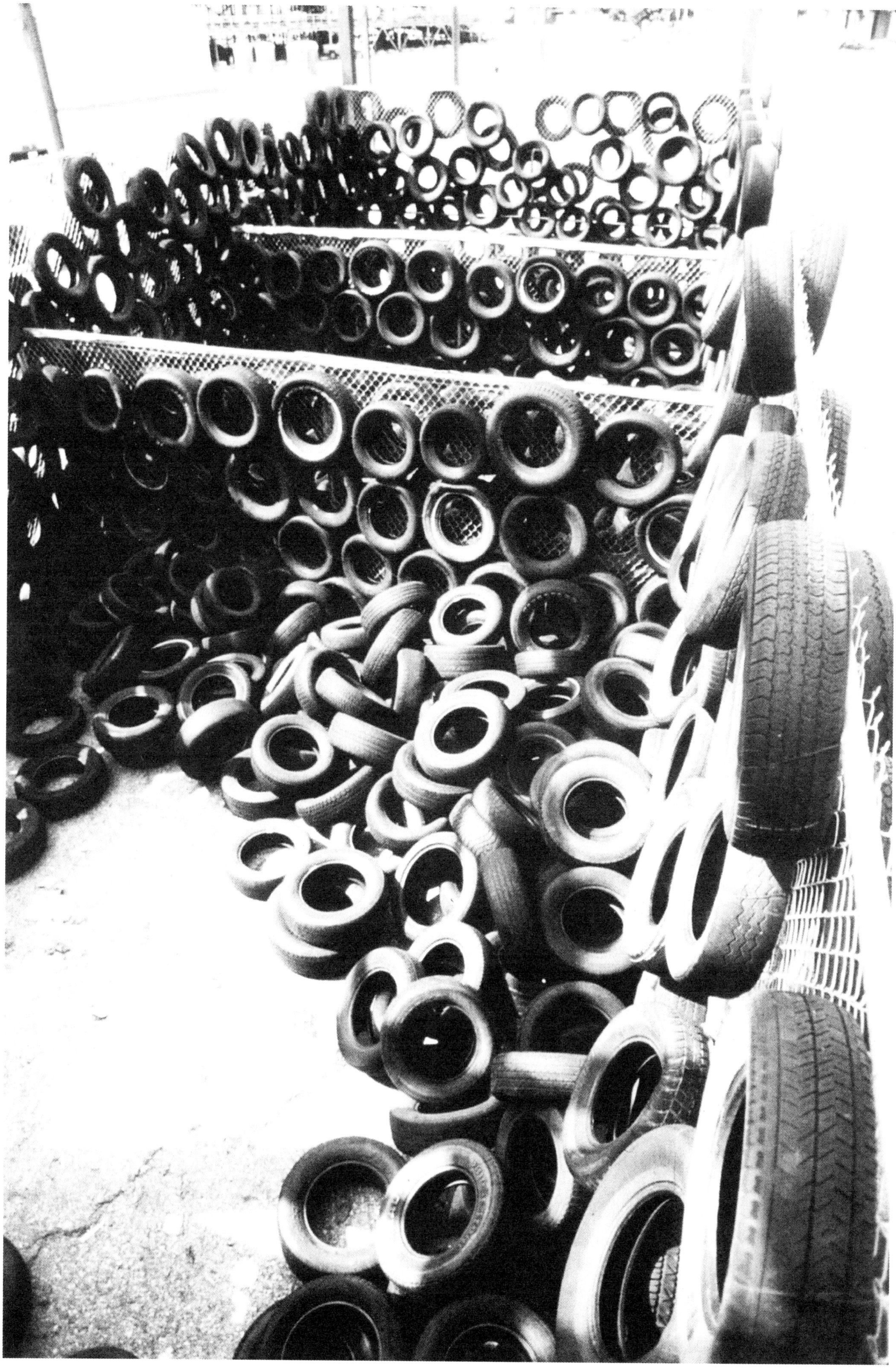

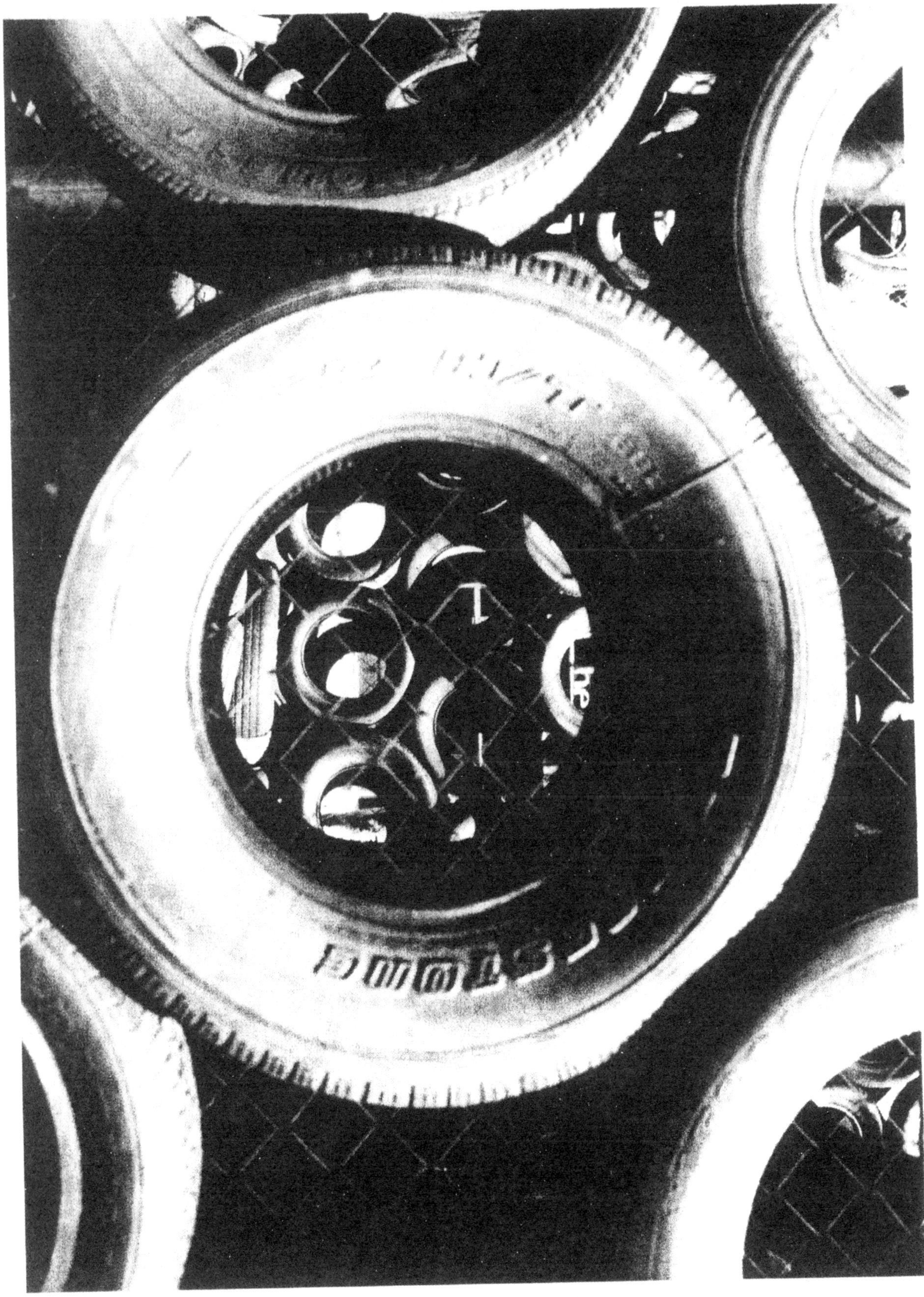

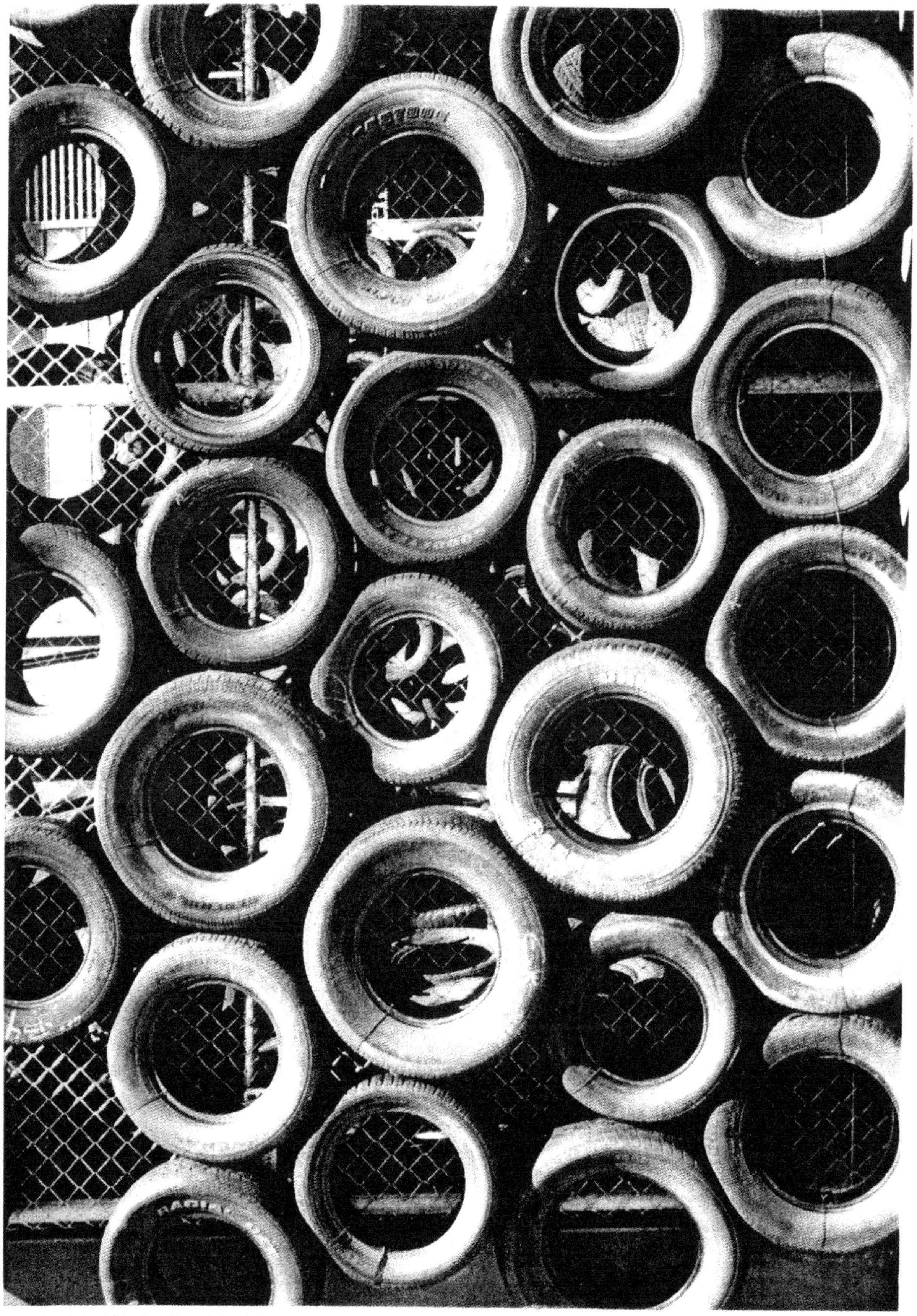

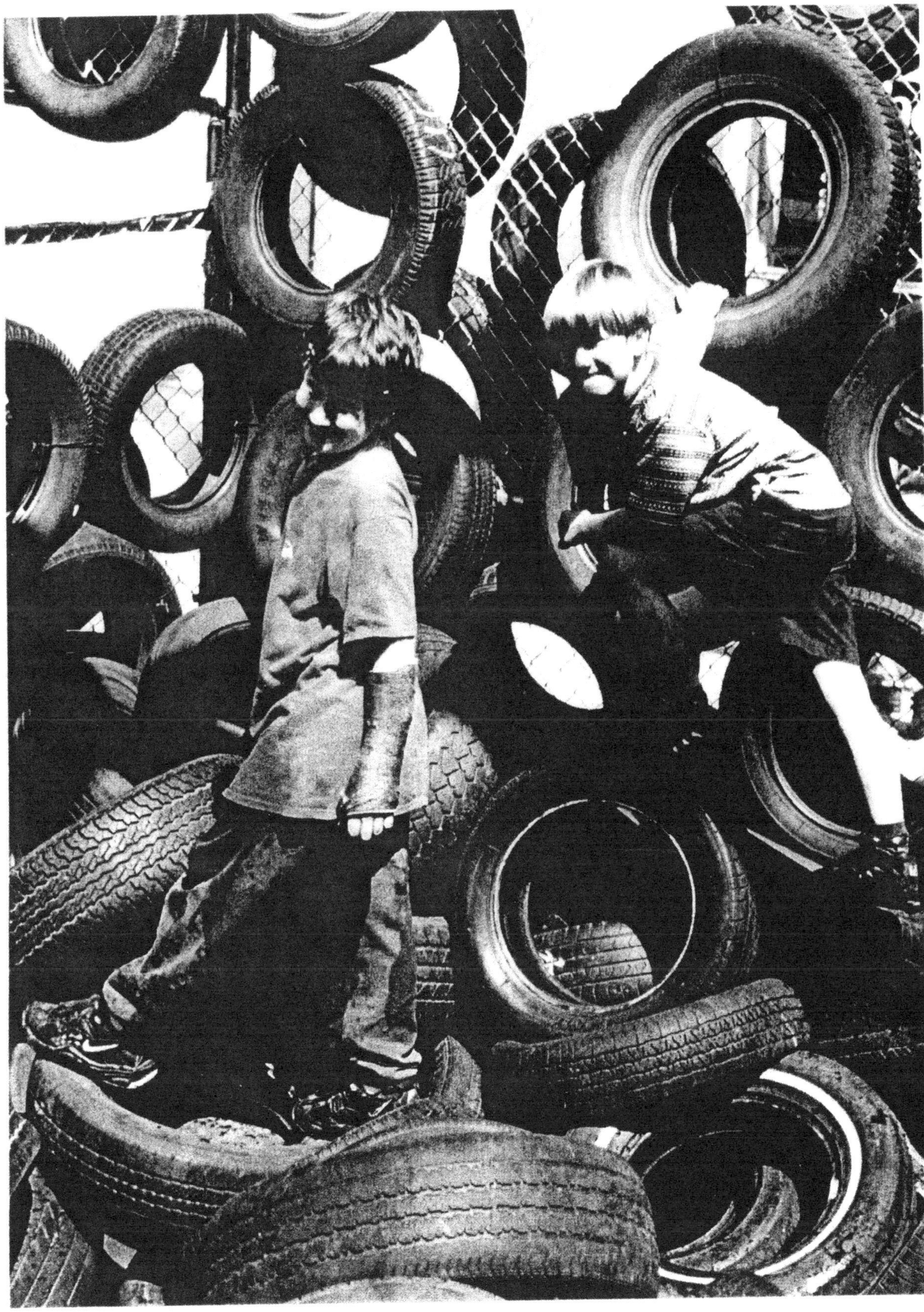

out of actions

ZWISCHEN PERFORMANCE UND OBJEKT 1949–1979

von Paul Schimmel,
The Museum of Contemporary Art, Los Angeles

mit Essays von

Kristine Stiles
Guy Brett
Hubert Klocker
Shinichiro Osaki
Paul Schimmel

Herausgeber
der deutschen Ausgabe
Peter Noever / MAK

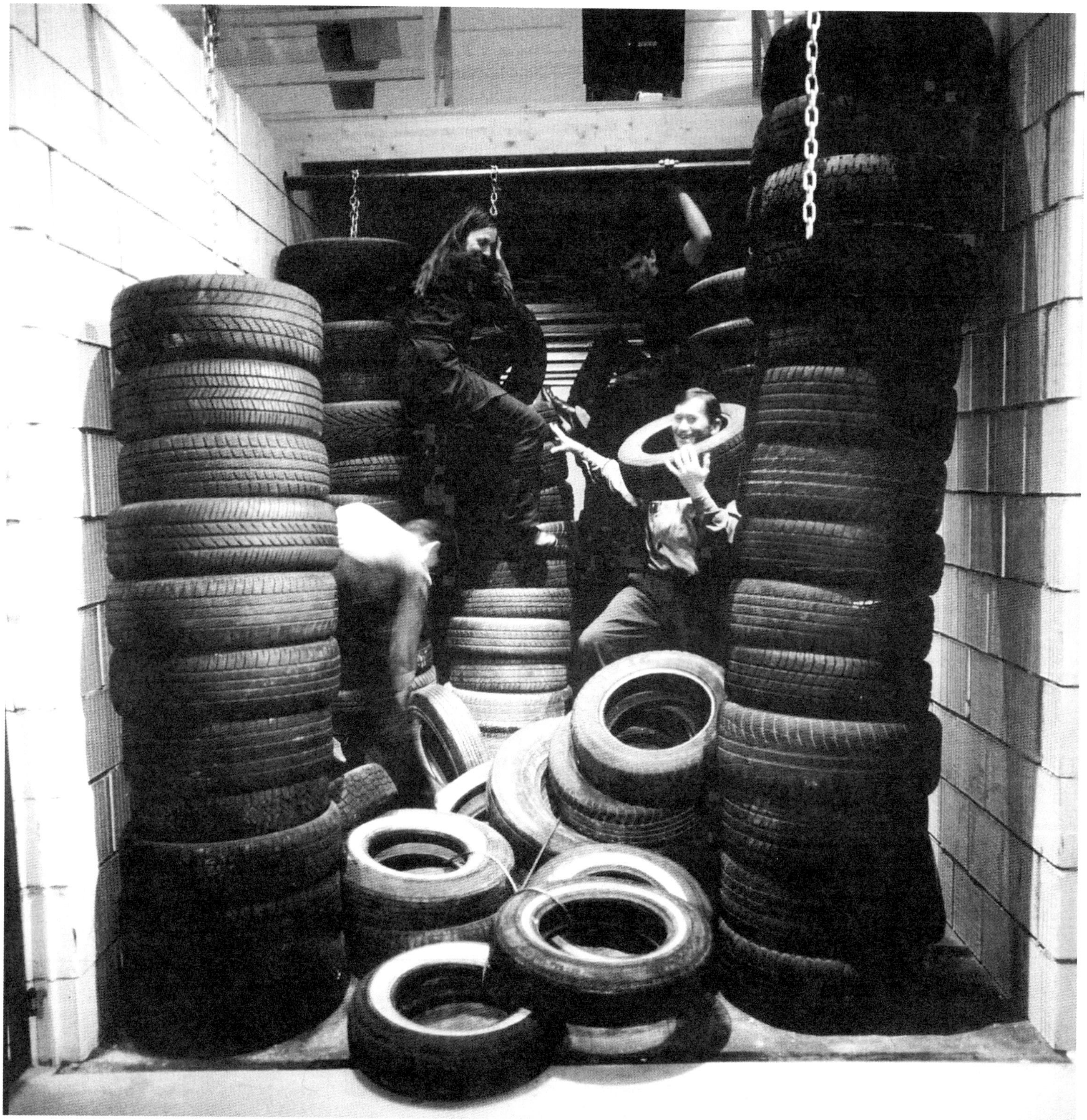

1998

NOTE ON YARD

YARD is a typical example of an artform of the late 1950s and early 1960s called an "Environment" (that is, a surrounding).

Since its first presentation in New York in 1961, YARD has been reinvented differently around the world nine times. This version in Vienna was designed to accommodate a corridor built in advance by MAK, and has never existed before. It will be dismantled at the end of the current exhibition. According to the first principle of the Environmental genre, it must always change.

The second principle of the Environmental genre has been, since the 1950s, that some other persons than the artist, friends, a sponsor, a public small or large, shall be invited to enter it physically, and to move its parts (here the loose tires on the floor) at will. YARD is not "visual art" for eyes alone; it involves the full spectrum of senses in participation.

Please feel free to enter YARD and proceed through the corridor. Take care that the tires are dirty and must be traversed attentatively. You are welcome, but know that you enter on your own responsibility.

— ALLAN KAPROW, 1998
(Courtesy Wolfgang Feelisch, Remscheid)

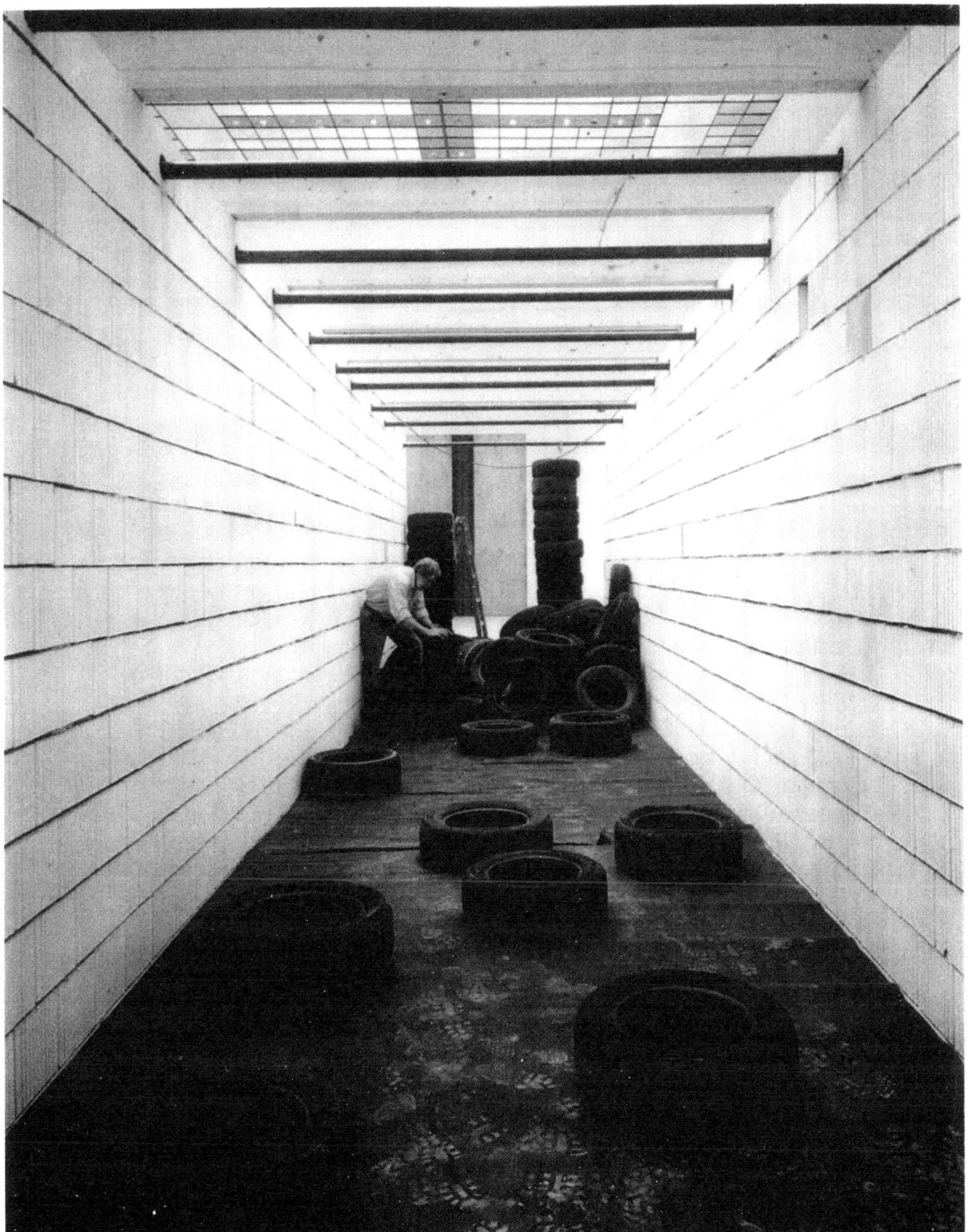

Naples, Castel Sant'Elmo, July 3rd - September 28th 2003
Opening: July 3rd 2003 6pm
Click HERE for an on-line schedule of events...

PRESS RELEASE

Much excitement is being generated by the exhibition **Living Theatre / LABYRINTHS OF THE IMAGINARY** at the Castel Sant'Elmo in Naples from July 3rd to September 28th 2003, one of the most significant events of the summer season of the international cultural and artistic scene.
The exhibition, curated by Judith Malina, Hanon Reznikov, Lorenzo Mango and Giuseppe Morra, has been organised by the regional government of Campania as part of the *Annali delle Arti* project, directed by Achille Bonito Oliva and curated by Eduardo Cicelyn, and the *Soprintendenza Speciale per il Polo Museale Napoletano* together with the Fondazione Morra.
For the opening on July 3rd at 6pm Aldo Loris Rossi will present the section by Luigi Castellano / LUCA *Immagini di un Segno* ("Images of a Sign"). This will be followed at 8pm by an atmospheric piano concert on the Piazzale delle Armi, **Suono Segno Gesto** ("Sound Sign Gesture"), with the participation of the composers Daniele Lombardi, Sylvano Bussotti, Giancarlo Cardini and Maestro Antonio Ballista.
The exhibition aims to give an account of the extraordinary artistic and cultural phenomenon that is the Living Theatre, a name which itself shows the idea of a theatre which opens itself up to life, politics and change, without ever giving up its search into and experiments with new forms of language. That of the Living Theatre is an extraordinary adventure in theatre, art and life which, having begun in the 1950s under the auspices of Julian Beck and Judith Malina, spread throughout the entire second half of the twentieth century, marking that century notably and continuing to do so, as can be seen from the premiere in this occasion of **Enigmi,** their most recent show (September 27th, a world premiere).
The 14th century Angevin castle will be the beautiful setting for this journey into the fascinating world of the Living Theatre. The journey passes though a series of objects which bear witness to a creative process more than a simple act of documentation. The image of a labyrinth signifies an artistic itinerary made up of many different elements, different tensions, ideas and ideals, of creative pathways, of life choices. The exhibition is a reconstruction of the Living Theatre's journey in the form of a visual narrative, using materials from their archives (photos, newspaper articles, posters and programmes from their shows) accompanied by the projection of video materials and films made of some of the company's most important shows.

One particularly important part of the event is the first large-scale exhibition in Italy of Julian Beck's paintings. Painted in the 1940s and 50s, these pictures show the importance of Beck's work as an "action painter" which would later find an outlet in the theatre.
Alongside the Living Theatre material, other events will testify to the group's interdisciplinary nature and their desire to put together different intelligences and art forms. One section of the exhibition will document these movements, from that of the "happening" to body art, from to Viennese aktionism to conceptual art, all creating a kind of ideal background against which to read the Living Theatre's theatrical work. Since theatre is "alive", as the Living Theatre has taught us and continues to teach us, it obviously needs to have contacts, actions, events, moments in which art immediately creates action.
Works of artists including Baldo Diodato, Ugo Dossi, Al Hansen, Jean-Jacques Lebel, Gina Pane, Luca Maria Patella, Vettor Pisani, Robert Rauschenberg, Errico Ruotolo and Rudolf Schwarzkogler will be exhibited.
One of the octagonal rooms will be the setting for The Well-Tuned Piano in The Magenta Lights, an atmospheric sound and light installation by La Monte Young and Marian Zazeela, with the DVD video-projection of a live concert lasting seven hours (Italian premiere).

The following works will be installed in some of the chambers of the castle: a homage to luigi castellano / LUCA, an installation by Hermann Nitsch, *Beck / ett* - a sound/video environment by Roberto Paci Dalò. Allan Kaprow will reconstruct the *YARD* Environment.

A 250-page bilingual Italian/English catalogue will also be published for the occasion, with essays by Achille Bonito Oliva, Matteo D'Ambrosio, Judith Malina, Lorenzo Mango, Jonas Mekas and Hanon Reznikov, illustrated in colour and including an audio CD containing a number of pieces of experimental music from the Alga Marghen label.

P. 2 TO: BEPPE MORRA

Plan for "YARD" (9th version

SEA OF OLD TIRES. BUILDING SMALL TOWERS AND WALLS OF TIRES.

USING ANY TIRE, THROWING IT TO TOPPLE TOWERS OR WALLS.

BUILDING OTHER TOWERS AND WALLS

CONTINUING BUILDING AND TOPPLING AS LONG AS DESIRED.

—AK, 2003

(TO be translated into Italian and posted near "Yard")

Dirt moved from one space to another
("treasures" at bottom?)
(bread + jam?) (used tires?)
(small tables with food or wood in space?)
* (passage with dirt along it)(fire hazard?)
* (shovels brooms to gather dirt in buckets)
* (space divided by 2 plastic curtains)
* (curtains have splits in them)
* (walls of concrete blocks plus soiled bread (?)
* (tables with wine?)
* (stones on floor);

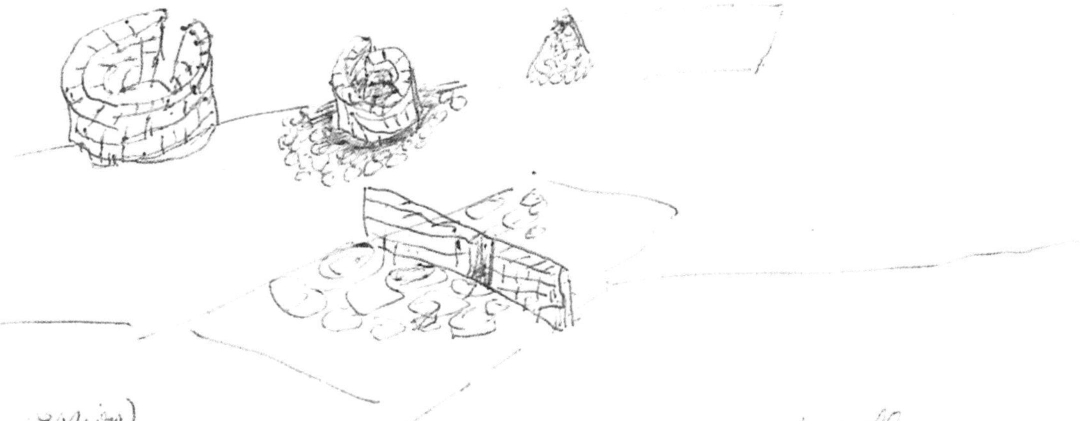

YARD (9th version)

Sea of old tires. Building towers and walls of tires.
(See drawing) Using any tire[s], throwing it ~~at tower~~ to topple tower or wall. ~~Rebuilding~~ Building another tower or wall; Continuing building and toppling as long as desired.

— AK

a b frames in stairs

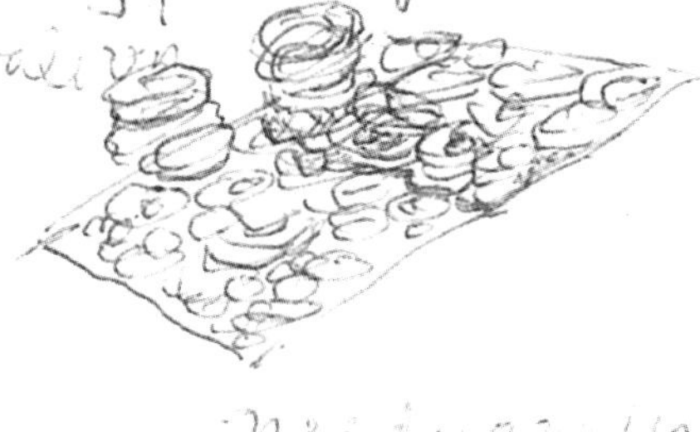

CIAO

Required used tires; 1 week to work

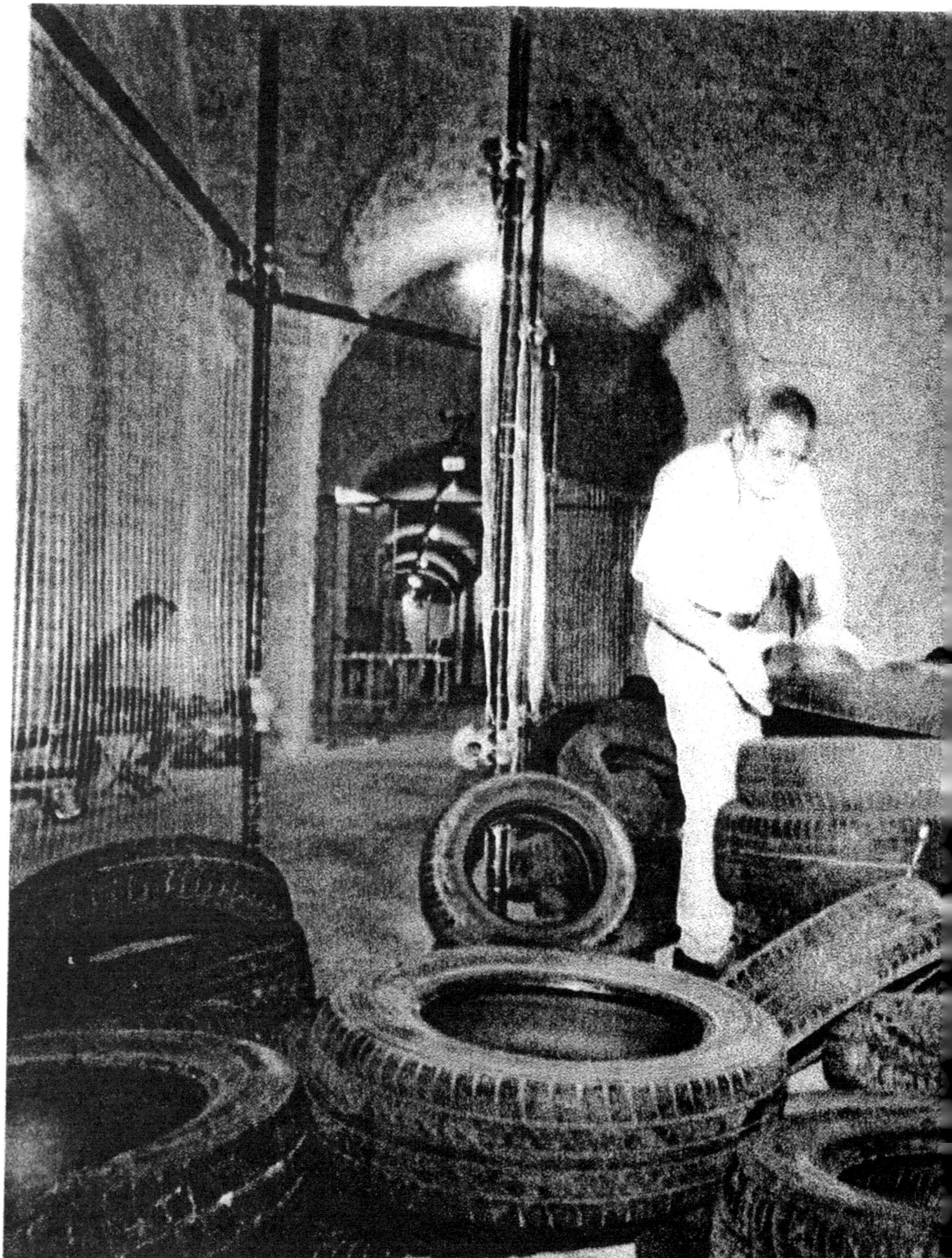

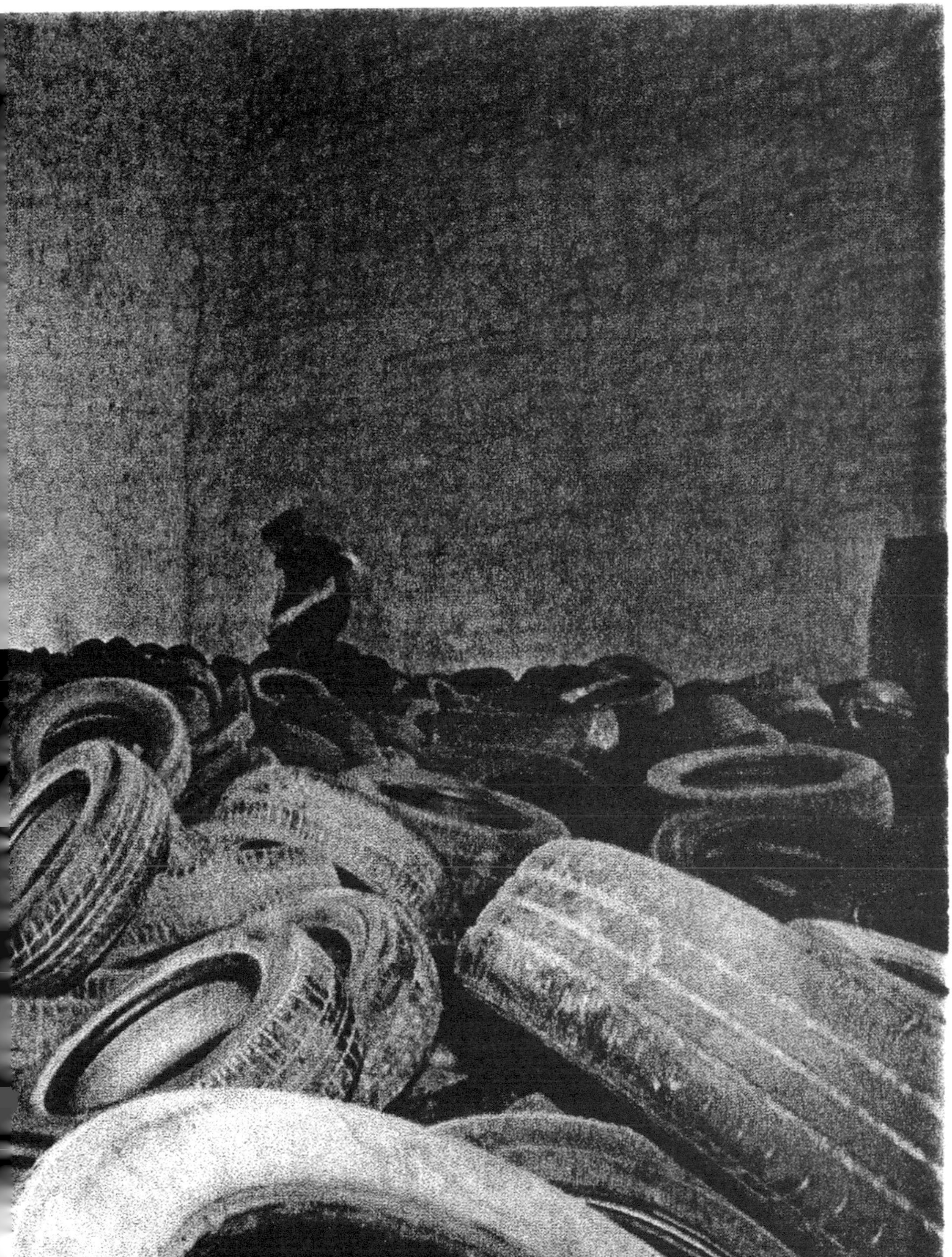

CRITICAL

HAPPENINGS, FLUXUS, PERFORMANCE, INTERMEDIA
and RUTGERS UNIVERSITY 1958–1972

MASS

Edited by GEOFFREY HENDRICKS

MASON GROSS ART GALLERIES, RUTGERS UNIVERSITY

MEAD ART MUSEUM, AMHERST COLLEGE

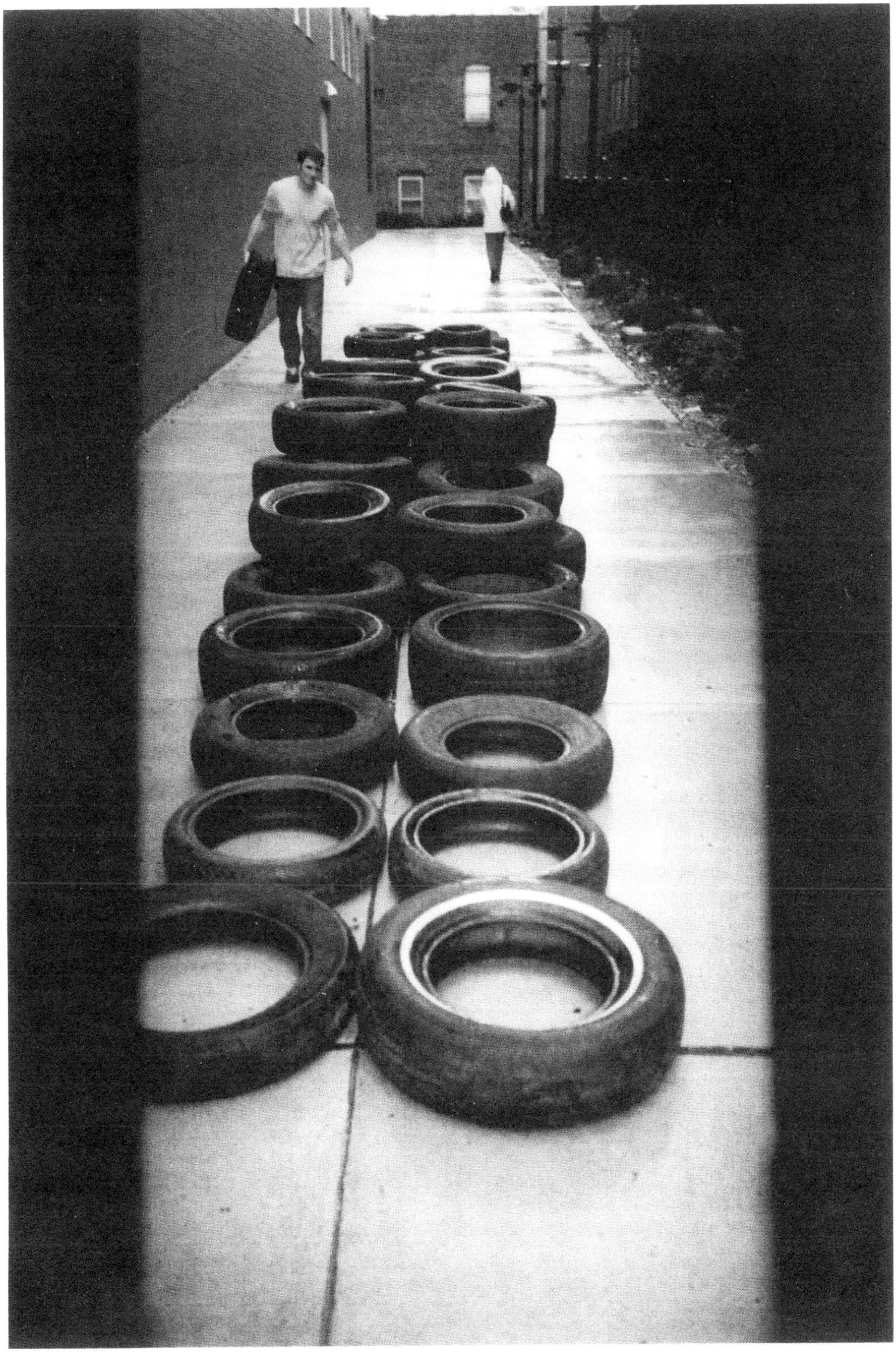

In going over the installation of the show with Sur, I realized the small room beyond the office needed an installation rather than more small work & documents on the wall, and Allan Kaprow's environment "Yard" (1961) which he had
done in a revised form in Naples last summer could look great. The original was
the garden (back yard) of the Martha Jackson Gallery filled with old rubber tires. The sculpture in the garden (objects what ever) wrapped with tar paper. I
spoke with Allan who said that every time the piece was done again it was a new version. He would think about it and call me back.
Some hours later he called back and proposed:
CARPETS (Version 10 of "Yard")
Picture to yourself a carpet sales person with the layers of carpets building
up, each row getting less. Then start to move tires out into the environment
as carpets, layer after layer. He said get a lot of tires, a lease calculations are that 400-450 are plenty for the space). Sur has down a
source of tires that can be delivered Tuesday or Wednesday.
I see the piece with the walls and floors all covered with tar paper rolled down, walls stapled on) and then the tires filling the room with the layers getting progressively less, up to just below the windows. It would be an
environment that people could climb up, but because of the rest of the show there, the "placing of the carpets would probably have to wait until Allan was
here in early November, when a "carpet or two or three" could be taken over to
Livingston or where ever.
Questions:
Could you two (recruit others if needed) get rolls of tar paper, enough to cover the room and have it ready (walls covered) for tires to arrive Tuesday?
(or Wednesday?) Tuesday would probably be better for a lot will be happening on
Wednesday. We have the tires lined up (Ideal Scrap Tires) and Blade (that's

his name) will drop them off when I say, but need to get back to him soon.

Think this will be a nice energetic component to the show.

Did the cases get over yesterday?

Phil Corner arrives tomorrow. Ready for a busy week.

Geoff

Уметност, живот и пометња | 47. Октобарски салон

Београд, 29. септембар – 5. новембар 2006

Art, Life & Confusion | 47th October Salon

Belgrade, September 29 – November 5, 2006

Art, Life & Confusion | 47th October Salon

Curated by René Block and Barbara Heinrich

Assistant to the Curators: Aleksandra Estela Bjelica Mladenović

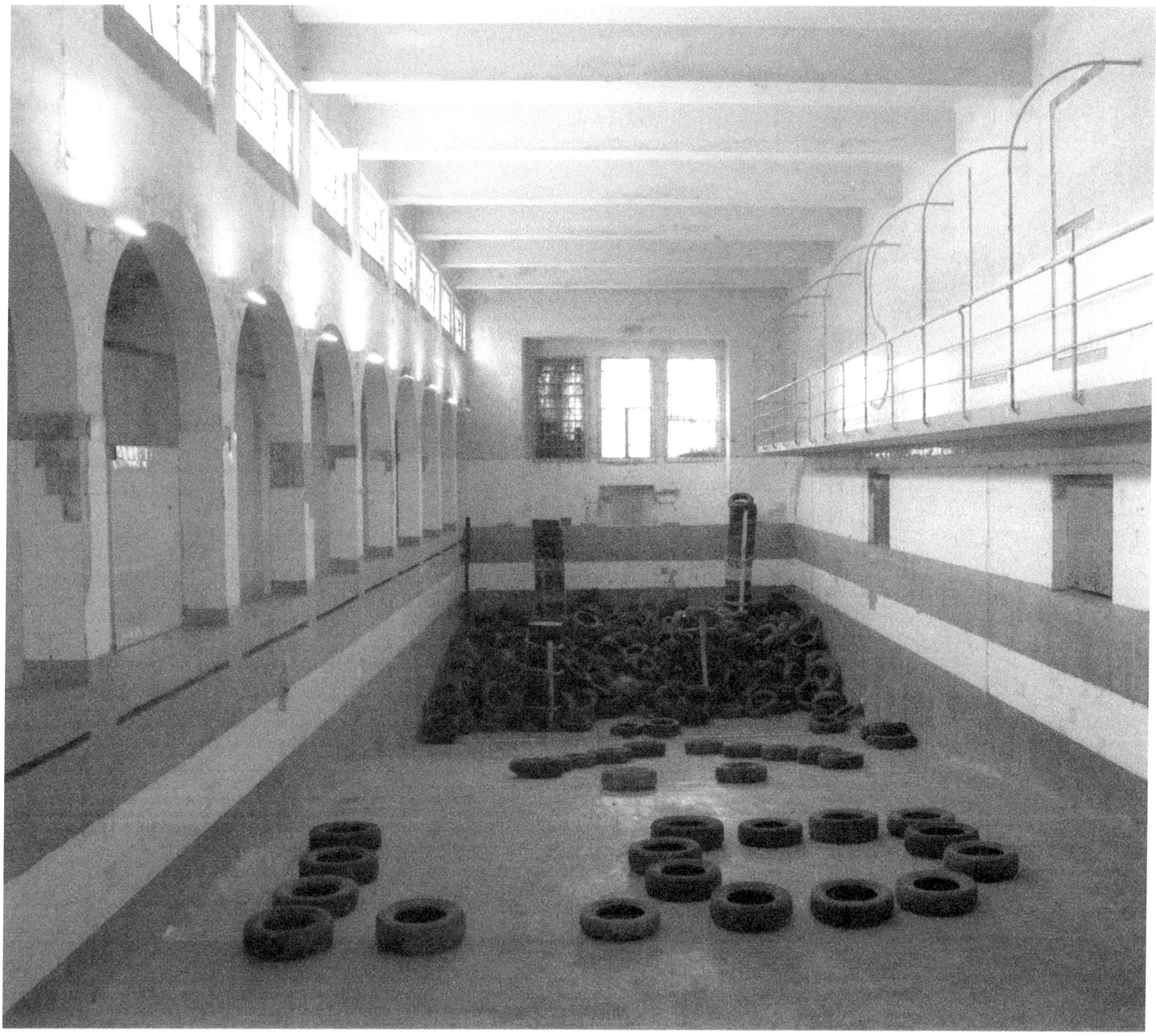

1
Кључни експеримент није био једноставно изналажење нових уметничких жанрова по којима је тај период обично познат, већ увиђање секуларизације целокупне уметничке ситуације: *жанра, оквира, публике и сврхе.*
2
Кључни потез у експерименту био је помак уметности од познатих контекста, атељеа, музеја, концертних дворана, позоришта, итд, до било ког другог места у стварном свету.
3
Разне врсте перформанса постале су делотворни начини да се изађе на крај са овим помаком у стварну околину. Перформанс је *чињење*, не глума у позоришту: на пример, преношење намештаја тек да би се пренео, или због селидбе у нови стан.
4
Структурни модели за експеримент били су стварни (не само имплицитни) процеси: на пример, сезонске промене; храна која се узгаја, припрема, једе, вари и користи као ђубриво; мисли које се преносе, преображавају и спроводе у дело.
5
Могуће границе између уметности налик животу, и остатка живота, намерно су замагљене. Није било важно где је уметност, а где живот, где једно, или друго „почиње", или где се „завршава". Такве дистинкције биле су само привремене.
6
Типична уметничка публика и критичари, навикли на одлажење на изложбе, концерте и позоришне представе, постали су неважни. Уместо њих, постојале су мале групе путника на далеке локације, учесника у организованим догађањима, групе мислилаца у возовима, и уметника у њиховим областима уметности, саме за себе. Публика за ову уметност налик животу, која се управо рађала као публика, више није била идеална нити уједињена, већ је била разноврсна, покретна и конкретних интересовања, као и људи у стварном свету.
7
Уметност налик животу није напросто прикачила животу етикету „уметности". Она је била у континуитету са тим животом, преобликујући га, залазећи у њега, испитујући га, чак и трпећи га, али увек са пажњом. (То је извориште њеног хумора, када помније размотрите своју патњу, то може испасти прилично смешно...)
8
Сврха уметности налик животу била је терапеутска: реинтегрисање појединачне стварности коју узимамо здраво за готово. Не само интелектуално, већ и непосредно, као искуства – у овом тренутку, у овој кући, код ове судопере...

Алан Капроу

Одломак из „The Real Experiment", Artforum, децембар 1983.

1
The key experiment was not simply the invention of new art genres by which the period is usually known, but the recognition of the secularization of the entire art situation: *genre, frame, public and purpose.*
2
The critical move in the experiment was the shift of art away from its familiar contexts, the studios, museums, concert halls, theatres etc., to anywhere else in the real world.
3
Various performative modes became the effective way to deal with this shift to the actual environment. Performing was *doing* something, not acting in theatre — moving furniture, for example, just to do it, or because you were changing apartments.
4
The structural models for the experiment were real (not merely implicit) processes: for example, seasonal changes; food that is grown, prepared, eaten, digested and composted; thoughts that are transmitted, converted and put into action.
5
The possible boundaries between lifelike art and the rest of life were kept intentionally blurred. Where the art was located and where life was, when one or the other "began" and "ended," was of no importance. Such distinctions were merely provisional.
6
The typical art public and critic used to going to exhibitions, concerts and plays, became irrelevant. Instead, there were small groups of travellers to far-off sites, participants in organised events, thinkers on commuter trains and artists in their art by themselves. The emerging public for this lifelike art was no longer ideal and unified, but was diversified, mobile and particular in interests, like people in the real world.
7
Lifelike art did not merely label life as "art". It was continuous with that life, inflecting, probing, testing and even suffering it, but always attentively. (That's the source of its humour, when you look closely at your suffering, it can be pretty funny ...)
8
The purpose of lifelike art was therapeutic: to reintegrate the piecemeal reality we take for granted. Not just intellectually, but directly, as experience — in this moment, in this house, at this kitchen sink...

Allan Kaprow

Excerpt from "The Real Experiment", Artforum, December 1983

1927 – 2006 / Born in Atlantic City, New Jersey, USA, lived and worked

Allan KAPROW

KUNST ALS LEVEN | ART AS LIFE

10/02–22/04/2007

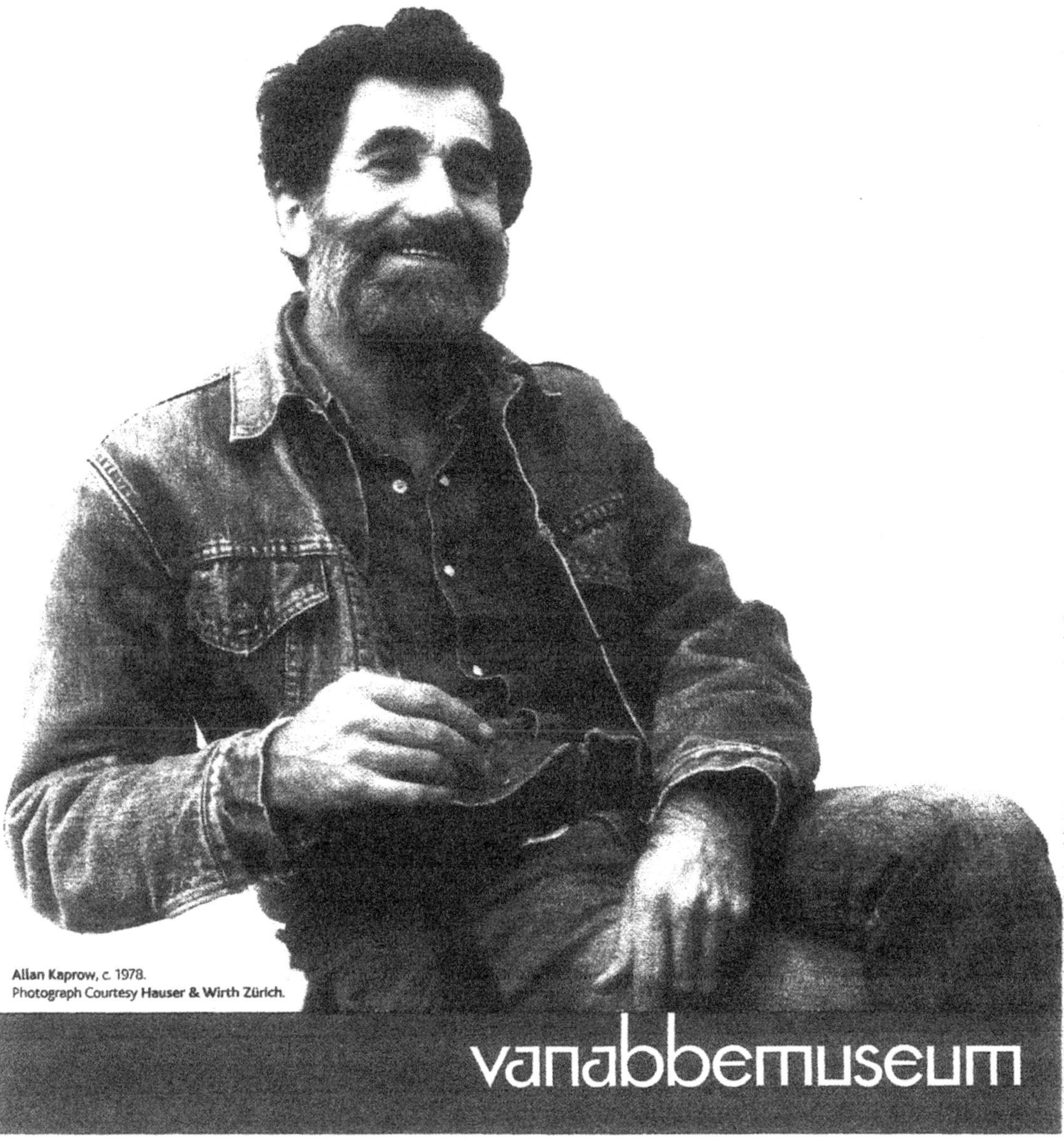

Allan Kaprow, c. 1978.
Photograph Courtesy Hauser & Wirth Zürich.

vanabbemuseum

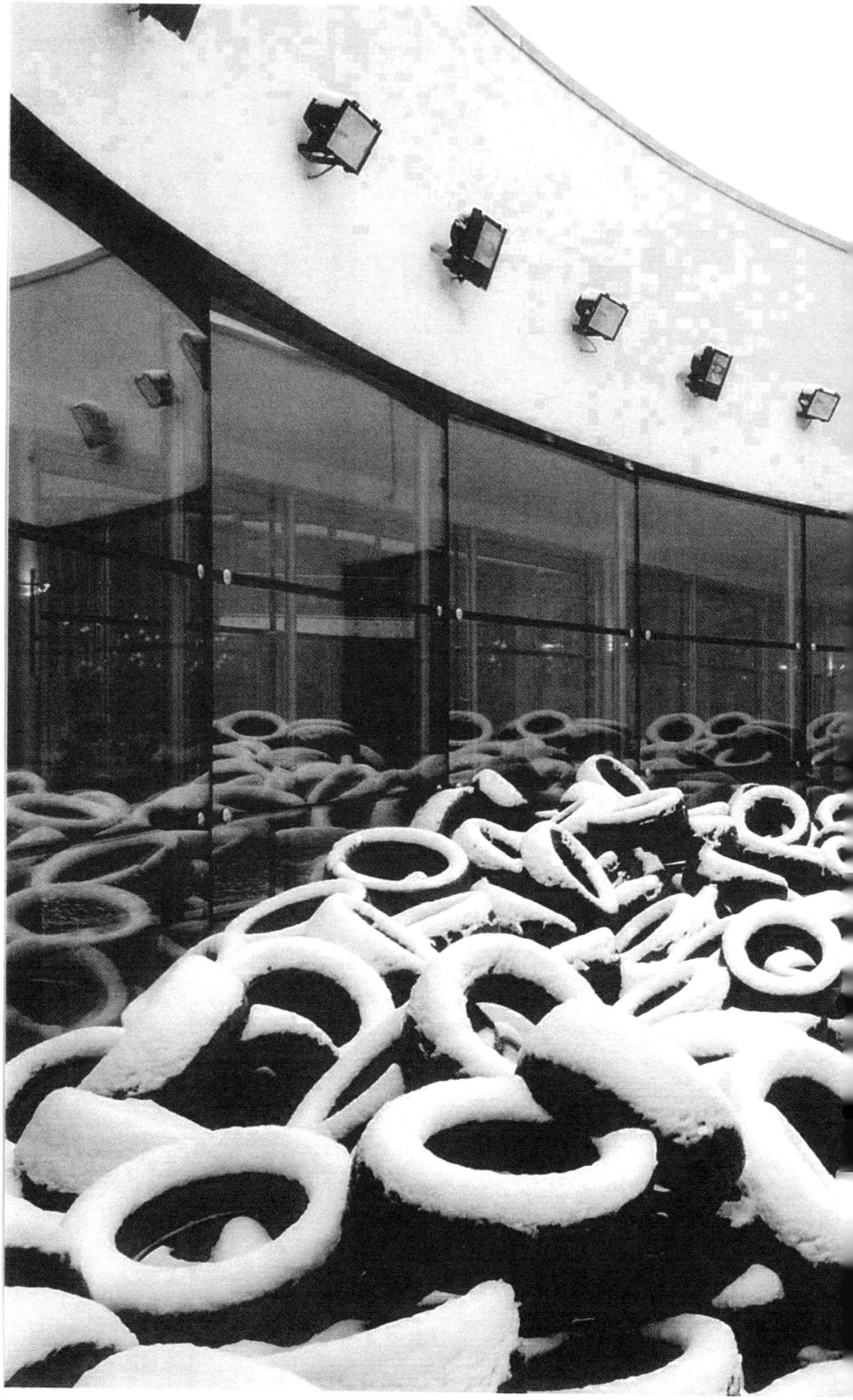

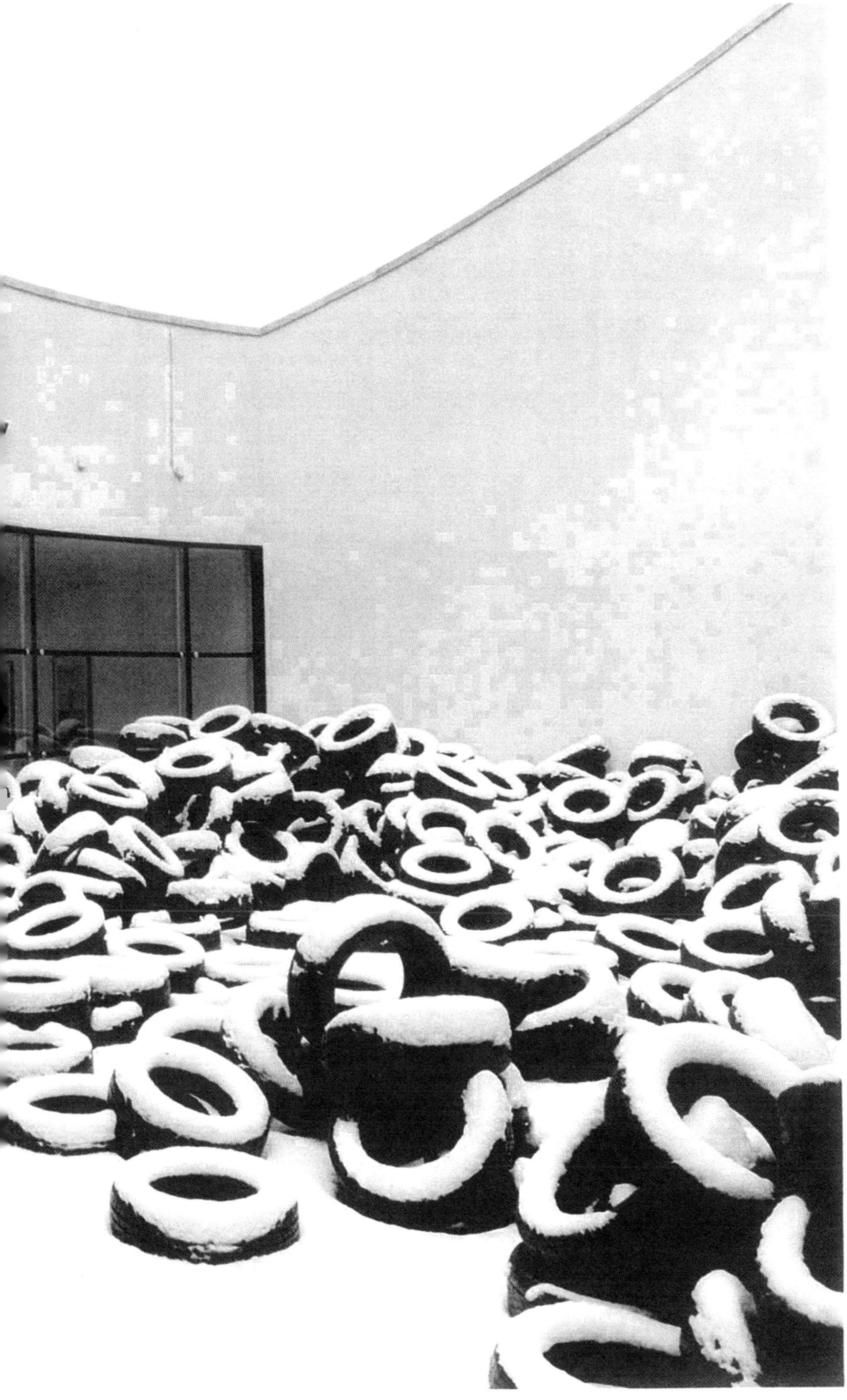

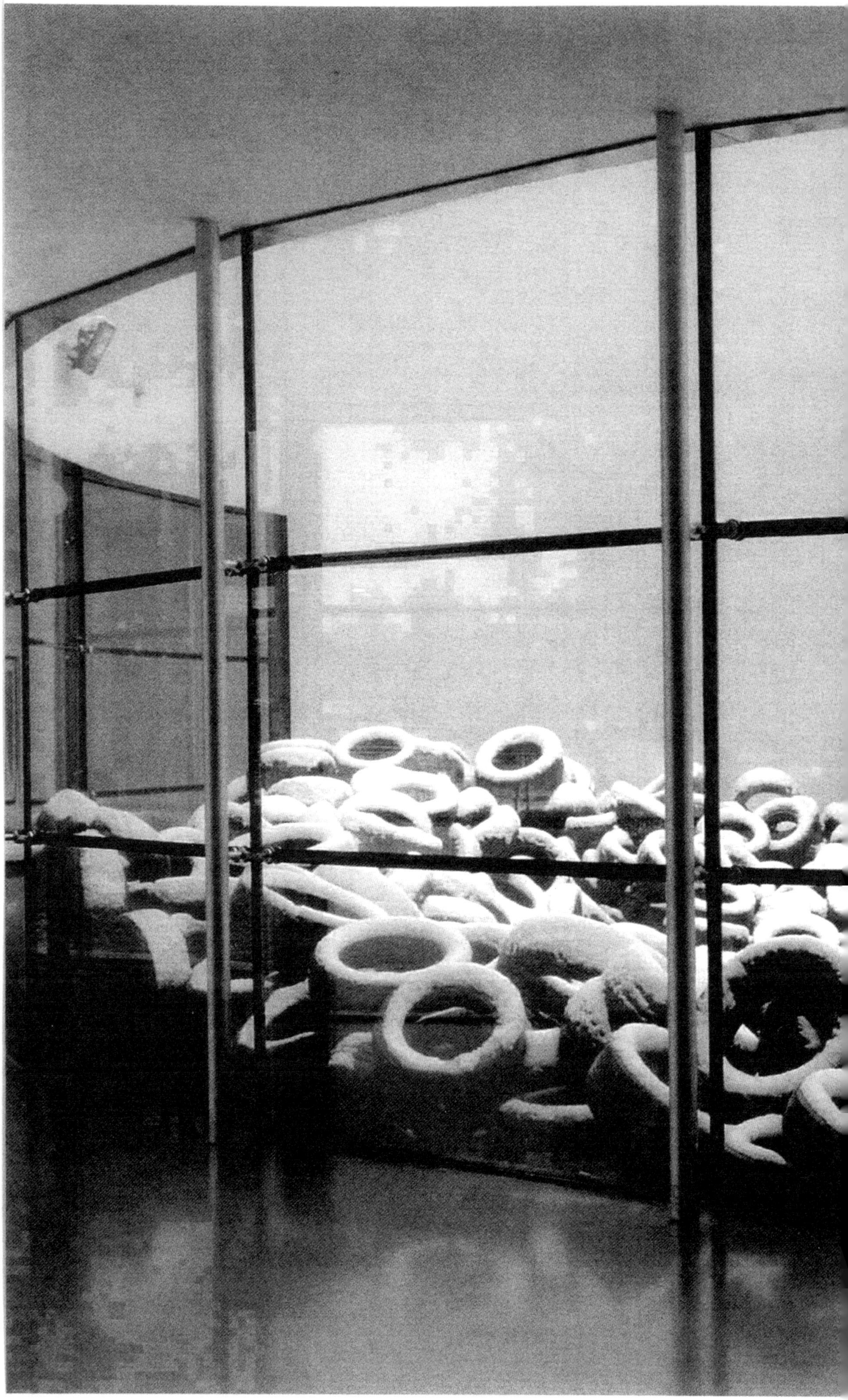

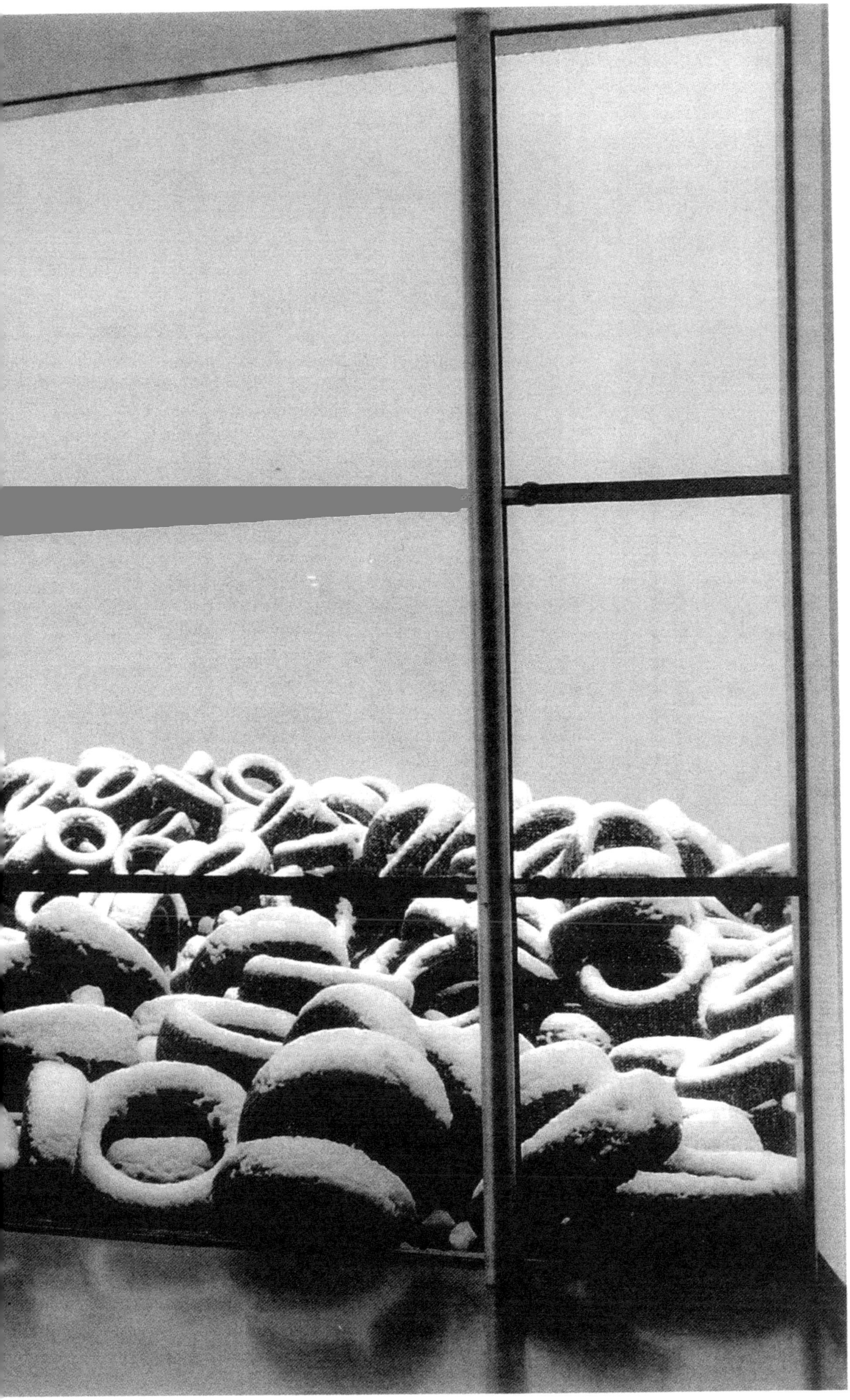

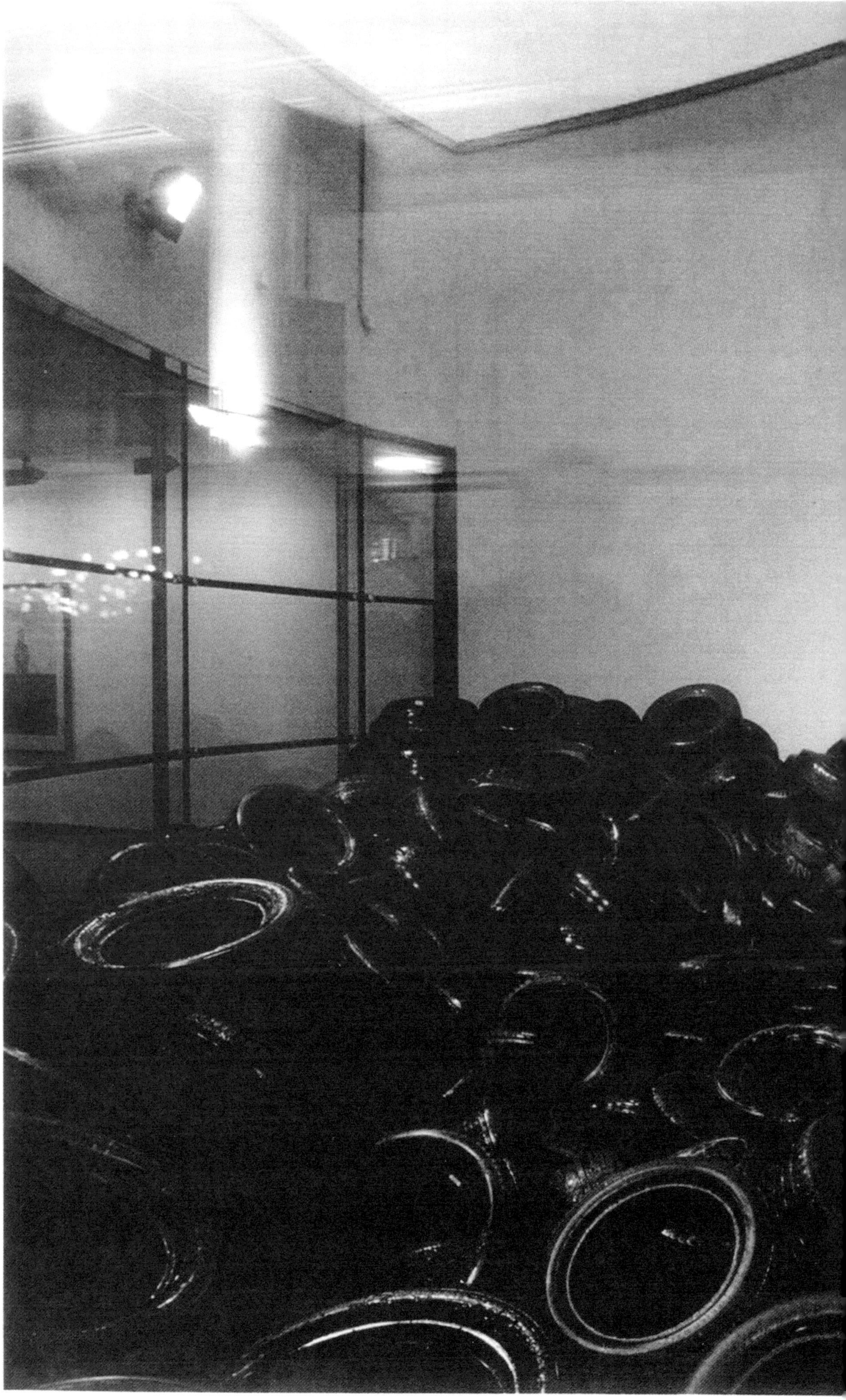

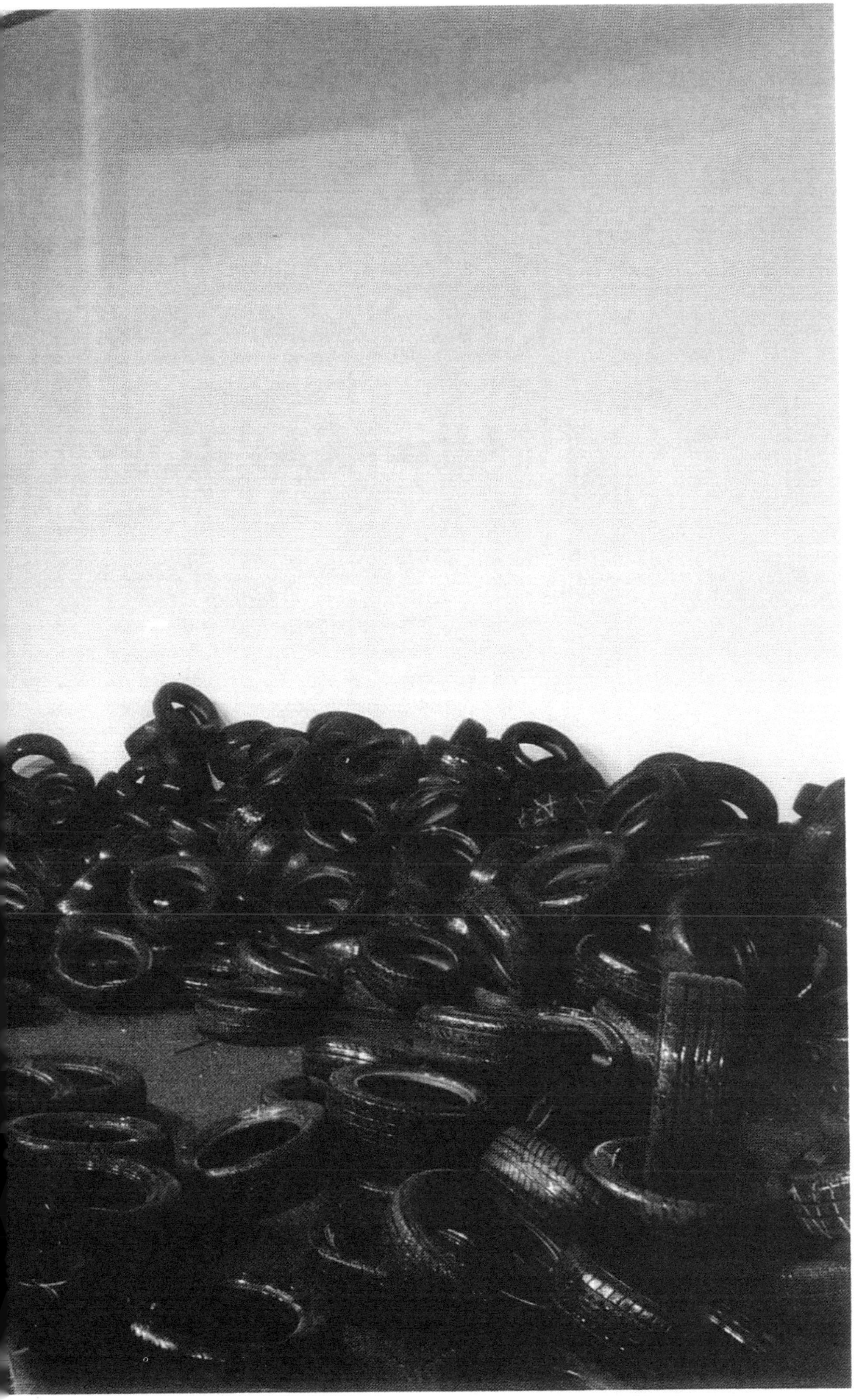

vanabbemuseum

BILDERDIJKLAAN 10 ▶ P.O. BOX 235 ▶ NL-5600 AE EINDHO
T +31 [0] 40 238 1000 ▶ F +31 [0] 40 246 0680
E INFO@VANABBEMUSEUM.NL ▶ WWW.VANABBEMUSEUM.N

Allan KAPROW

Kunst als leven | Art as Li

10/02–22/04/2007

Kaprow, vader van de 'happenings' en de 'beroemdste onbeke
is in april 2006 overleden. Het **Van Abbemuseum** organiseert
met het **Haus der Kunst** in München de eerste grote Europese
Ook tijdens de opening wordt een happening uitgevoerd.

Kaprow, the father of the 'happenings' and the 'most famous
died in April 2006. In association with the **Haus der Kunst** in M
Abbemuseum is organising the first largest European solo pre
work. During the opening a happening will also take place.

U bent van harte welkom op de opening op zaterdag 10 februari van 15:00 tot 18:00 uur.
Welkomstwoord door **Charles Esche** en conservator van de tentoonstelling **Eva Meyer-Hermann** om 16:00 uur.

You are cordially in
opening on Saturda
from 15:00 to 18:0
Word of welcome b
and exhibition cura
Eva Meyer-Herma

Onderwijs en cultuur

Cultuur 2000

Deze tentoonstelling wordt mede mogelijk gemaakt door de **Andy W**
Cultuur 2000 programma van de Europese Unie. | This exhibition is
with support of the **Culture 2000** programme of the European Union.

THERLANDS

TPG Post

Port betaald
Port payé
Pays-Bas

enaar'
verking
ntatie.

rtist',
Van
of his

e
y 10,

Esche

) PM.

to:

n for the **Visual Arts**. Het project is uitgevoerd in het raamwerk van **TRANSFORM** en met de steun van het
y the **Andy Warhol Foundation for the Visual Arts**. The project is part of the framework of **TRANSFORM**

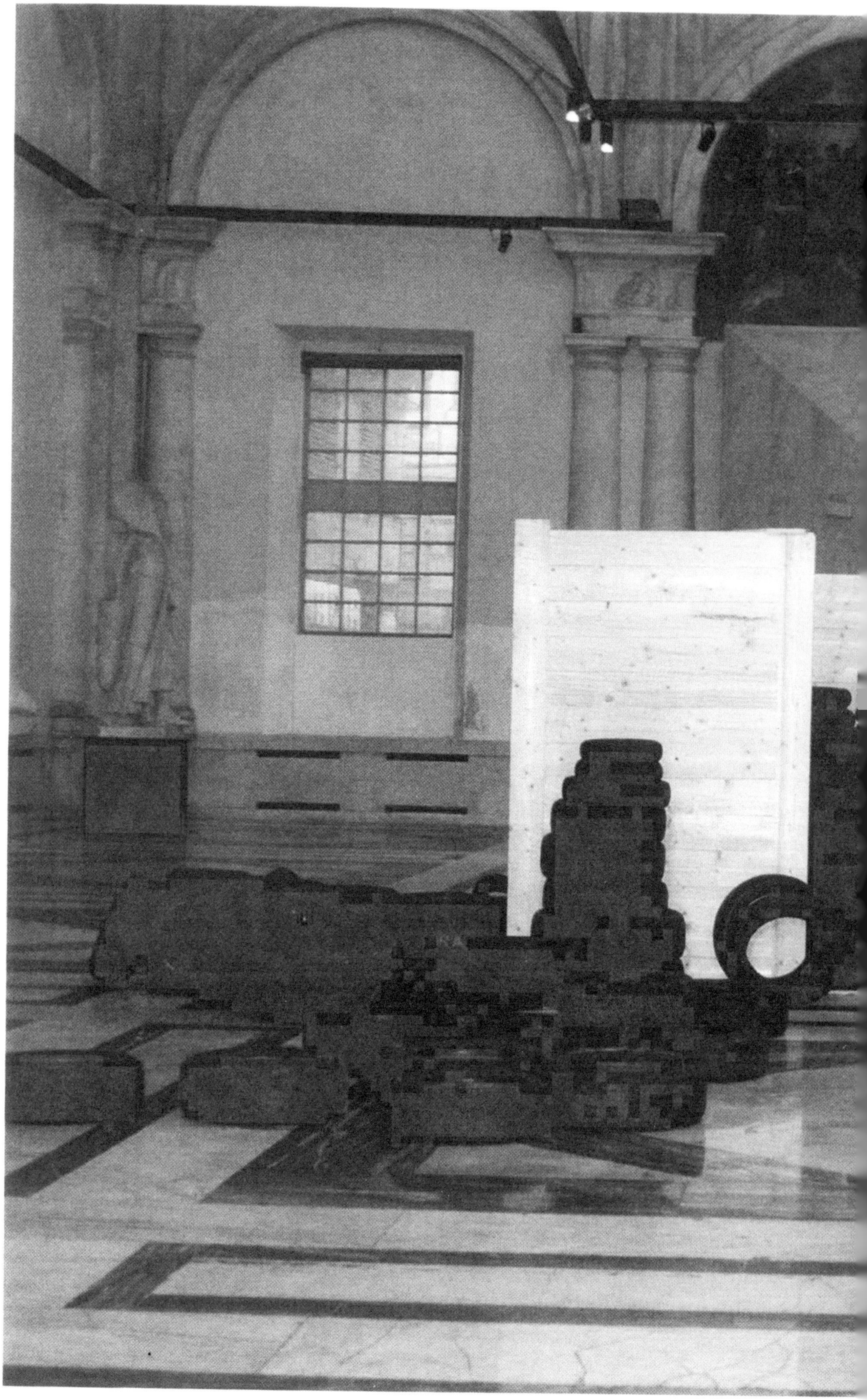

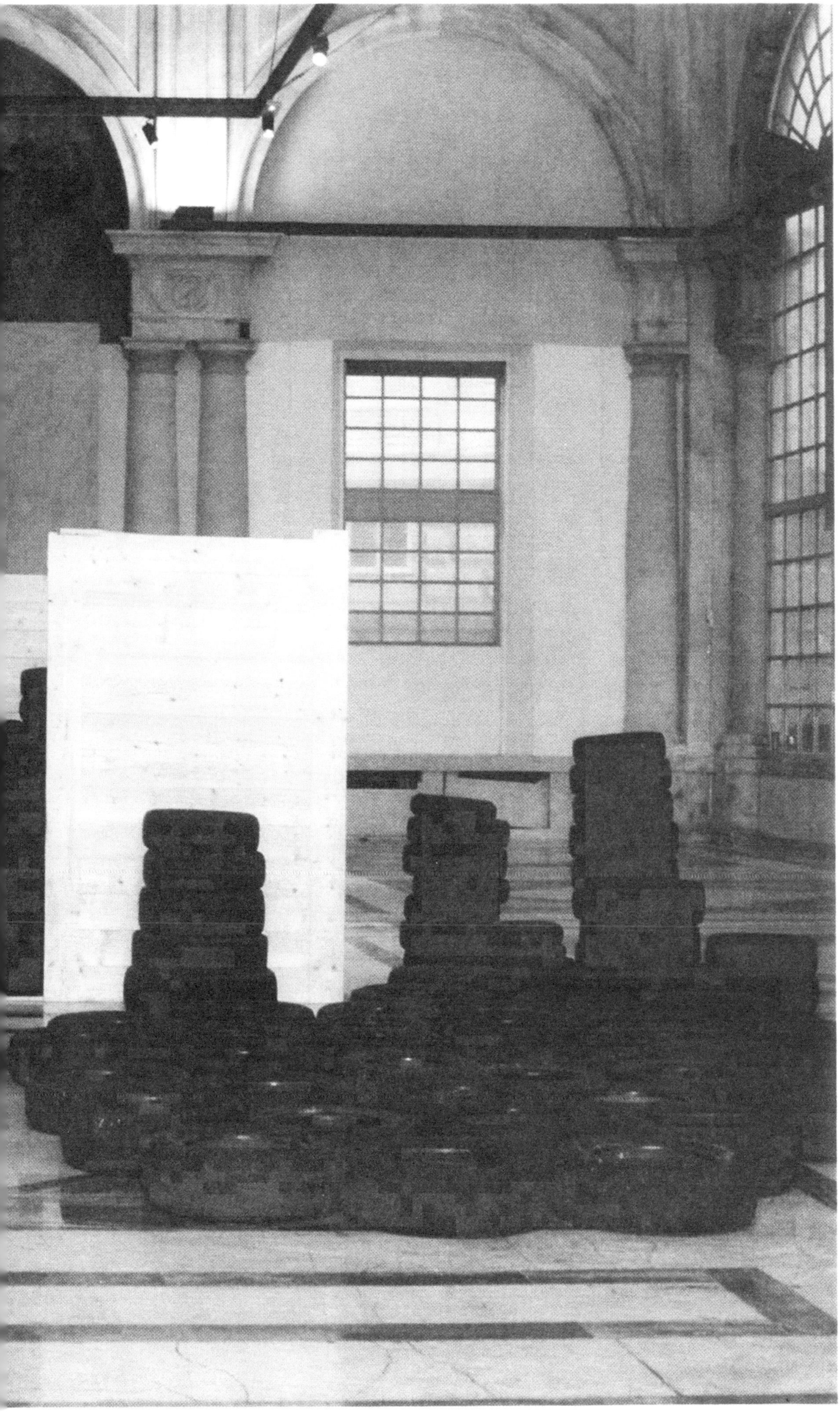

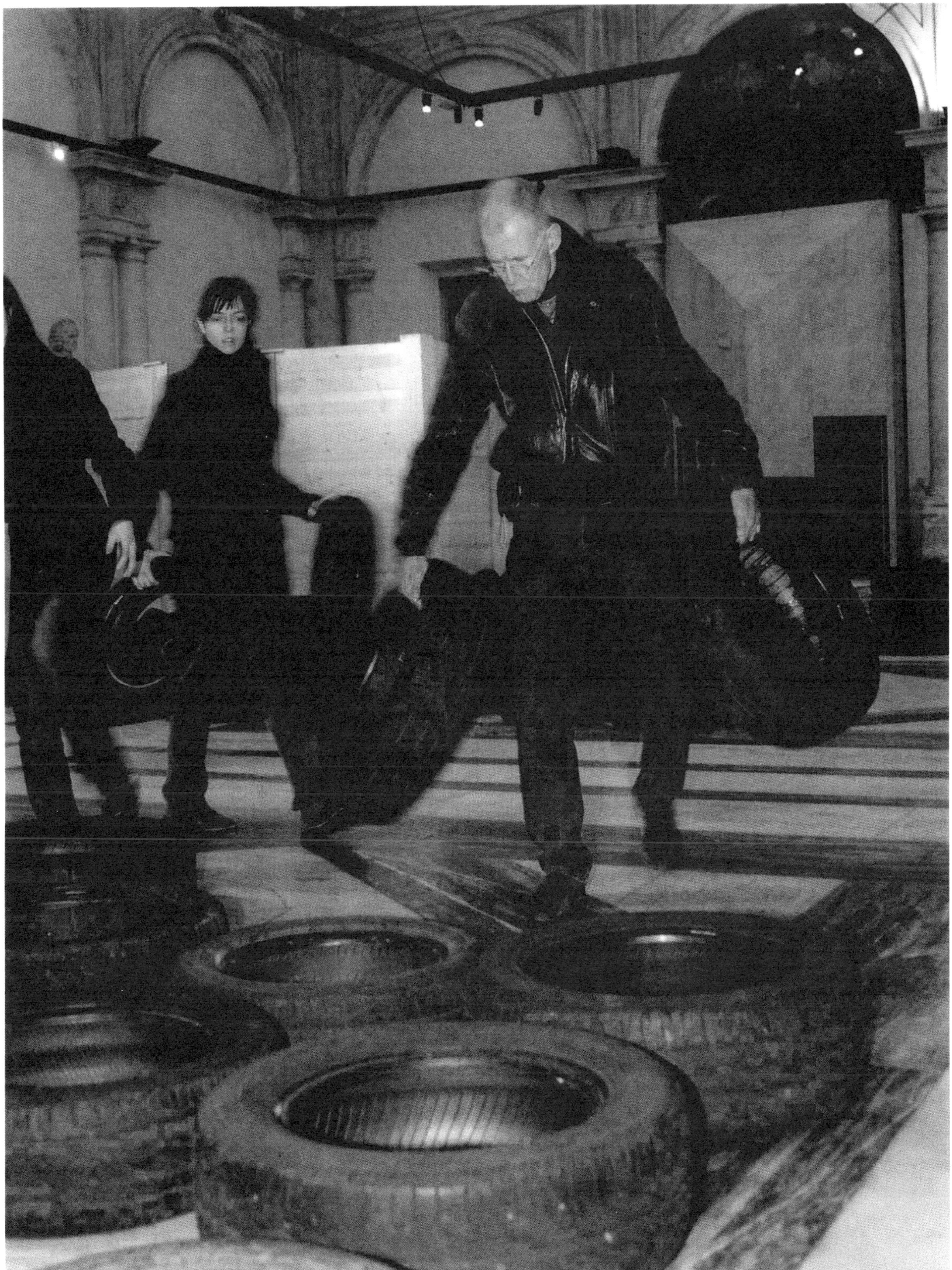

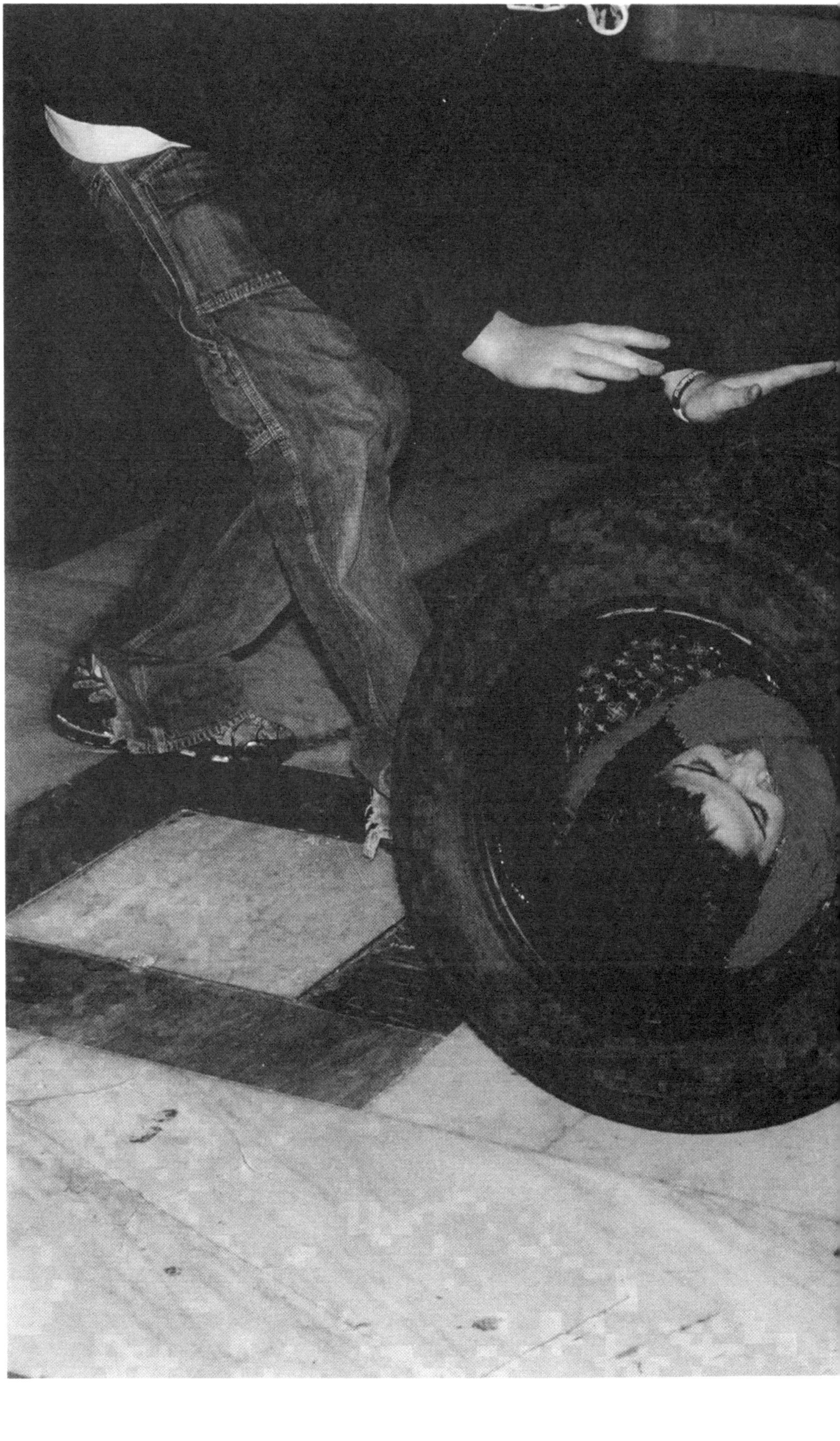

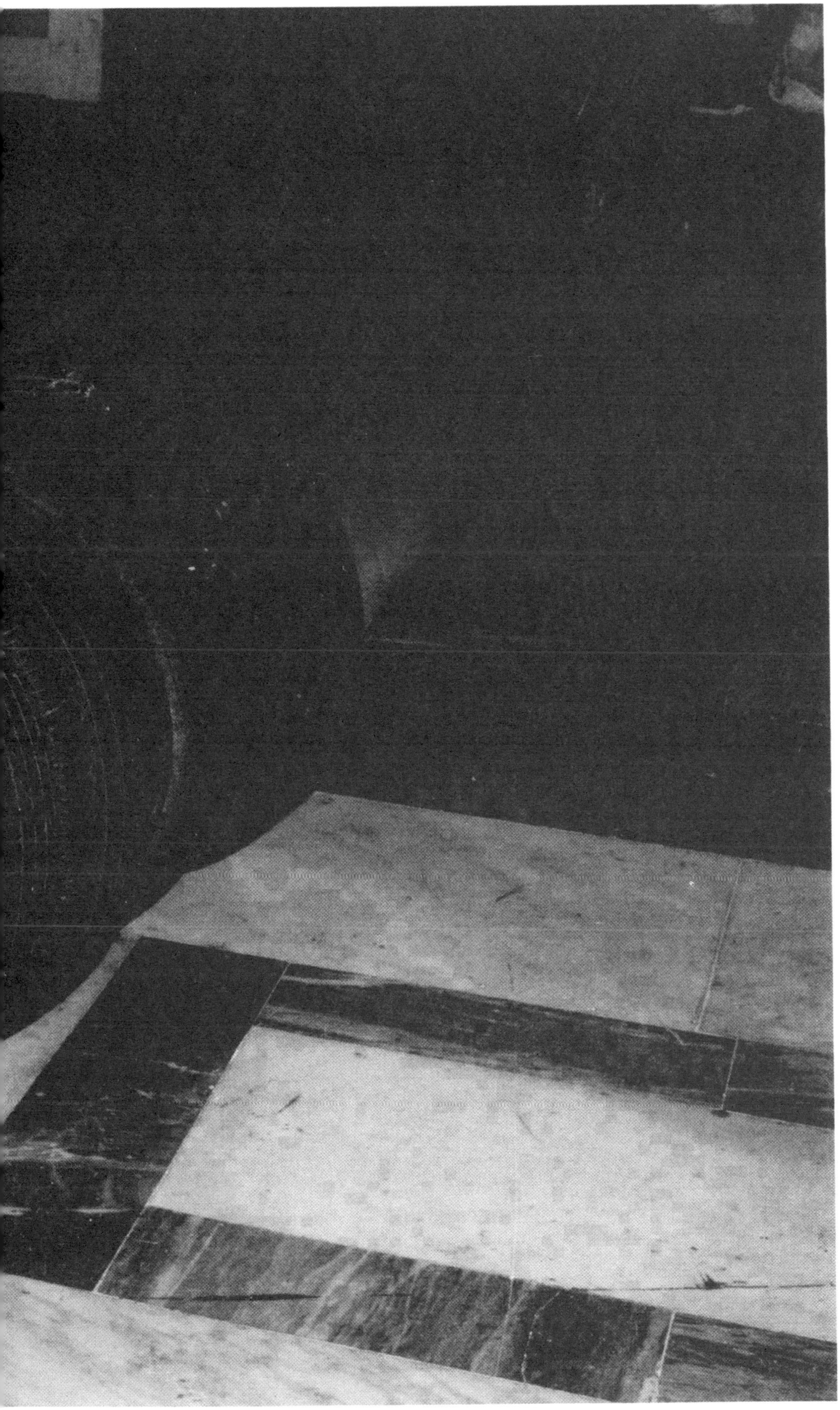

SOME OBSERVATIONS ON CONTEMPORARY ART

WE ARE BEGINNING to see clearly now that in the last decade or so the several categories of the plastic arts have become increasingly indistinguishable. What separates a large drawing from a painting, a construction from a collage or sculpture, and so forth, is not at all easy to define. A kind of interchange is occurring which, besides blurring traditional outlines, is producing a new set of forms that in turn are reconditioning our experience.

Though individual points of view vary, I feel there has been a shift in general from a concern for the work of art as a thing to be possessed, i.e., a valuable object upon which highly specialized care has been lavished, to the work of art as a situation, an action, an environment or an event.

More often than not, the result is fragile, as though it had emerged spontaneously, composed of mixed "mediums" that usually do not belong to "art," but to industry, the household, nature, the ash can and the hardware store. Its shape is sprawling and irregular, sometimes made up of units that are infinitely rearrangeable, expandable and reduceable to adjust to different areas, which gives the whole an ambiguous, fluid existence. Added to this seeming lack of professional definition (and therefore respectability), is the rawness or immediacy of impulse present in the manner some of these artists use their materials, or, in other cases where the touch is more delicate, the indifference to the "beauty" of craftsman-like arrangement. Not only have permanence and skill largely been given up in the literal finished product, but this implies philosophically greater preoccupation with **the changeable** as a raison d'etre.

The structural principle of these works can best be conveyed by the term "extension." Changeableness being what it is, one thing may become another, which may extend to another ad infinitum. Unrestricted to paint on canvas, these may literally include: anything. Space is no longer pictorial but actual (and sometimes both), and sound, odors, artificial light, movement and time are now utilized. Hence, extension as an organic function is meant to embrace the whole world of experience.

These agglomerates may grow, as if they were some self-energized being, into rooms-full and become in every sense of the word **environments** where the spectator is a real part, i.e., a participant rather than a passive observer. And in their most extended form, the environments have gone the next step to "happenings," events in a given time in which, put simply, "things happen" according to flexible scores and where theoretically the participant becomes even more actively engaged. (This present exhibition, for practical reasons, cannot show the more fully developed aspects of this new art, but even so, certain rudiments of it can be recognized by the sensitive visitor.)

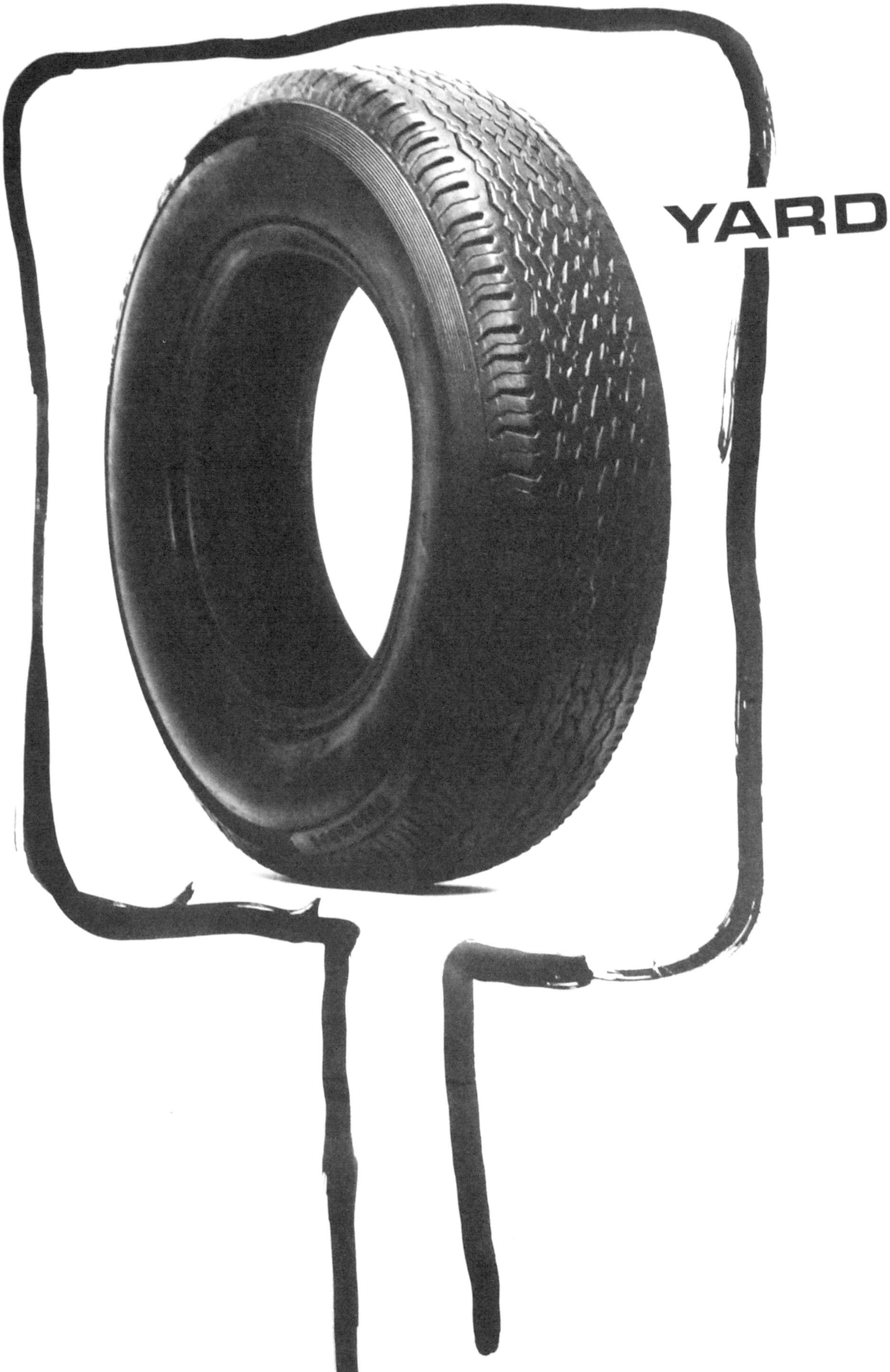
YARD